DOCTOR WHO

STAR TREK

THE NEXT GENERATION

D1198862

Written by **Scott & David Tipton**

Painted Art by **J.K. Woodward**

Pencils by **Gordon Purcell**

Letters by **Shawn Lee** and **Tom B. Long**

Series Editorial Assist by **Jacen Smith**

Series Edits by **Denton J. Tipton**

Cover by **J.K. Woodward**

Collection Edits by **Justin Eisinger** and **Alonzo Simon**

Collection Design by **Robbie Robbins**

Special thanks to Risa Kessler and John Van Citters of CBS Consumer Products, and Kate Bush, Georgie Britton, Caroline Skinner, Denise Paul, and Ed Casey at BBC Worldwide for their invaluable assistance.

IDW founded by Ted Adams, Alex Garner, Kris Oprisko, and Robbie Robbins |

ISBN: 978-1-61377-551-6   16 15 14 13   2 3 4 5

IDW®

Ted Adams, CEO & Publisher
Greg Goldstein, President & COO
Robbie Robbins, EVP/Sr. Graphic Artist
Chris Ryall, Chief Creative Officer/Editor-in-Chief
Matthew Ruzicka, CPA, Chief Financial Officer
Alan Payne, VP of Sales
Dirk Wood, VP of Marketing
Lorelei Bunjes, VP of Digital Services

Become our fan on Facebook **facebook.com/idwpublishing**
Follow us on Twitter **@idwpublishing**
Check us out on YouTube **youtube.com/idwpublishing**
www.IDWPUBLISHING.com

STAR TREK: THE NEXT GENERATION / DOCTOR WHO: ASSIMILATION², VOLUME 2. SEPTEMBER 2013. SECOND PRINTING. STAR TREK ® and © 2013 CBS Studios, Inc. All Rights Reserved. STAR TREK and related marks are trademarks of CBS Studios, Inc. IDW Publishing authorized user. All rights reserved. BBC, DOCTOR WHO (word marks, logos and devices) and TARDIS are trade marks of the British Broadcasting Corporation and are used under license. BBC logo © BBC 1996. Doctor Who logo © BBC 2009. TARDIS image © BBC 1963. Cybermen image © BBC/Kit Pedler/Gerry Davis 1966. © 2013 Idea and Design Works, LLC. All Rights Reserved. The IDW logo is registered in the U.S. Patent and Trademark Office. IDW Publishing, a division of Idea and Design Works, LLC. Editorial offices: 5080 Santa Fe St., San Diego, CA 92109. Any similarities to persons living or dead are purely coincidental. With the exception of artwork used for review purposes, none of the contents of this publication may be reprinted without the permission of Idea and Design Works, LLC. Printed in Korea.
IDW Publishing does not read or accept unsolicited submissions of ideas, stories, or artwork.

Originally published as STAR TREK: THE NEXT GENERATION / DOCTOR WHO: ASSIMILATION² Issues #5–8.

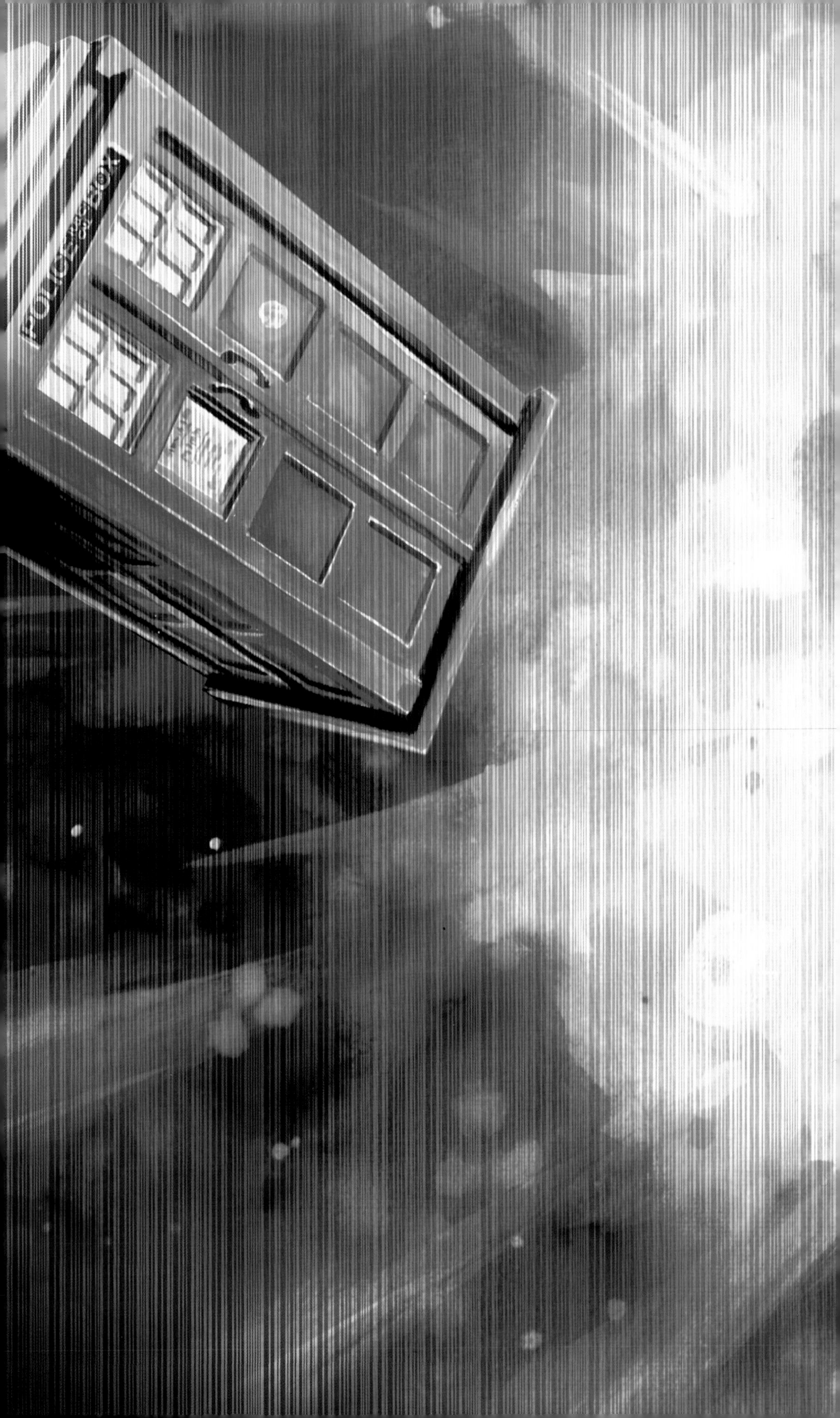
POLICE BOX

ASSIMILATION²

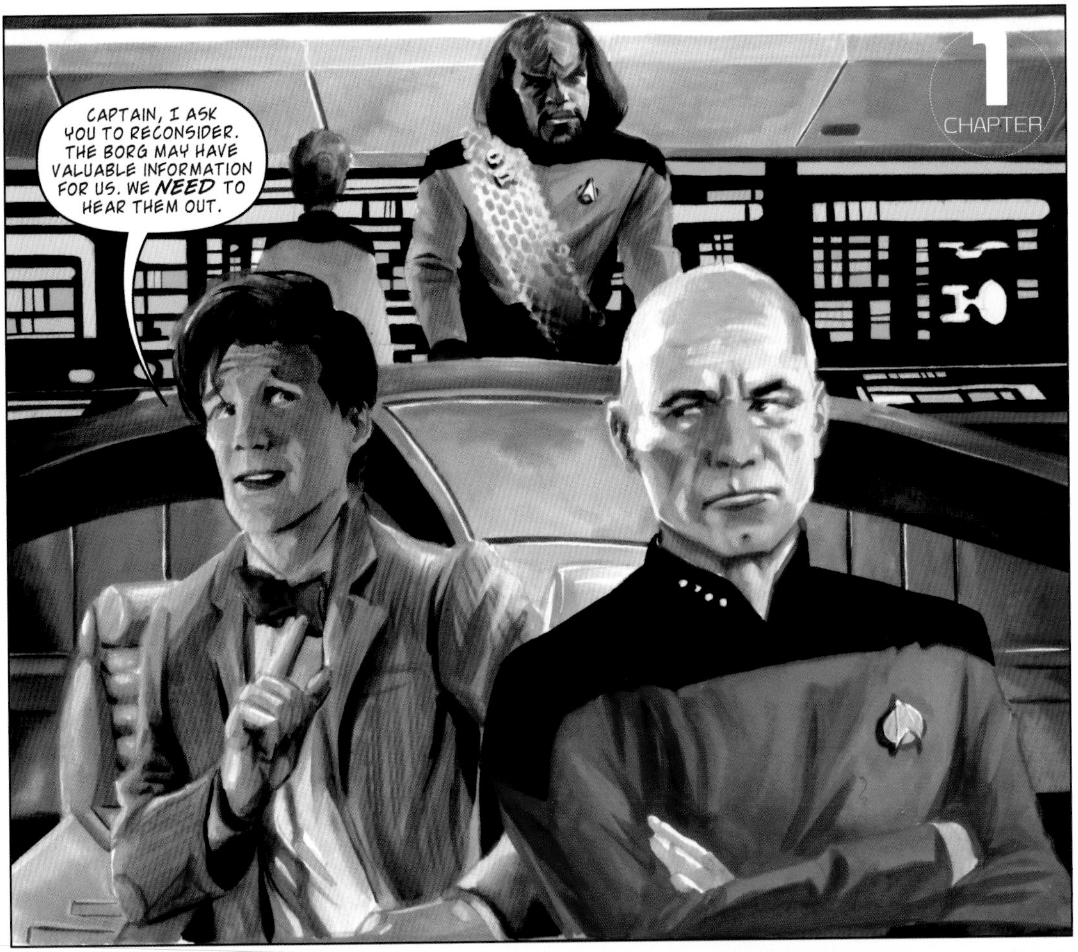
1
CHAPTER
CAPTAIN, I ASK YOU TO RECONSIDER. THE BORG MAY HAVE VALUABLE INFORMATION FOR US. WE *NEED* TO HEAR THEM OUT.

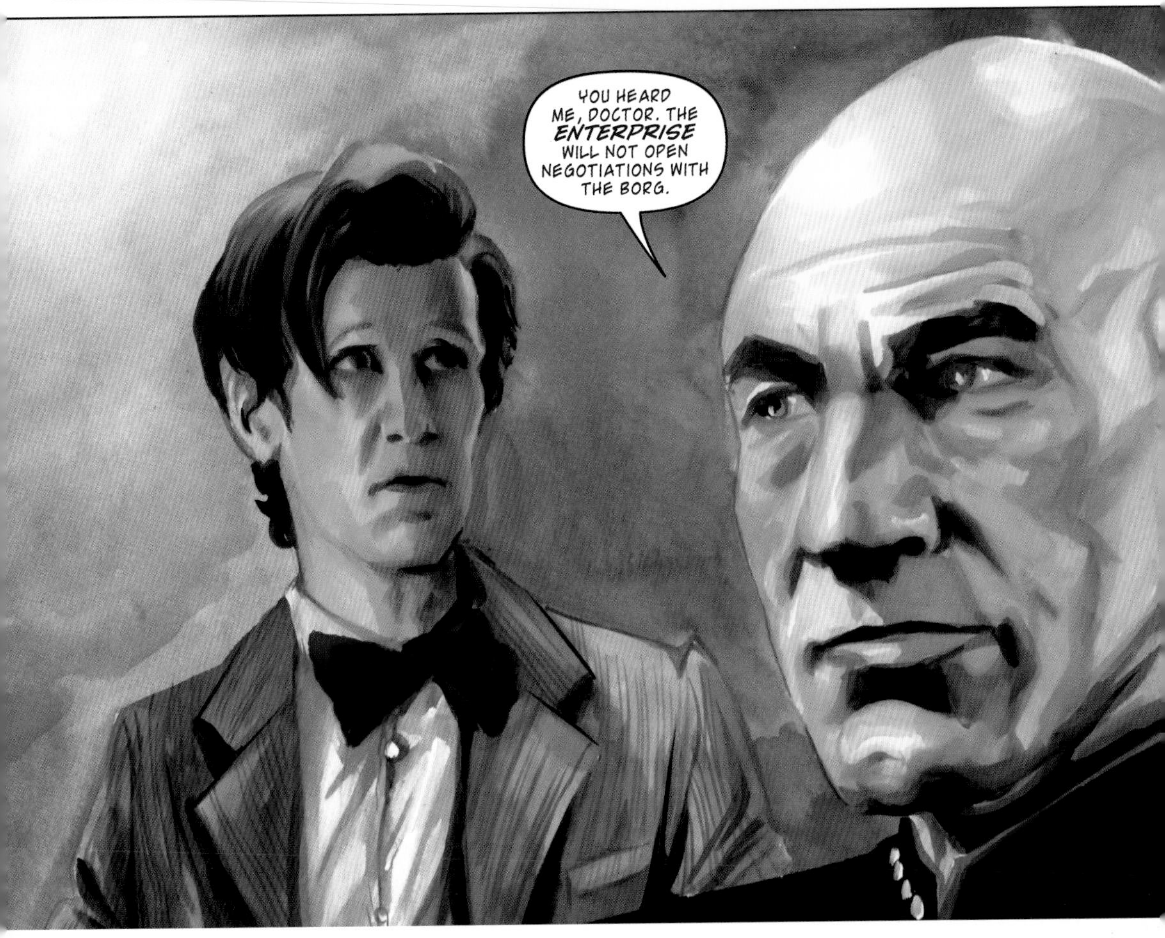
YOU HEARD ME, DOCTOR. THE *ENTERPRISE* WILL NOT OPEN NEGOTIATIONS WITH THE BORG.

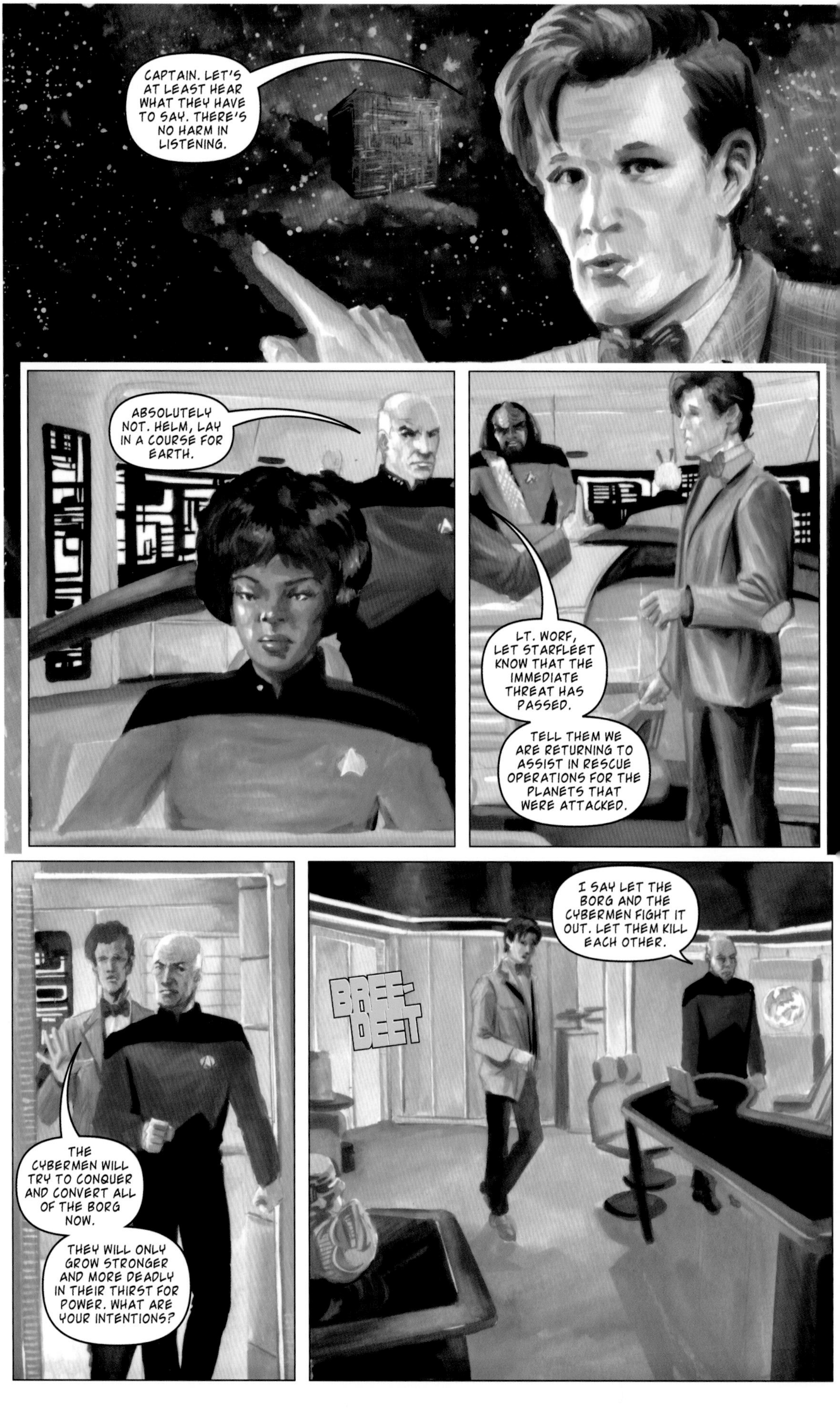

CAPTAIN. LET'S AT LEAST HEAR WHAT THEY HAVE TO SAY. THERE'S NO HARM IN LISTENING.
ABSOLUTELY NOT. HELM, LAY IN A COURSE FOR EARTH.
LT. WORF, LET STARFLEET KNOW THAT THE IMMEDIATE THREAT HAS PASSED.
TELL THEM WE ARE RETURNING TO ASSIST IN RESCUE OPERATIONS FOR THE PLANETS THAT WERE ATTACKED.
THE CYBERMEN WILL TRY TO CONQUER AND CONVERT ALL OF THE BORG NOW.
THEY WILL ONLY GROW STRONGER AND MORE DEADLY IN THEIR THIRST FOR POWER. WHAT ARE YOUR INTENTIONS?
BREE-DEET
I SAY LET THE BORG AND THE CYBERMEN FIGHT IT OUT. LET THEM KILL EACH OTHER.

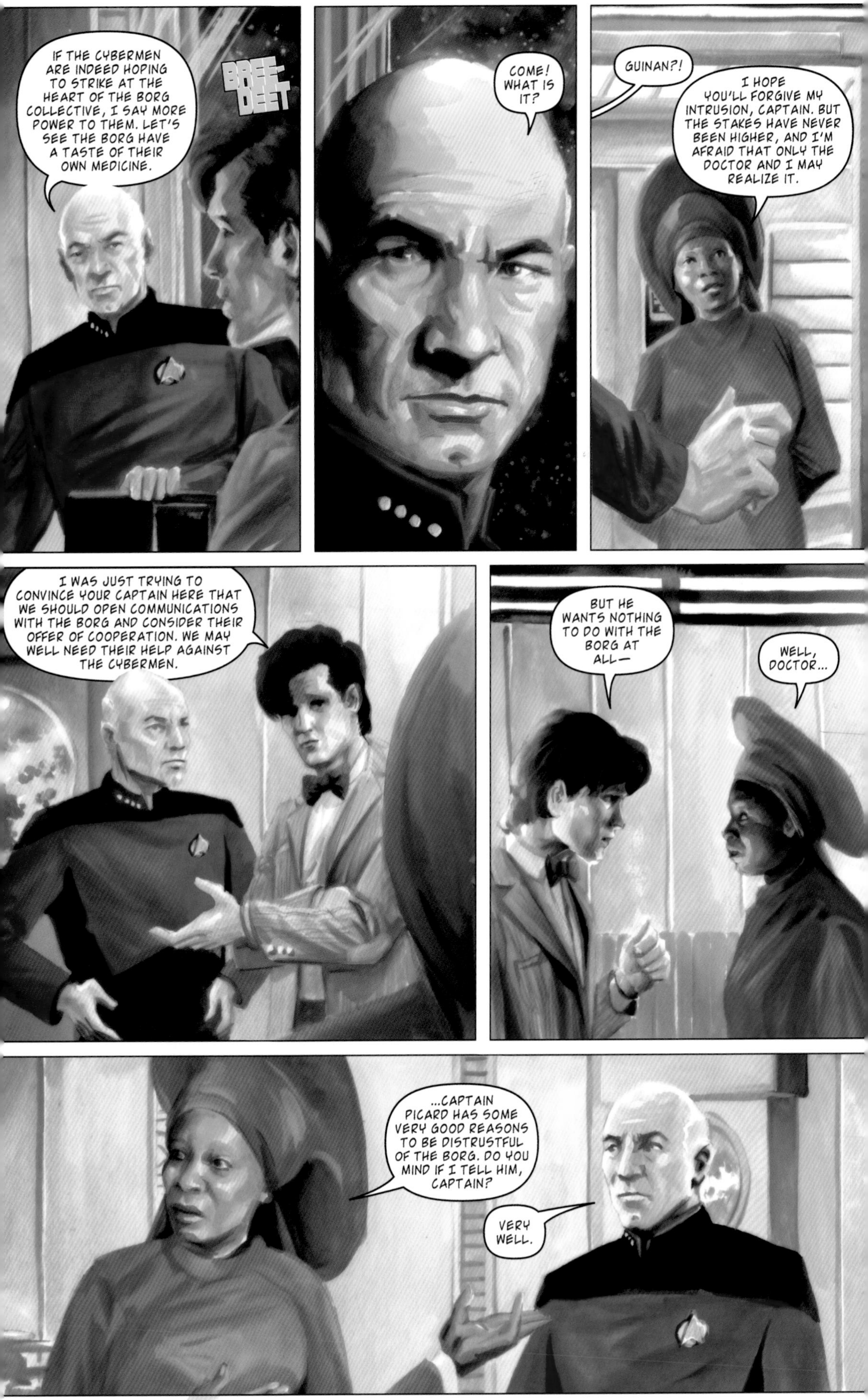

IF THE CYBERMEN ARE INDEED HOPING TO STRIKE AT THE HEART OF THE BORG COLLECTIVE, I SAY MORE POWER TO THEM. LET'S SEE THE BORG HAVE A TASTE OF THEIR OWN MEDICINE.
BREE-DEET
COME! WHAT IS IT?
GUINAN?!
I HOPE YOU'LL FORGIVE MY INTRUSION, CAPTAIN. BUT THE STAKES HAVE NEVER BEEN HIGHER, AND I'M AFRAID THAT ONLY THE DOCTOR AND I MAY REALIZE IT.
I WAS JUST TRYING TO CONVINCE YOUR CAPTAIN HERE THAT WE SHOULD OPEN COMMUNICATIONS WITH THE BORG AND CONSIDER THEIR OFFER OF COOPERATION. WE MAY WELL NEED THEIR HELP AGAINST THE CYBERMEN.
BUT HE WANTS NOTHING TO DO WITH THE BORG AT ALL—
WELL, DOCTOR...
...CAPTAIN PICARD HAS SOME VERY GOOD REASONS TO BE DISTRUSTFUL OF THE BORG. DO YOU MIND IF I TELL HIM, CAPTAIN?
VERY WELL.

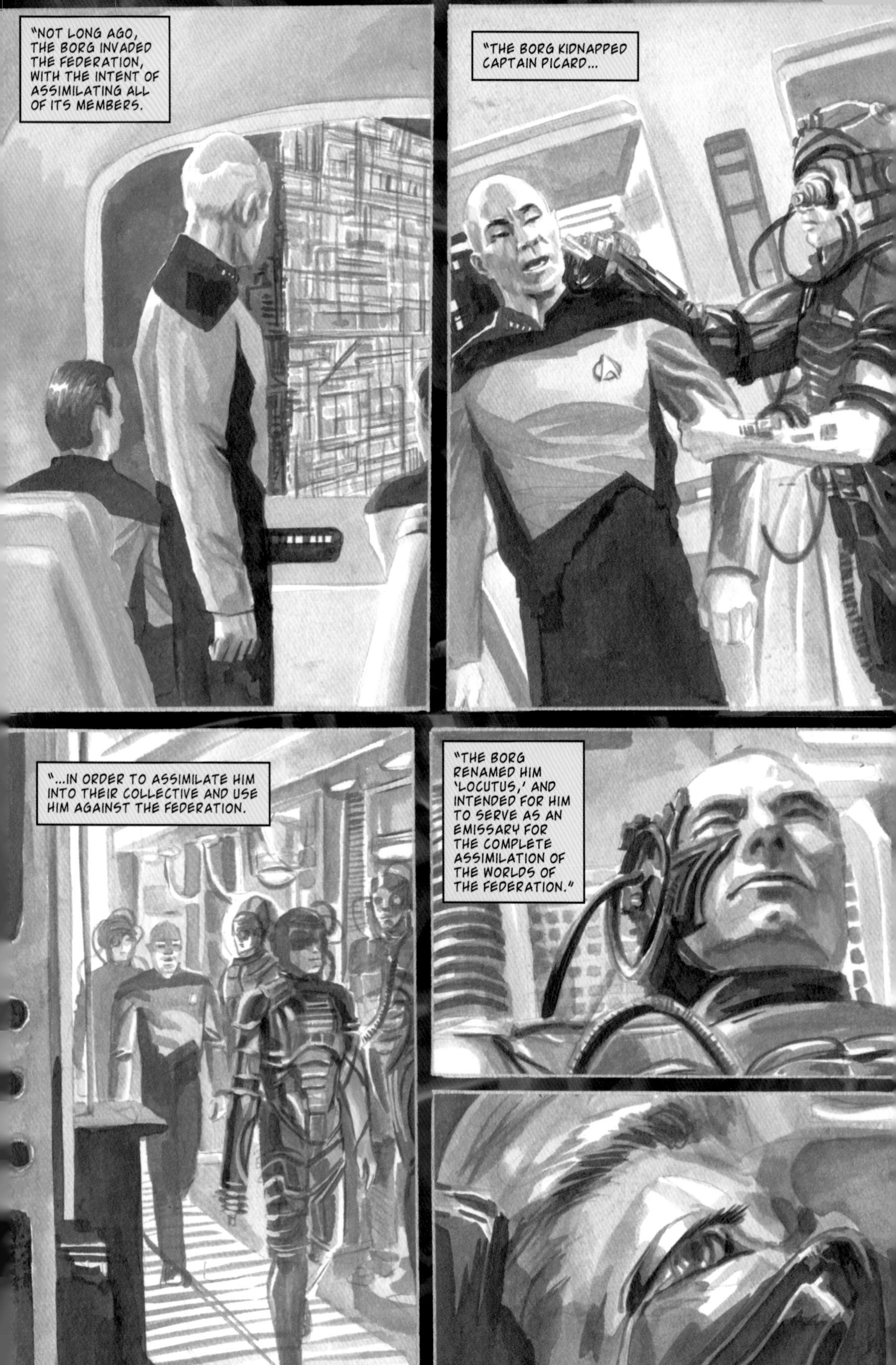
"NOT LONG AGO, THE BORG INVADED THE FEDERATION, WITH THE INTENT OF ASSIMILATING ALL OF ITS MEMBERS.
"THE BORG KIDNAPPED CAPTAIN PICARD...
"...IN ORDER TO ASSIMILATE HIM INTO THEIR COLLECTIVE AND USE HIM AGAINST THE FEDERATION.
"THE BORG RENAMED HIM 'LOCUTUS,' AND INTENDED FOR HIM TO SERVE AS AN EMISSARY FOR THE COMPLETE ASSIMILATION OF THE WORLDS OF THE FEDERATION."

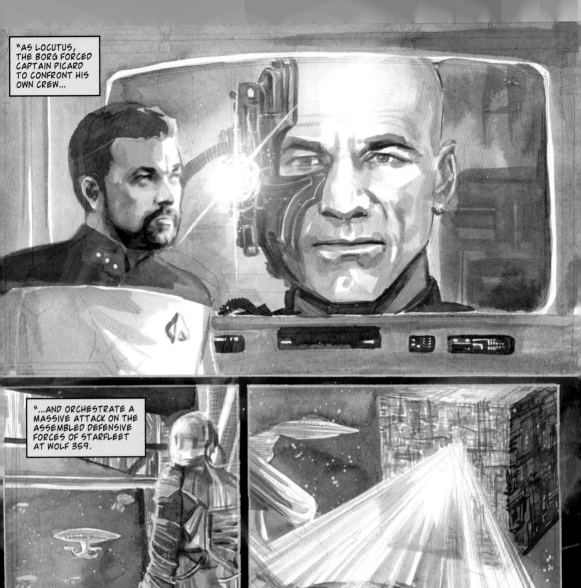

"AS LOCUTUS, THE BORG FORCED CAPTAIN PICARD TO CONFRONT HIS OWN CREW...

"...AND ORCHESTRATE A MASSIVE ATTACK ON THE ASSEMBLED DEFENSIVE FORCES OF STARFLEET AT WOLF 359.

"THE BORG USED CAPTAIN PICARD'S KNOWLEDGE OF STARFLEET TACTICS AND WEAKNESSES AGAINST THEM. THE LOSSES WERE STAGGERING. THOUSANDS DIED.

"AFTER DEFEATING THE STARFLEET TASK FORCE, THE BORG HEADED DIRECTLY TO EARTH."

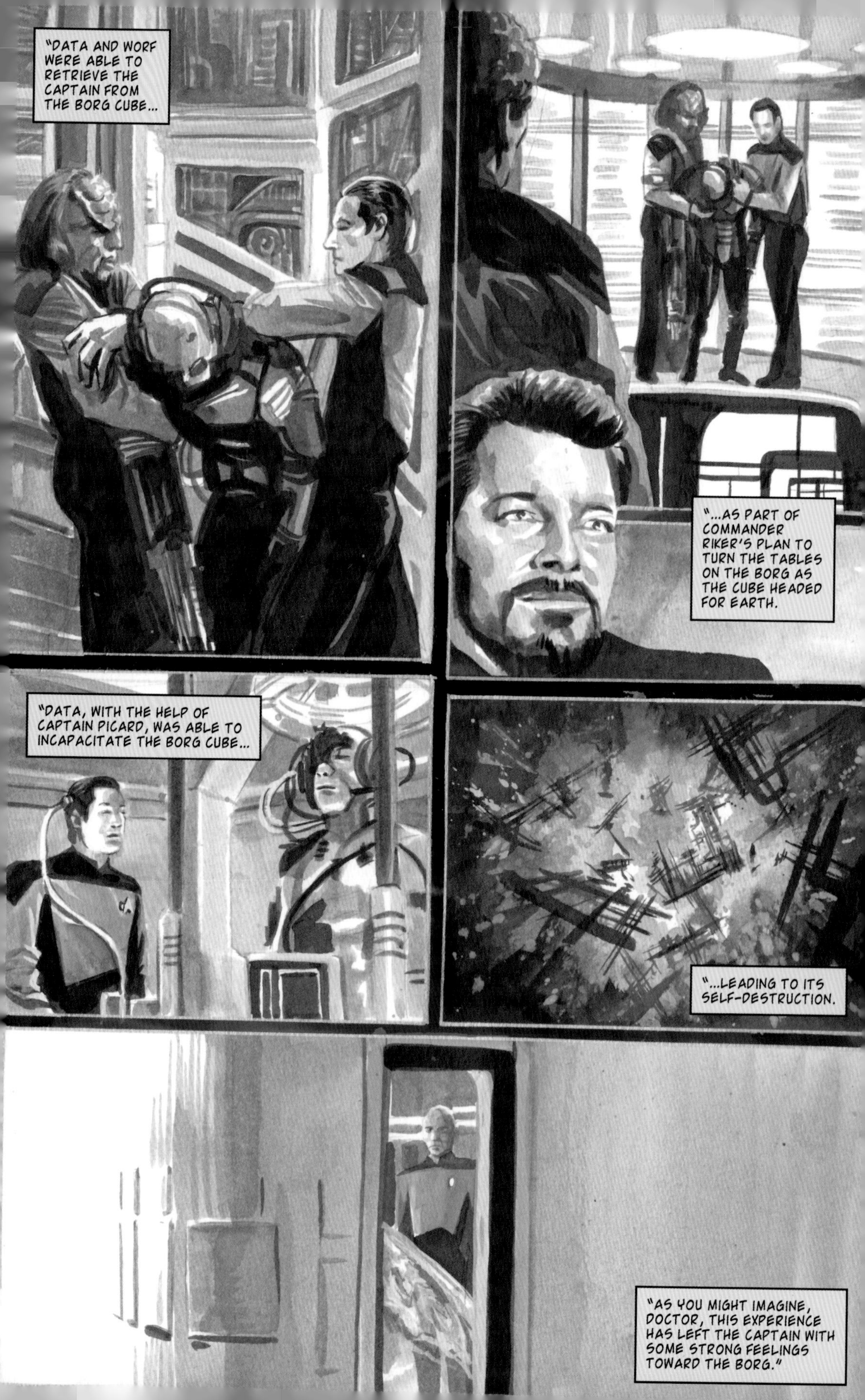
"DATA AND WORF WERE ABLE TO RETRIEVE THE CAPTAIN FROM THE BORG CUBE...
"...AS PART OF COMMANDER RIKER'S PLAN TO TURN THE TABLES ON THE BORG AS THE CUBE HEADED FOR EARTH.
"DATA, WITH THE HELP OF CAPTAIN PICARD, WAS ABLE TO INCAPACITATE THE BORG CUBE...
"...LEADING TO ITS SELF-DESTRUCTION.
"AS YOU MIGHT IMAGINE, DOCTOR, THIS EXPERIENCE HAS LEFT THE CAPTAIN WITH SOME STRONG FEELINGS TOWARD THE BORG."

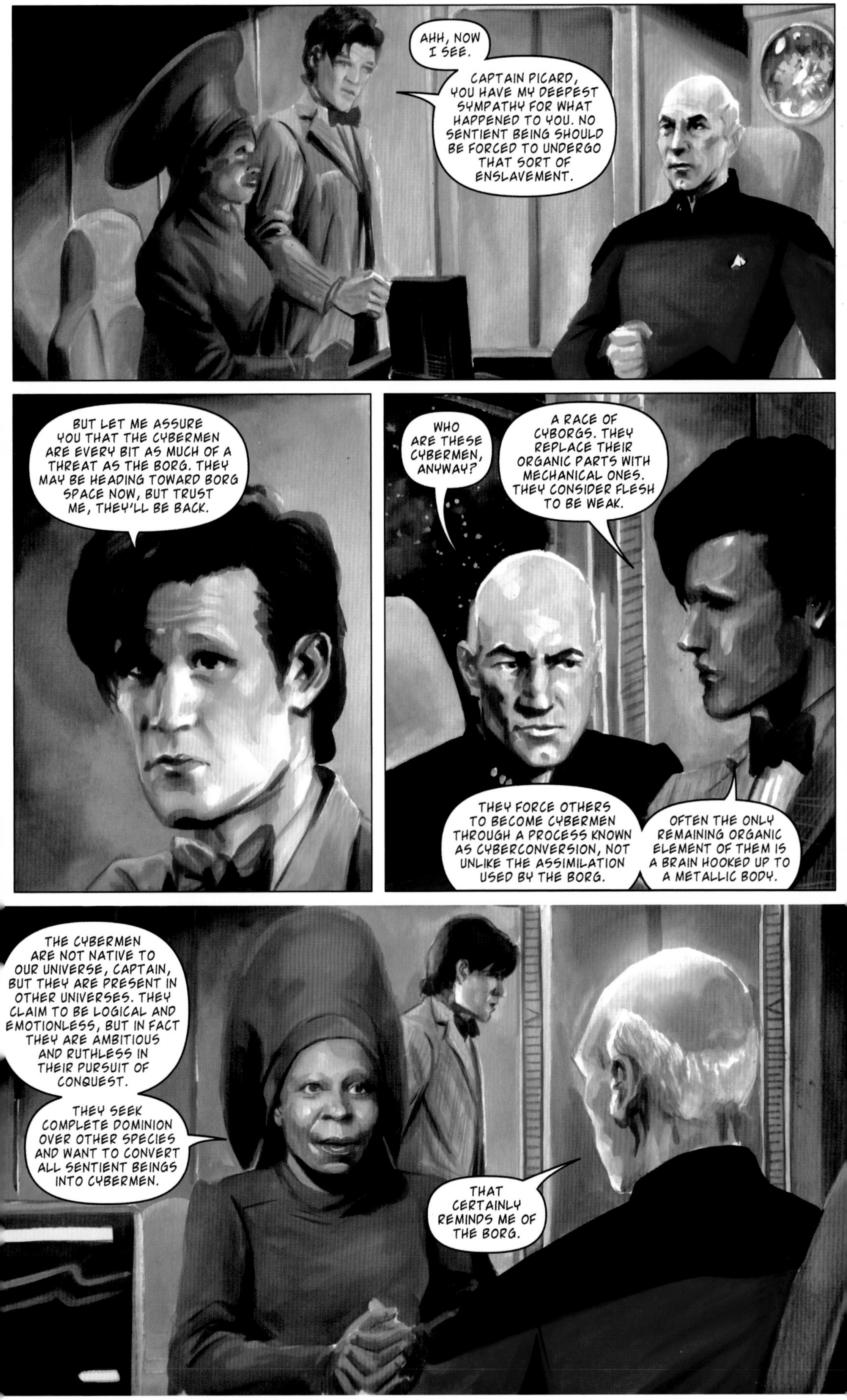
AHH, NOW I SEE.
CAPTAIN PICARD, YOU HAVE MY DEEPEST SYMPATHY FOR WHAT HAPPENED TO YOU. NO SENTIENT BEING SHOULD BE FORCED TO UNDERGO THAT SORT OF ENSLAVEMENT.
BUT LET ME ASSURE YOU THAT THE CYBERMEN ARE EVERY BIT AS MUCH OF A THREAT AS THE BORG. THEY MAY BE HEADING TOWARD BORG SPACE NOW, BUT TRUST ME, THEY'LL BE BACK.
WHO ARE THESE CYBERMEN, ANYWAY?
A RACE OF CYBORGS. THEY REPLACE THEIR ORGANIC PARTS WITH MECHANICAL ONES. THEY CONSIDER FLESH TO BE WEAK.
THEY FORCE OTHERS TO BECOME CYBERMEN THROUGH A PROCESS KNOWN AS CYBERCONVERSION, NOT UNLIKE THE ASSIMILATION USED BY THE BORG.
OFTEN THE ONLY REMAINING ORGANIC ELEMENT OF THEM IS A BRAIN HOOKED UP TO A METALLIC BODY.
THE CYBERMEN ARE NOT NATIVE TO OUR UNIVERSE, CAPTAIN, BUT THEY ARE PRESENT IN OTHER UNIVERSES. THEY CLAIM TO BE LOGICAL AND EMOTIONLESS, BUT IN FACT THEY ARE AMBITIOUS AND RUTHLESS IN THEIR PURSUIT OF CONQUEST.
THEY SEEK COMPLETE DOMINION OVER OTHER SPECIES AND WANT TO CONVERT ALL SENTIENT BEINGS INTO CYBERMEN.
THAT CERTAINLY REMINDS ME OF THE BORG.

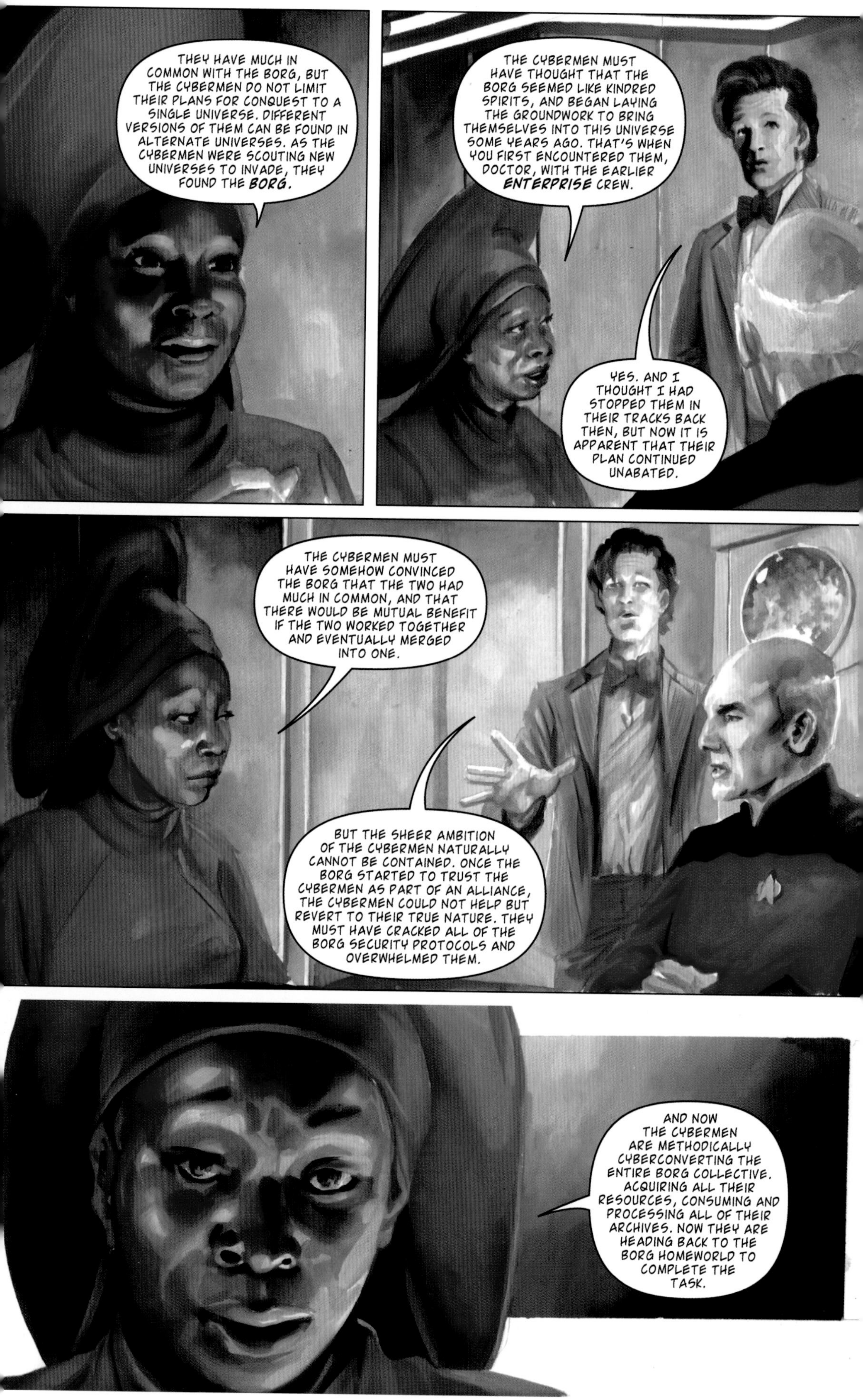
THEY HAVE MUCH IN COMMON WITH THE BORG, BUT THE CYBERMEN DO NOT LIMIT THEIR PLANS FOR CONQUEST TO A SINGLE UNIVERSE. DIFFERENT VERSIONS OF THEM CAN BE FOUND IN ALTERNATE UNIVERSES. AS THE CYBERMEN WERE SCOUTING NEW UNIVERSES TO INVADE, THEY FOUND THE **BORG.**
THE CYBERMEN MUST HAVE THOUGHT THAT THE BORG SEEMED LIKE KINDRED SPIRITS, AND BEGAN LAYING THE GROUNDWORK TO BRING THEMSELVES INTO THIS UNIVERSE SOME YEARS AGO. THAT'S WHEN YOU FIRST ENCOUNTERED THEM, DOCTOR, WITH THE EARLIER ***ENTERPRISE*** CREW.
YES. AND I THOUGHT I HAD STOPPED THEM IN THEIR TRACKS BACK THEN, BUT NOW IT IS APPARENT THAT THEIR PLAN CONTINUED UNABATED.
THE CYBERMEN MUST HAVE SOMEHOW CONVINCED THE BORG THAT THE TWO HAD MUCH IN COMMON, AND THAT THERE WOULD BE MUTUAL BENEFIT IF THE TWO WORKED TOGETHER AND EVENTUALLY MERGED INTO ONE.
BUT THE SHEER AMBITION OF THE CYBERMEN NATURALLY CANNOT BE CONTAINED. ONCE THE BORG STARTED TO TRUST THE CYBERMEN AS PART OF AN ALLIANCE, THE CYBERMEN COULD NOT HELP BUT REVERT TO THEIR TRUE NATURE. THEY MUST HAVE CRACKED ALL OF THE BORG SECURITY PROTOCOLS AND OVERWHELMED THEM.
AND NOW THE CYBERMEN ARE METHODICALLY CYBERCONVERTING THE ENTIRE BORG COLLECTIVE. ACQUIRING ALL THEIR RESOURCES, CONSUMING AND PROCESSING ALL OF THEIR ARCHIVES. NOW THEY ARE HEADING BACK TO THE BORG HOMEWORLD TO COMPLETE THE TASK.

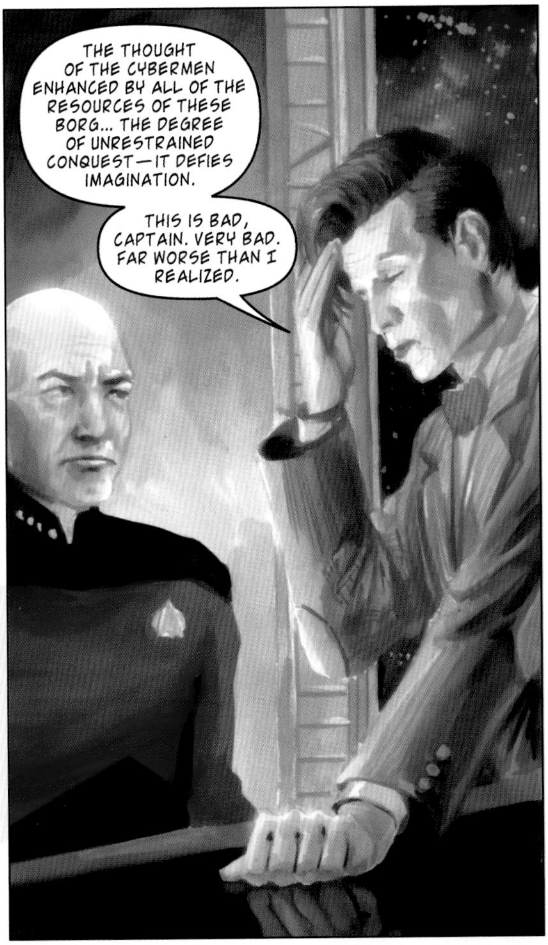
THE THOUGHT OF THE CYBERMEN ENHANCED BY ALL OF THE RESOURCES OF THESE BORG... THE DEGREE OF UNRESTRAINED CONQUEST—IT DEFIES IMAGINATION.
THIS IS BAD, CAPTAIN. VERY BAD. FAR WORSE THAN I REALIZED.

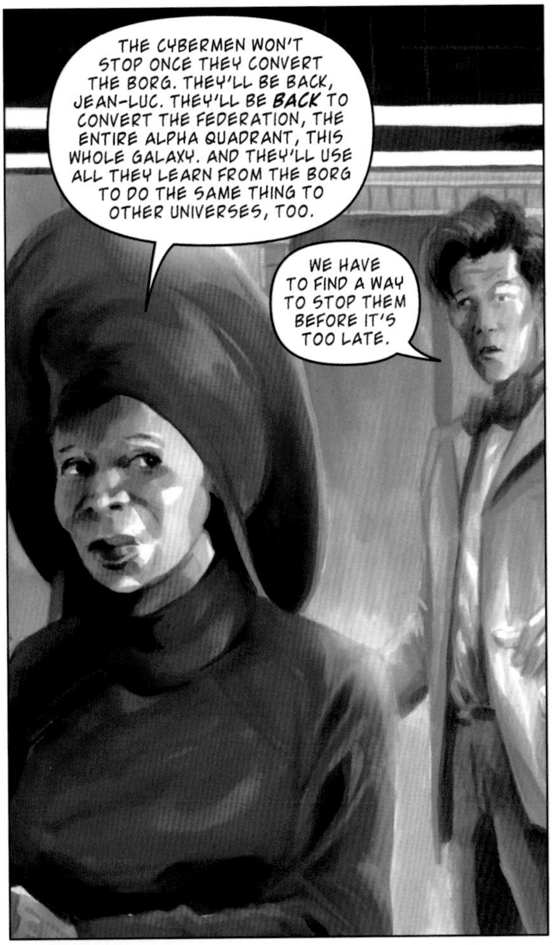
THE CYBERMEN WON'T STOP ONCE THEY CONVERT THE BORG. THEY'LL BE BACK, JEAN-LUC. THEY'LL BE ***BACK*** TO CONVERT THE FEDERATION, THE ENTIRE ALPHA QUADRANT, THIS WHOLE GALAXY. AND THEY'LL USE ALL THEY LEARN FROM THE BORG TO DO THE SAME THING TO OTHER UNIVERSES, TOO.
WE HAVE TO FIND A WAY TO STOP THEM BEFORE IT'S TOO LATE.

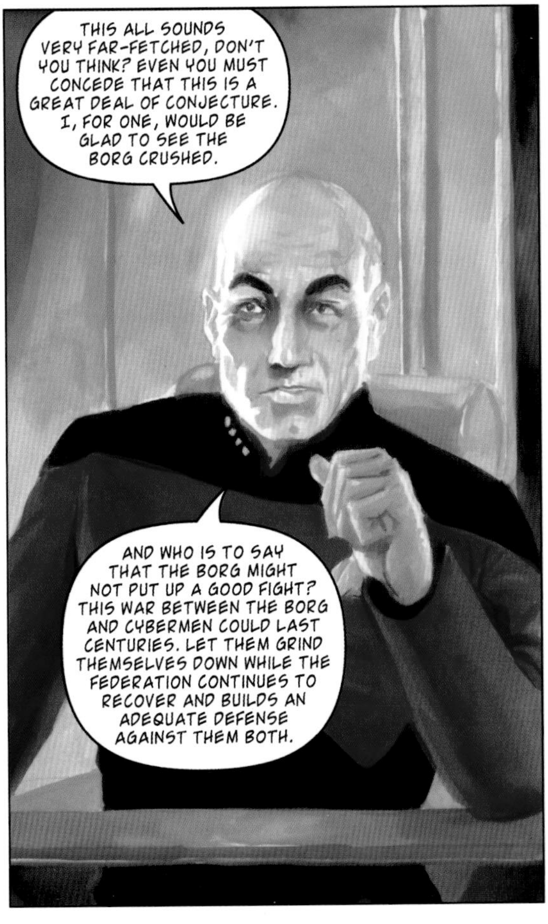
THIS ALL SOUNDS VERY FAR-FETCHED, DON'T YOU THINK? EVEN YOU MUST CONCEDE THAT THIS IS A GREAT DEAL OF CONJECTURE. I, FOR ONE, WOULD BE GLAD TO SEE THE BORG CRUSHED.
AND WHO IS TO SAY THAT THE BORG MIGHT NOT PUT UP A GOOD FIGHT? THIS WAR BETWEEN THE BORG AND CYBERMEN COULD LAST CENTURIES. LET THEM GRIND THEMSELVES DOWN WHILE THE FEDERATION CONTINUES TO RECOVER AND BUILDS AN ADEQUATE DEFENSE AGAINST THEM BOTH.

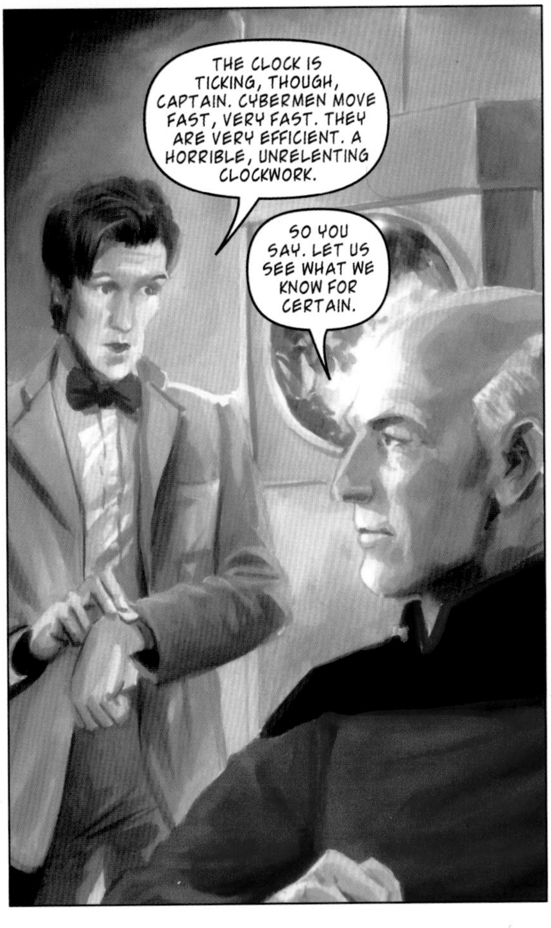
THE CLOCK IS TICKING, THOUGH, CAPTAIN. CYBERMEN MOVE FAST, VERY FAST. THEY ARE VERY EFFICIENT. A HORRIBLE, UNRELENTING CLOCKWORK.
SO YOU SAY. LET US SEE WHAT WE KNOW FOR CERTAIN.

MR. DATA, WHAT'S THE LATEST STATUS ON THE CYBERMAN FLEET?

I'VE CONFIRMED THEIR COURSE, SIR. THEY ARE HEADING DIRECTLY TOWARD BORG SPACE, TOWARD WHERE WE BELIEVE THE BORG HOMEWORLD TO BE.

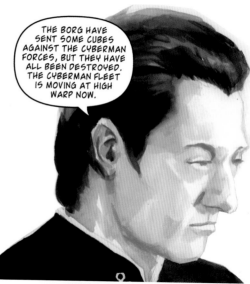

THE BORG HAVE SENT SOME CUBES AGAINST THE CYBERMAN FORCES, BUT THEY HAVE ALL BEEN DESTROYED. THE CYBERMAN FLEET IS MOVING AT HIGH WARP NOW.

DO YOU SEE, CAPTAIN? IT'S ALL FALLING INTO PLACE.

ACKNOWLEDGED, DATA. CONTINUE WITH OUR COURSE BACK TO EARTH.

WHAT?

DOCTOR, EVEN IF EVERYTHING THAT YOU AND GUINAN ARE TELLING ME IS TRUE, WHAT GOOD IS THE *ENTERPRISE* GOING TO BE AGAINST THAT CYBERMAN FLEET? WE WOULD BE LIKE A MOSQUITO AGAINST A HERD OF ELEPHANTS. I WON'T SACRIFICE THIS VESSEL TO CHASE YOUR THEORIES.

COURSE LAID IN, CAPTAIN.

WARP FIVE, ENSIGN. ENGAGE.

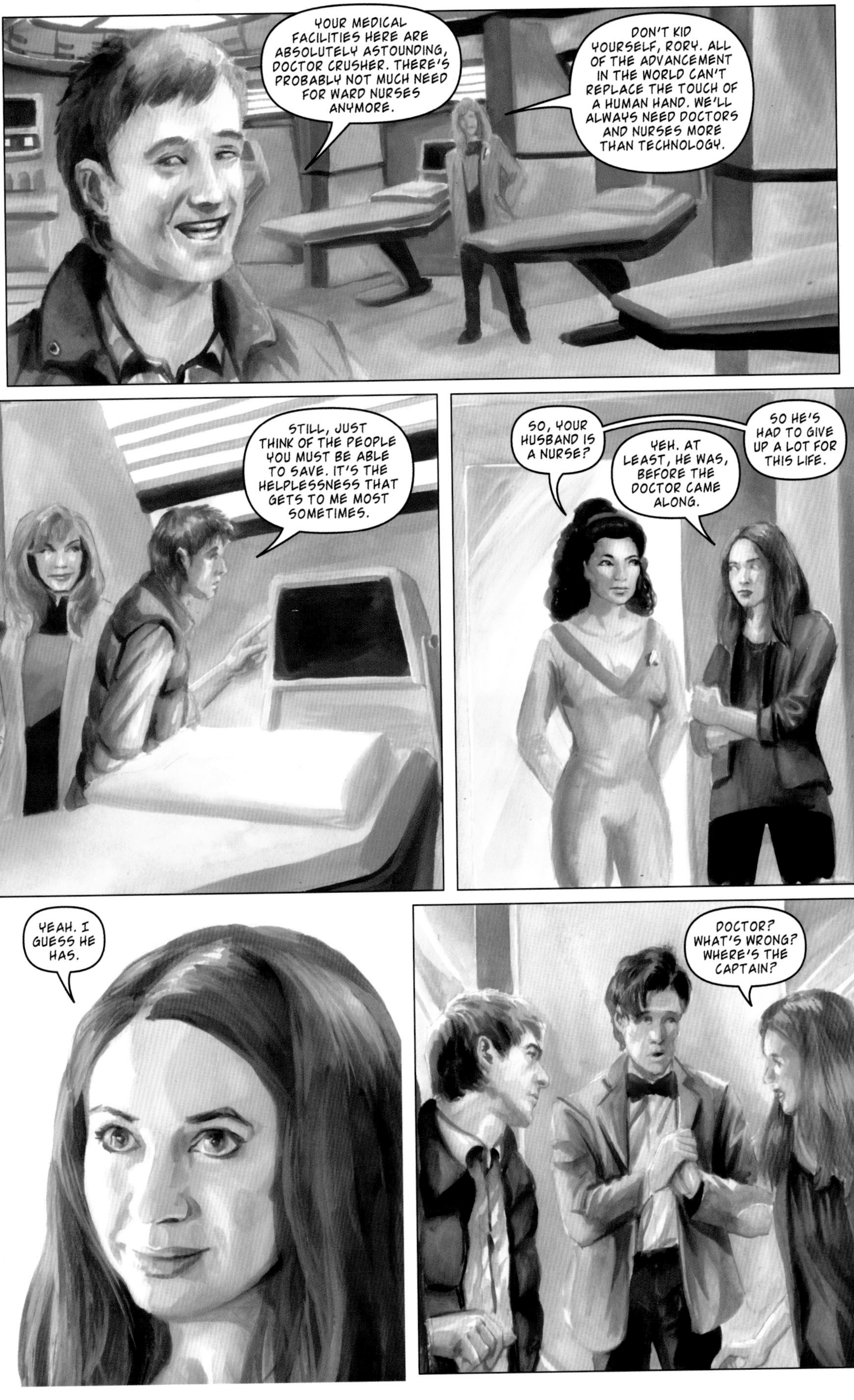
YOUR MEDICAL FACILITIES HERE ARE ABSOLUTELY ASTOUNDING, DOCTOR CRUSHER. THERE'S PROBABLY NOT MUCH NEED FOR WARD NURSES ANYMORE.
DON'T KID YOURSELF, RORY. ALL OF THE ADVANCEMENT IN THE WORLD CAN'T REPLACE THE TOUCH OF A HUMAN HAND. WE'LL ALWAYS NEED DOCTORS AND NURSES MORE THAN TECHNOLOGY.
STILL, JUST THINK OF THE PEOPLE YOU MUST BE ABLE TO SAVE. IT'S THE HELPLESSNESS THAT GETS TO ME MOST SOMETIMES.
SO, YOUR HUSBAND IS A NURSE?
YEH. AT LEAST, HE WAS, BEFORE THE DOCTOR CAME ALONG.
SO HE'S HAD TO GIVE UP A LOT FOR THIS LIFE.
YEAH. I GUESS HE HAS.
DOCTOR? WHAT'S WRONG? WHERE'S THE CAPTAIN?

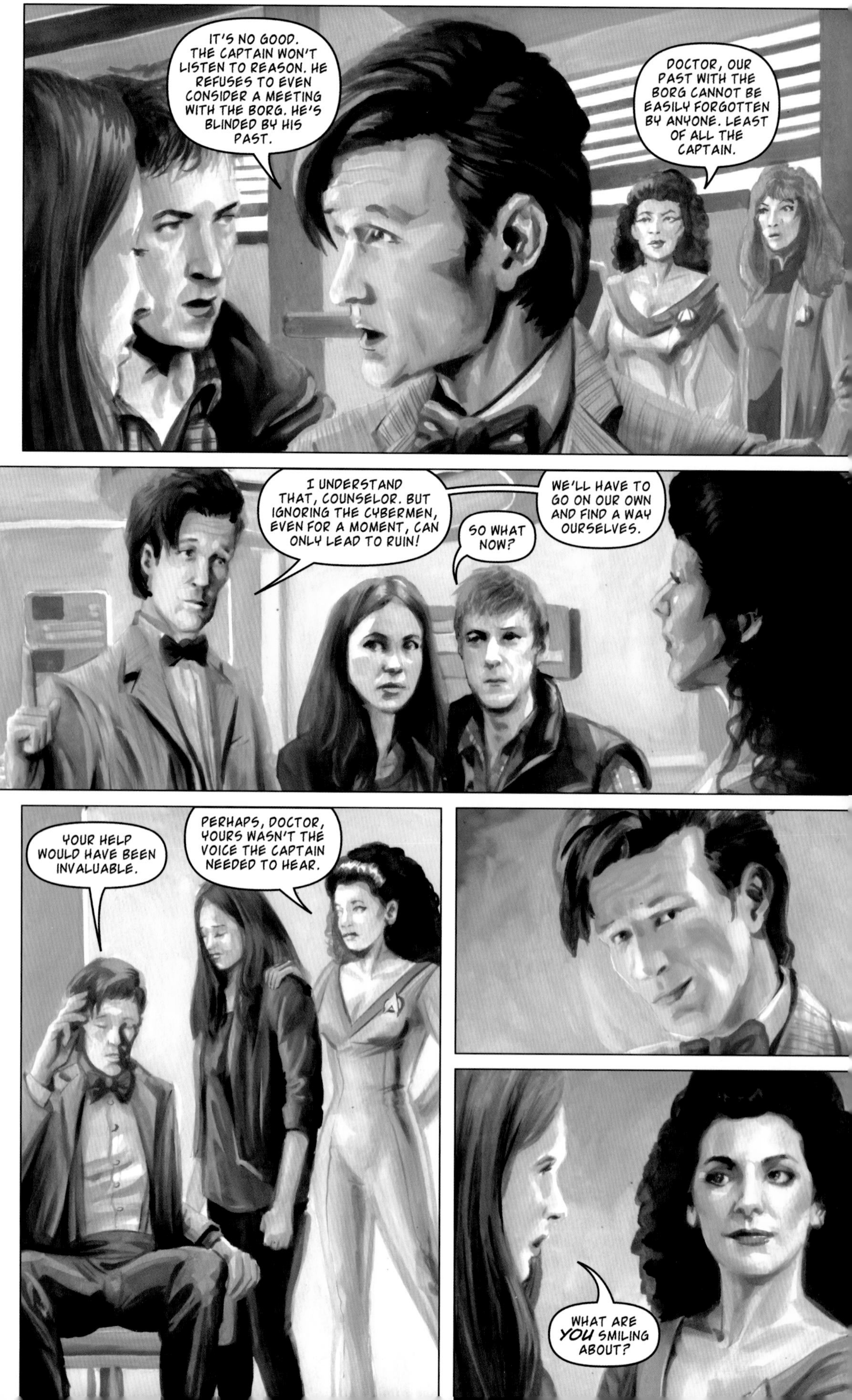
IT'S NO GOOD. THE CAPTAIN WON'T LISTEN TO REASON. HE REFUSES TO EVEN CONSIDER A MEETING WITH THE BORG. HE'S BLINDED BY HIS PAST.
DOCTOR, OUR PAST WITH THE BORG CANNOT BE EASILY FORGOTTEN BY ANYONE. LEAST OF ALL THE CAPTAIN.
I UNDERSTAND THAT, COUNSELOR. BUT IGNORING THE CYBERMEN, EVEN FOR A MOMENT, CAN ONLY LEAD TO RUIN!
WE'LL HAVE TO GO ON OUR OWN AND FIND A WAY OURSELVES.
SO WHAT NOW?
YOUR HELP WOULD HAVE BEEN INVALUABLE.
PERHAPS, DOCTOR, YOURS WASN'T THE VOICE THE CAPTAIN NEEDED TO HEAR.
WHAT ARE *YOU* SMILING ABOUT?

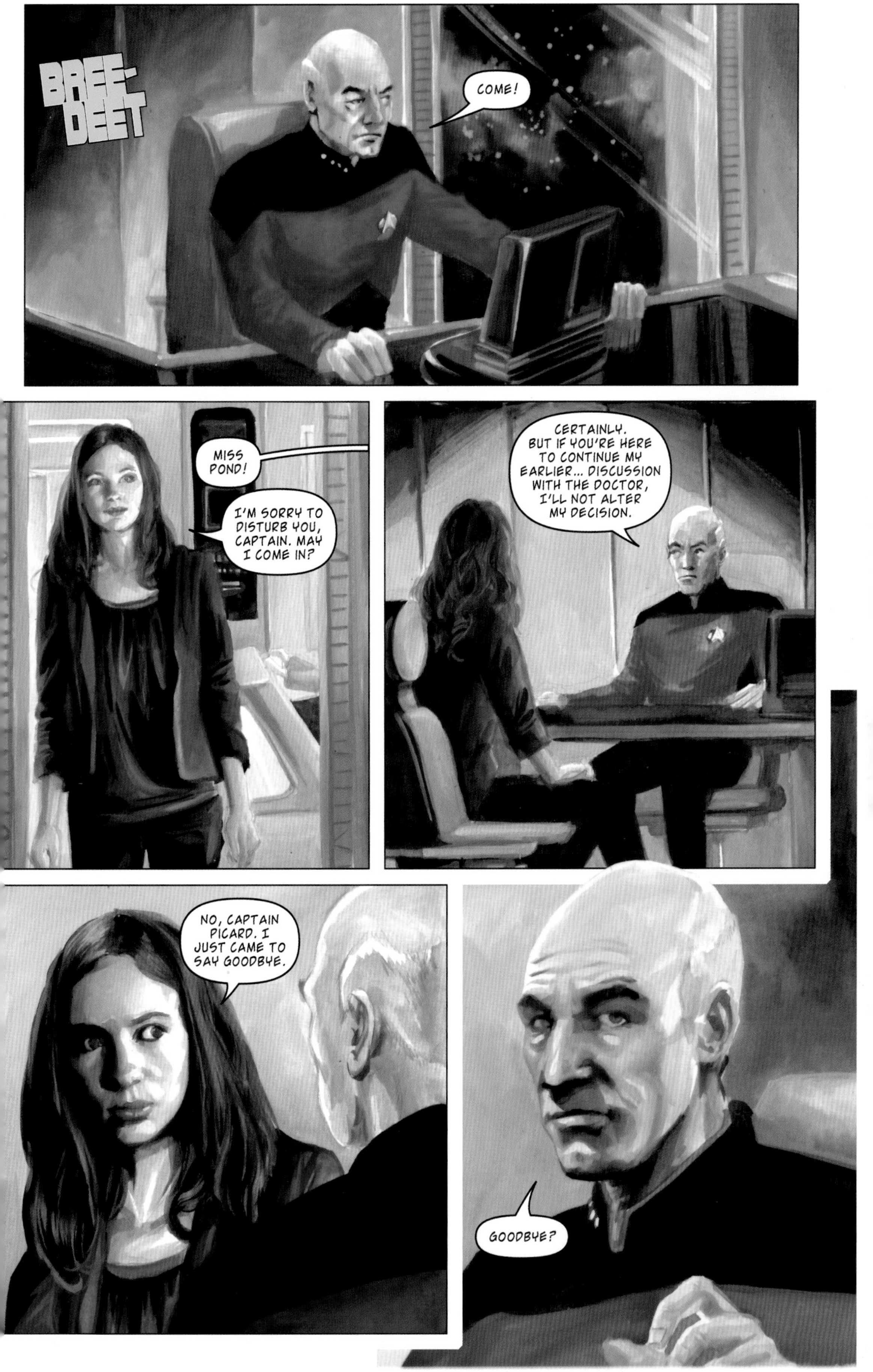
BREE-DEET
COME!
MISS POND!
I'M SORRY TO DISTURB YOU, CAPTAIN. MAY I COME IN?
CERTAINLY. BUT IF YOU'RE HERE TO CONTINUE MY EARLIER... DISCUSSION WITH THE DOCTOR, I'LL NOT ALTER MY DECISION.
NO, CAPTAIN PICARD. I JUST CAME TO SAY GOODBYE.
GOODBYE?

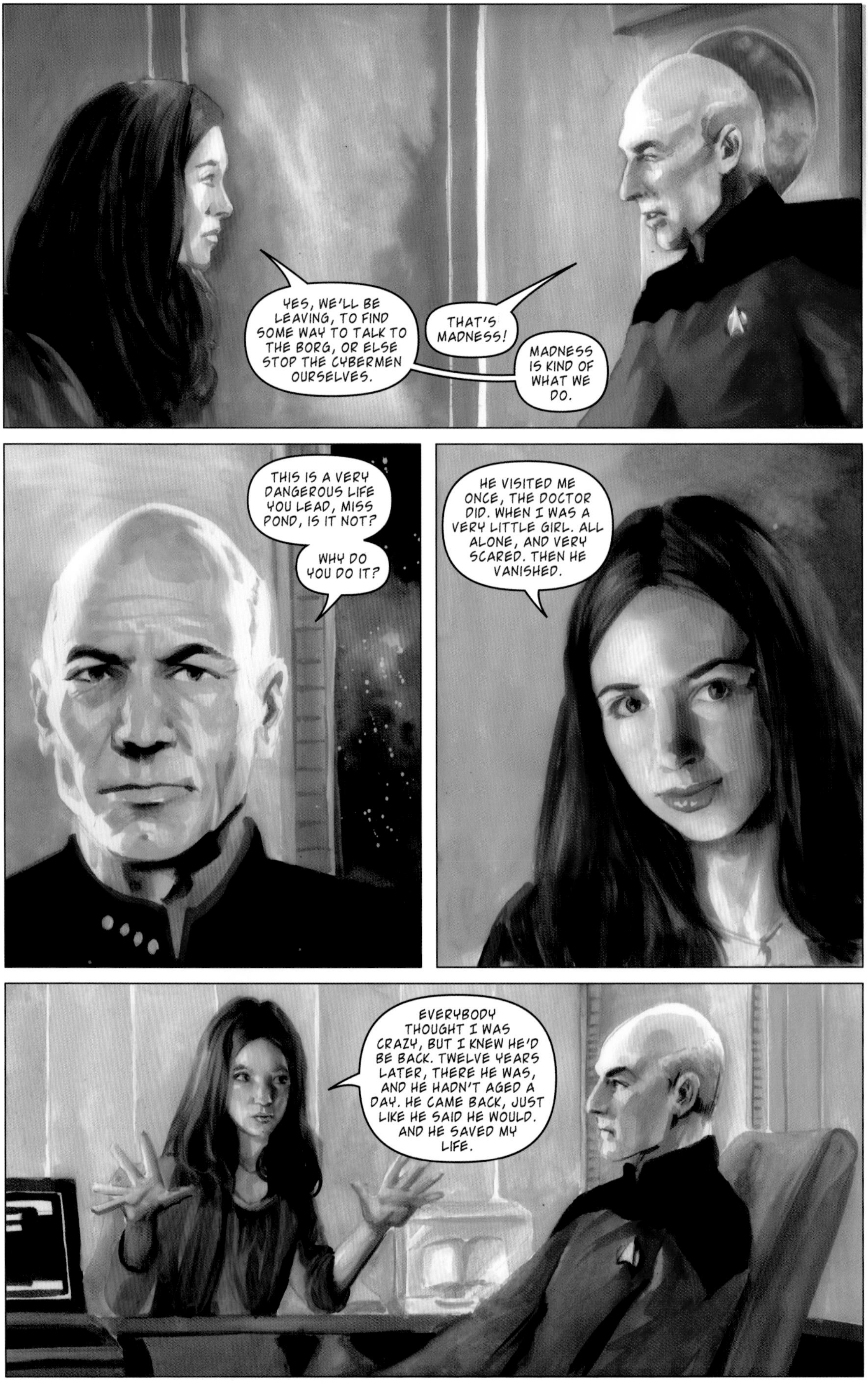
YES, WE'LL BE LEAVING, TO FIND SOME WAY TO TALK TO THE BORG, OR ELSE STOP THE CYBERMEN OURSELVES.
THAT'S MADNESS!
MADNESS IS KIND OF WHAT WE DO.
THIS IS A VERY DANGEROUS LIFE YOU LEAD, MISS POND, IS IT NOT?
WHY DO YOU DO IT?
HE VISITED ME ONCE, THE DOCTOR DID. WHEN I WAS A VERY LITTLE GIRL. ALL ALONE, AND VERY SCARED. THEN HE VANISHED.
EVERYBODY THOUGHT I WAS CRAZY, BUT I KNEW HE'D BE BACK. TWELVE YEARS LATER, THERE HE WAS, AND HE HADN'T AGED A DAY. HE CAME BACK, JUST LIKE HE SAID HE WOULD. AND HE SAVED MY LIFE.

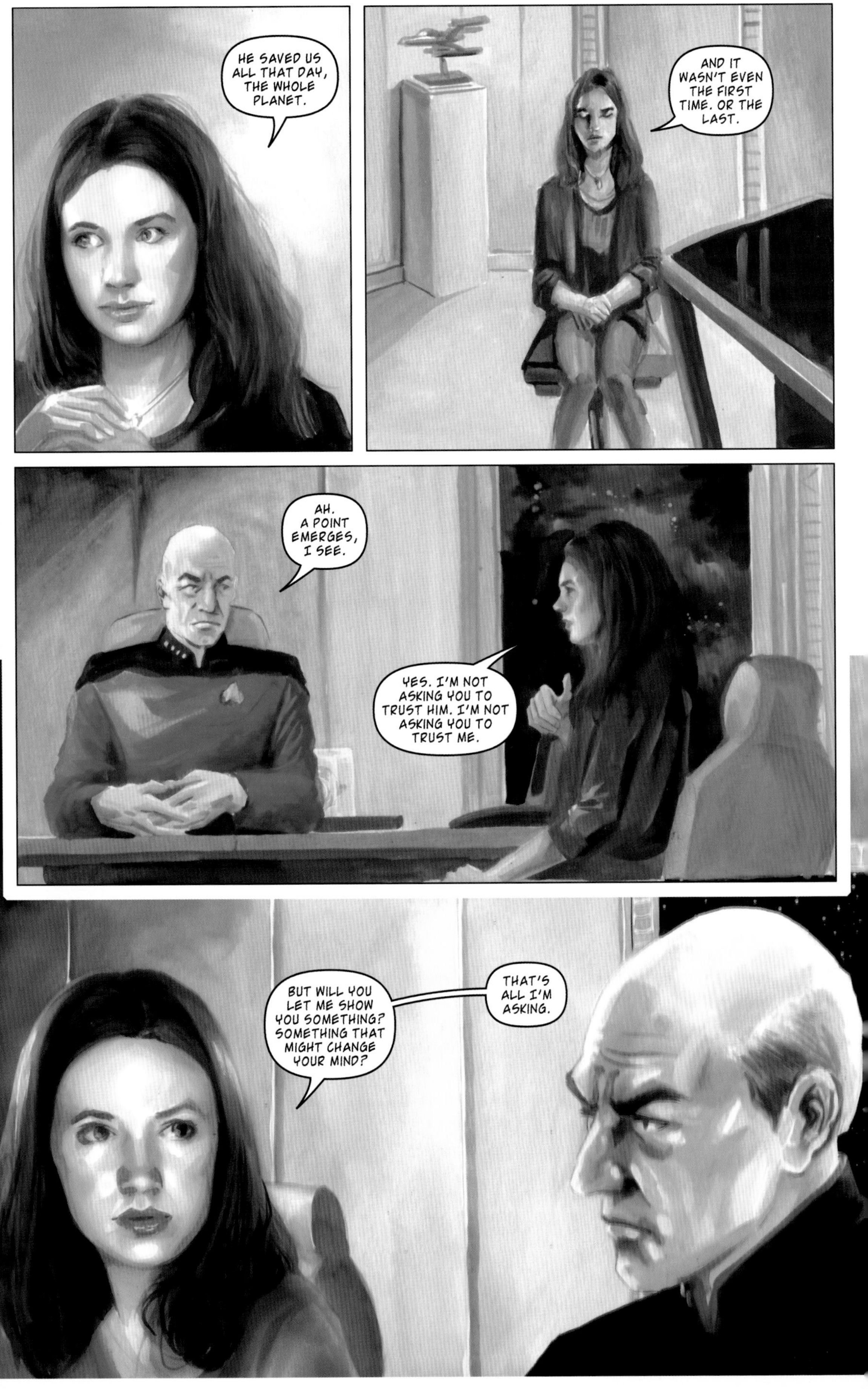
HE SAVED US ALL THAT DAY, THE WHOLE PLANET.
AND IT WASN'T EVEN THE FIRST TIME. OR THE LAST.
AH. A POINT EMERGES, I SEE.
YES. I'M NOT ASKING YOU TO TRUST HIM. I'M NOT ASKING YOU TO TRUST ME.
BUT WILL YOU LET ME SHOW YOU SOMETHING? SOMETHING THAT MIGHT CHANGE YOUR MIND?
THAT'S ALL I'M ASKING.

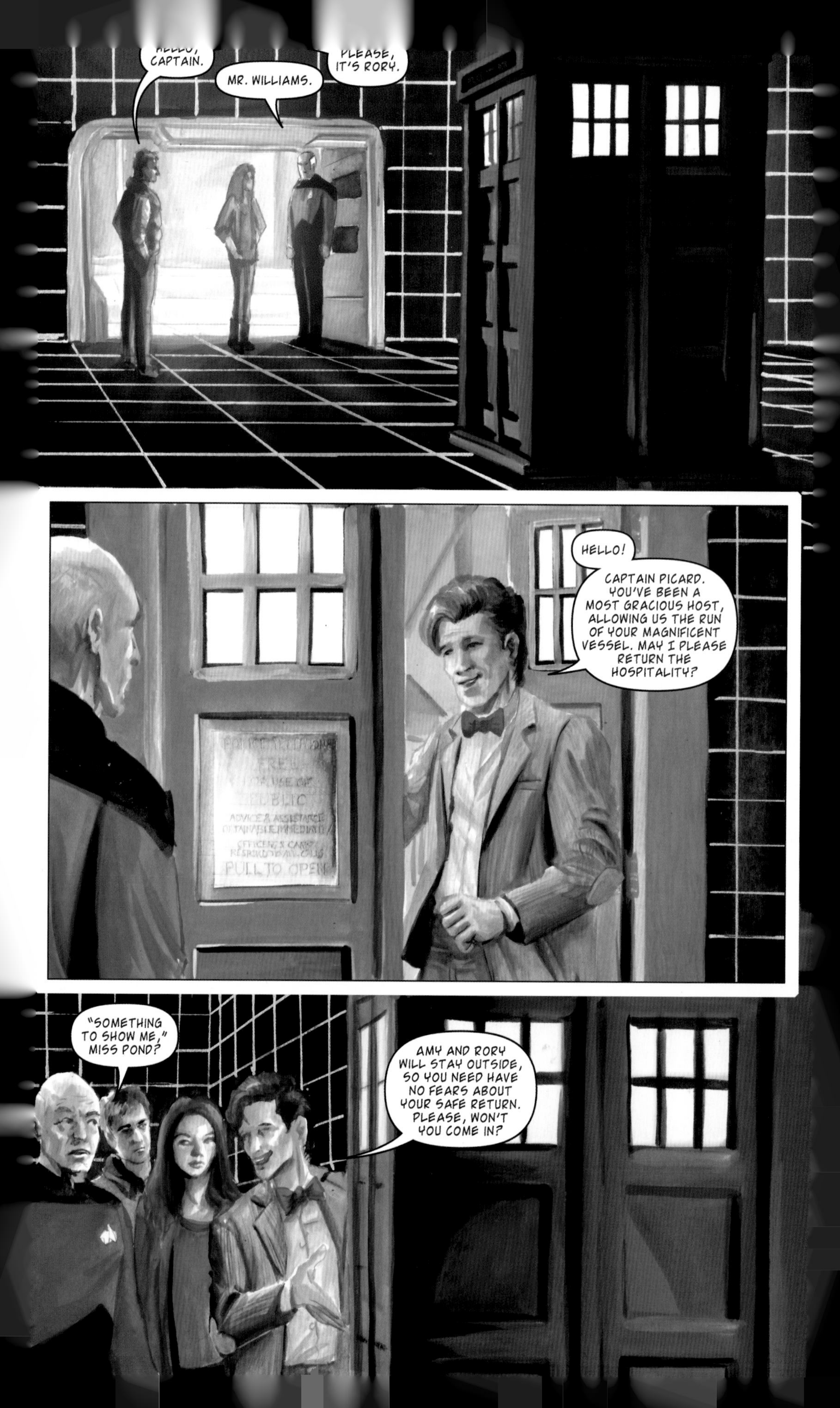

HELLO, CAPTAIN.
MR. WILLIAMS.
PLEASE, IT'S RORY.
HELLO!
CAPTAIN PICARD. YOU'VE BEEN A MOST GRACIOUS HOST, ALLOWING US THE RUN OF YOUR MAGNIFICENT VESSEL. MAY I PLEASE RETURN THE HOSPITALITY?
PULL TO OPEN
"SOMETHING TO SHOW ME," MISS POND?
AMY AND RORY WILL STAY OUTSIDE, SO YOU NEED HAVE NO FEARS ABOUT YOUR SAFE RETURN. PLEASE, WON'T YOU COME IN?

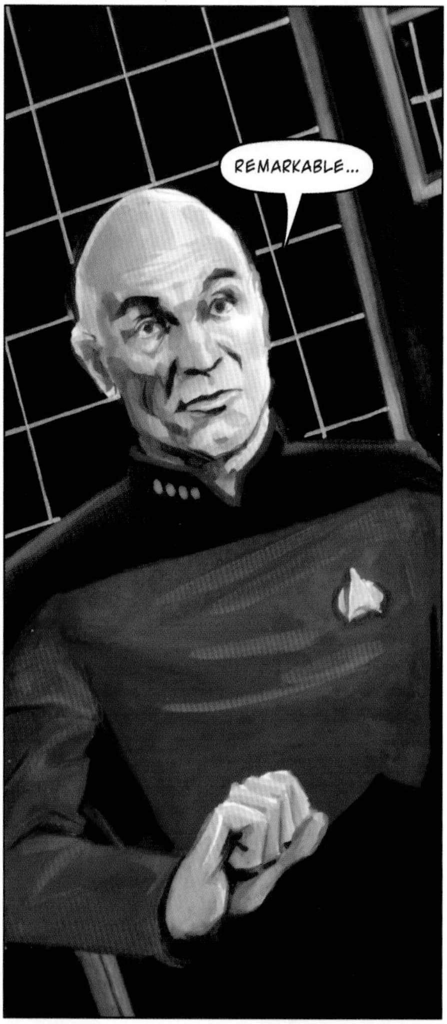
REMARKABLE...

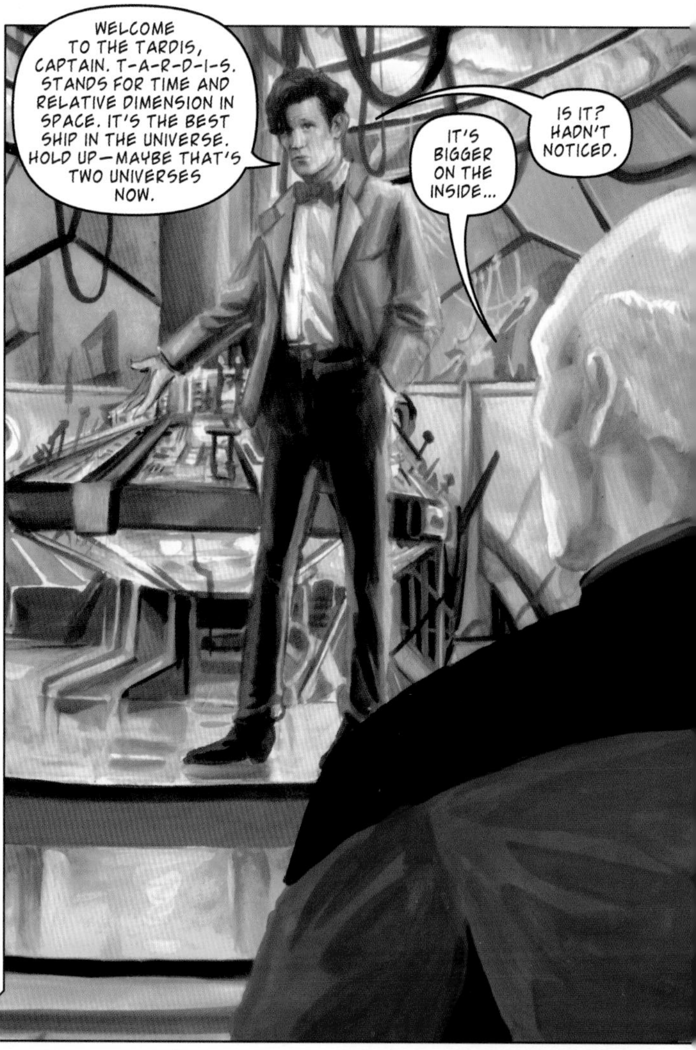
WELCOME TO THE TARDIS, CAPTAIN. T-A-R-D-I-S. STANDS FOR TIME AND RELATIVE DIMENSION IN SPACE. IT'S THE BEST SHIP IN THE UNIVERSE. HOLD UP—MAYBE THAT'S TWO UNIVERSES NOW.
IT'S BIGGER ON THE INSIDE...
IS IT? HADN'T NOTICED.

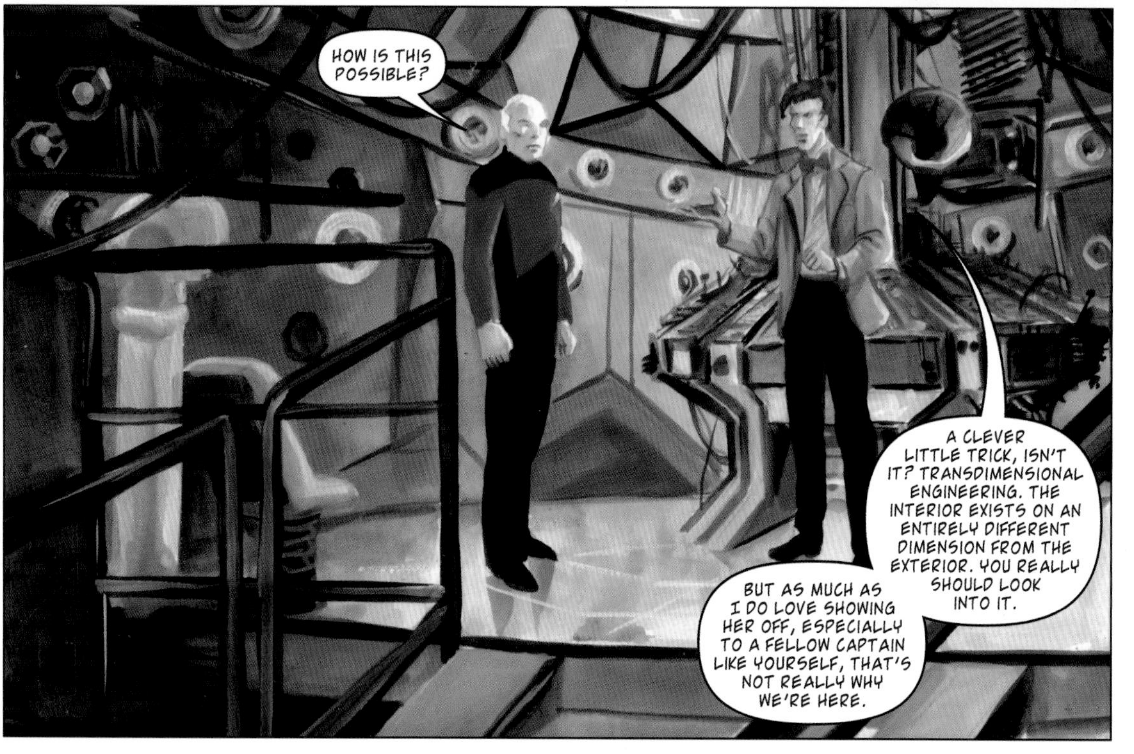
HOW IS THIS POSSIBLE?
A CLEVER LITTLE TRICK, ISN'T IT? TRANSDIMENSIONAL ENGINEERING. THE INTERIOR EXISTS ON AN ENTIRELY DIFFERENT DIMENSION FROM THE EXTERIOR. YOU REALLY SHOULD LOOK INTO IT.
BUT AS MUCH AS I DO LOVE SHOWING HER OFF, ESPECIALLY TO A FELLOW CAPTAIN LIKE YOURSELF, THAT'S NOT REALLY WHY WE'RE HERE.

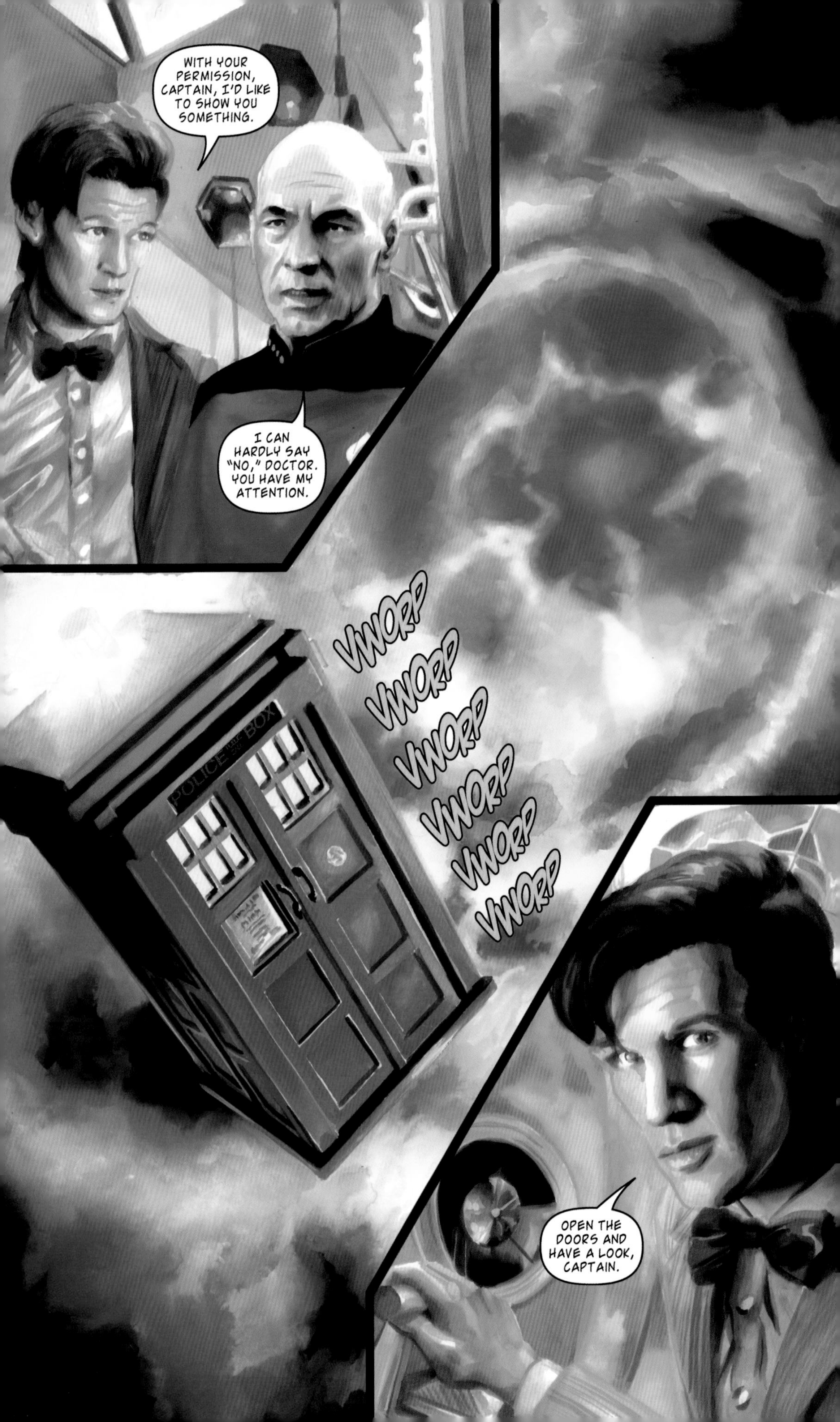
WITH YOUR PERMISSION, CAPTAIN, I'D LIKE TO SHOW YOU SOMETHING.
I CAN HARDLY SAY "NO," DOCTOR. YOU HAVE MY ATTENTION.
POLICE BOX
VWORP VWORP VWORP VWORP VWORP VWORP
OPEN THE DOORS AND HAVE A LOOK, CAPTAIN.

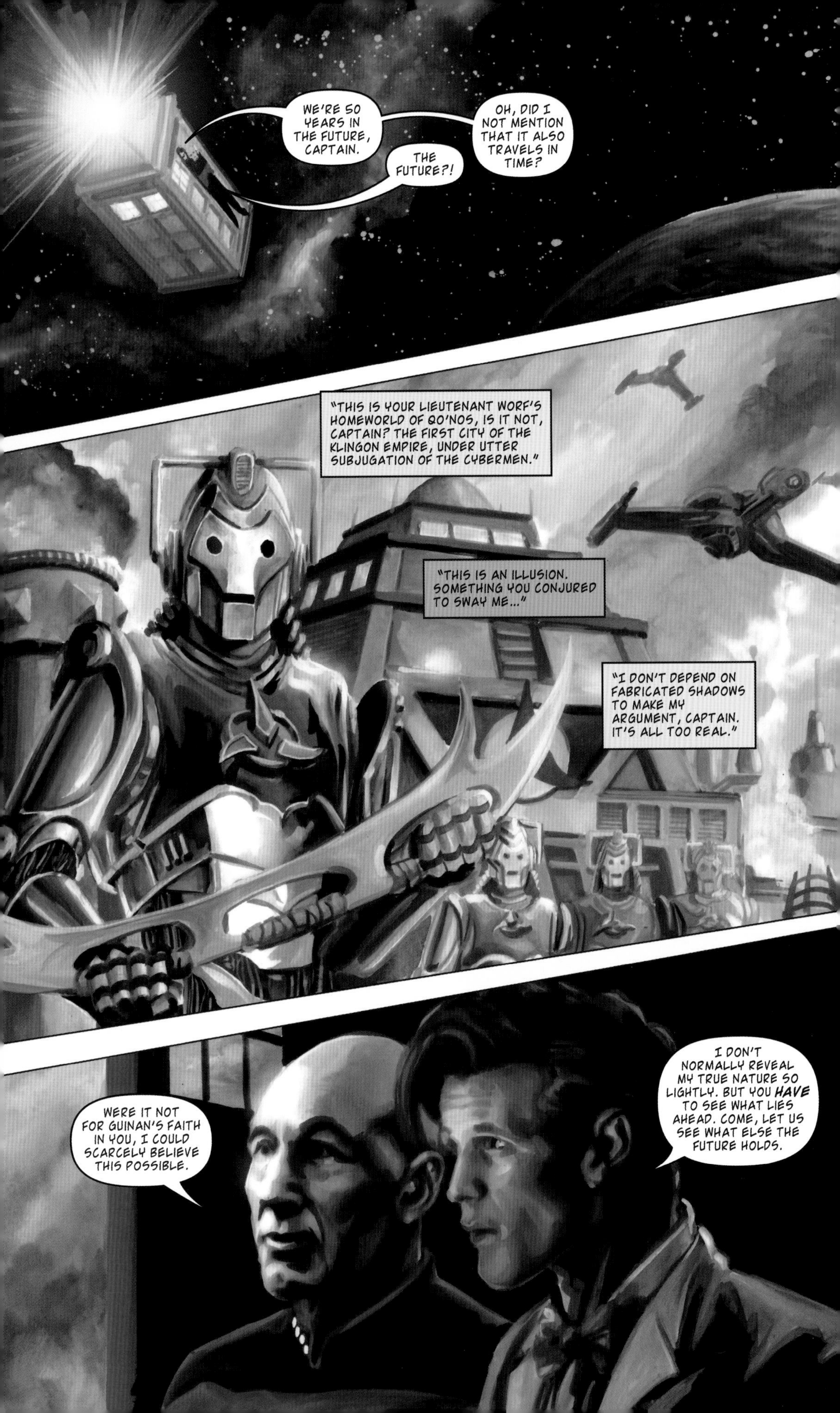
WE'RE 50 YEARS IN THE FUTURE, CAPTAIN.
THE FUTURE?!
OH, DID I NOT MENTION THAT IT ALSO TRAVELS IN TIME?
"THIS IS YOUR LIEUTENANT WORF'S HOMEWORLD OF QO'NOS, IS IT NOT, CAPTAIN? THE FIRST CITY OF THE KLINGON EMPIRE, UNDER UTTER SUBJUGATION OF THE CYBERMEN."
"THIS IS AN ILLUSION. SOMETHING YOU CONJURED TO SWAY ME..."
"I DON'T DEPEND ON FABRICATED SHADOWS TO MAKE MY ARGUMENT, CAPTAIN. IT'S ALL TOO REAL."
WERE IT NOT FOR GUINAN'S FAITH IN YOU, I COULD SCARCELY BELIEVE THIS POSSIBLE.
I DON'T NORMALLY REVEAL MY TRUE NATURE SO LIGHTLY. BUT YOU HAVE TO SEE WHAT LIES AHEAD. COME, LET US SEE WHAT ELSE THE FUTURE HOLDS.

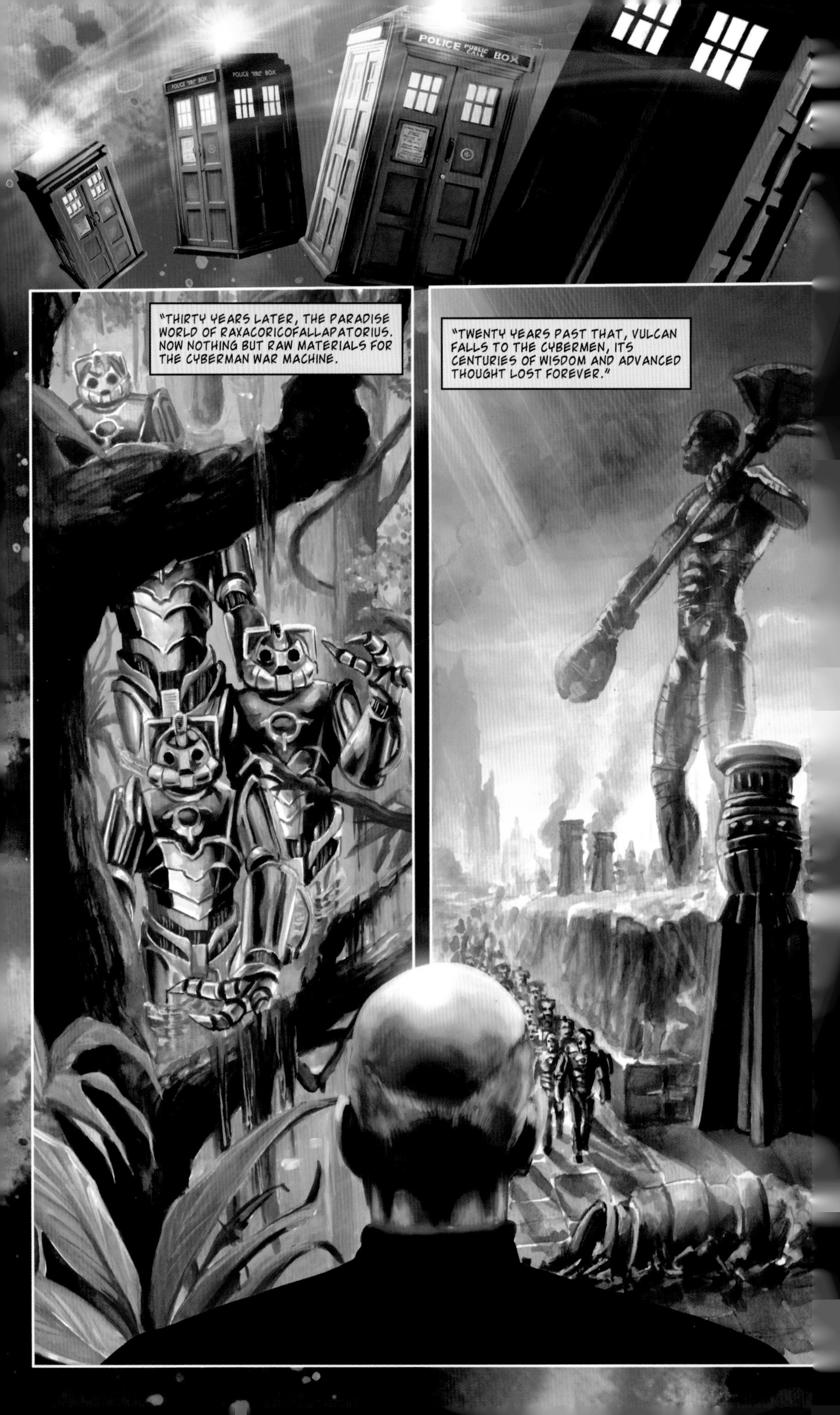
POLICE PUBLIC CALL BOX
"THIRTY YEARS LATER, THE PARADISE WORLD OF RAXACORICOFALLAPATORIUS. NOW NOTHING BUT RAW MATERIALS FOR THE CYBERMAN WAR MACHINE.
"TWENTY YEARS PAST THAT, VULCAN FALLS TO THE CYBERMEN, ITS CENTURIES OF WISDOM AND ADVANCED THOUGHT LOST FOREVER."

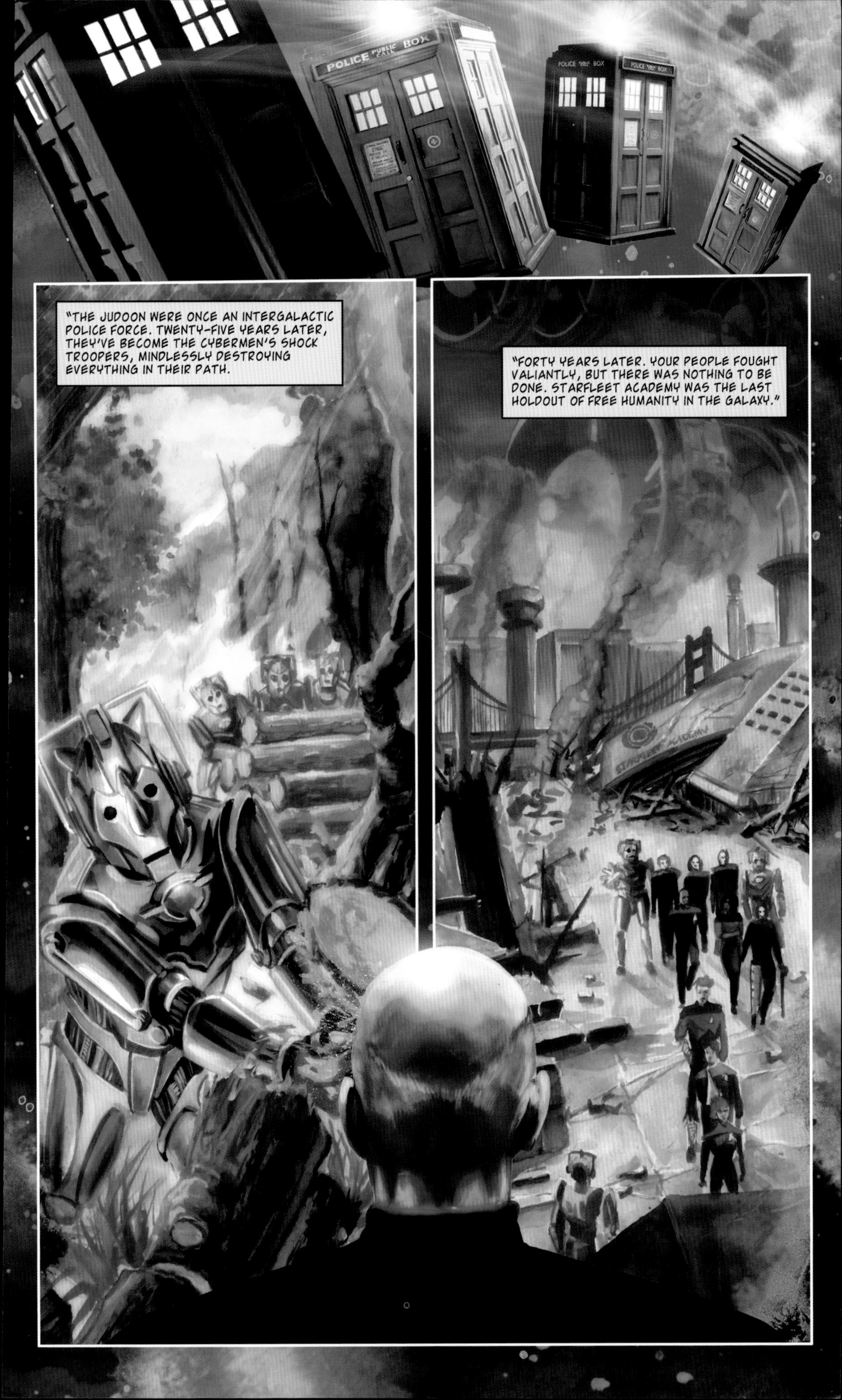
POLICE PUBLIC CALL BOX
"THE JUDOON WERE ONCE AN INTERGALACTIC POLICE FORCE. TWENTY-FIVE YEARS LATER, THEY'VE BECOME THE CYBERMEN'S SHOCK TROOPERS, MINDLESSLY DESTROYING EVERYTHING IN THEIR PATH.
"FORTY YEARS LATER. YOUR PEOPLE FOUGHT VALIANTLY, BUT THERE WAS NOTHING TO BE DONE. STARFLEET ACADEMY WAS THE LAST HOLDOUT OF FREE HUMANITY IN THE GALAXY."

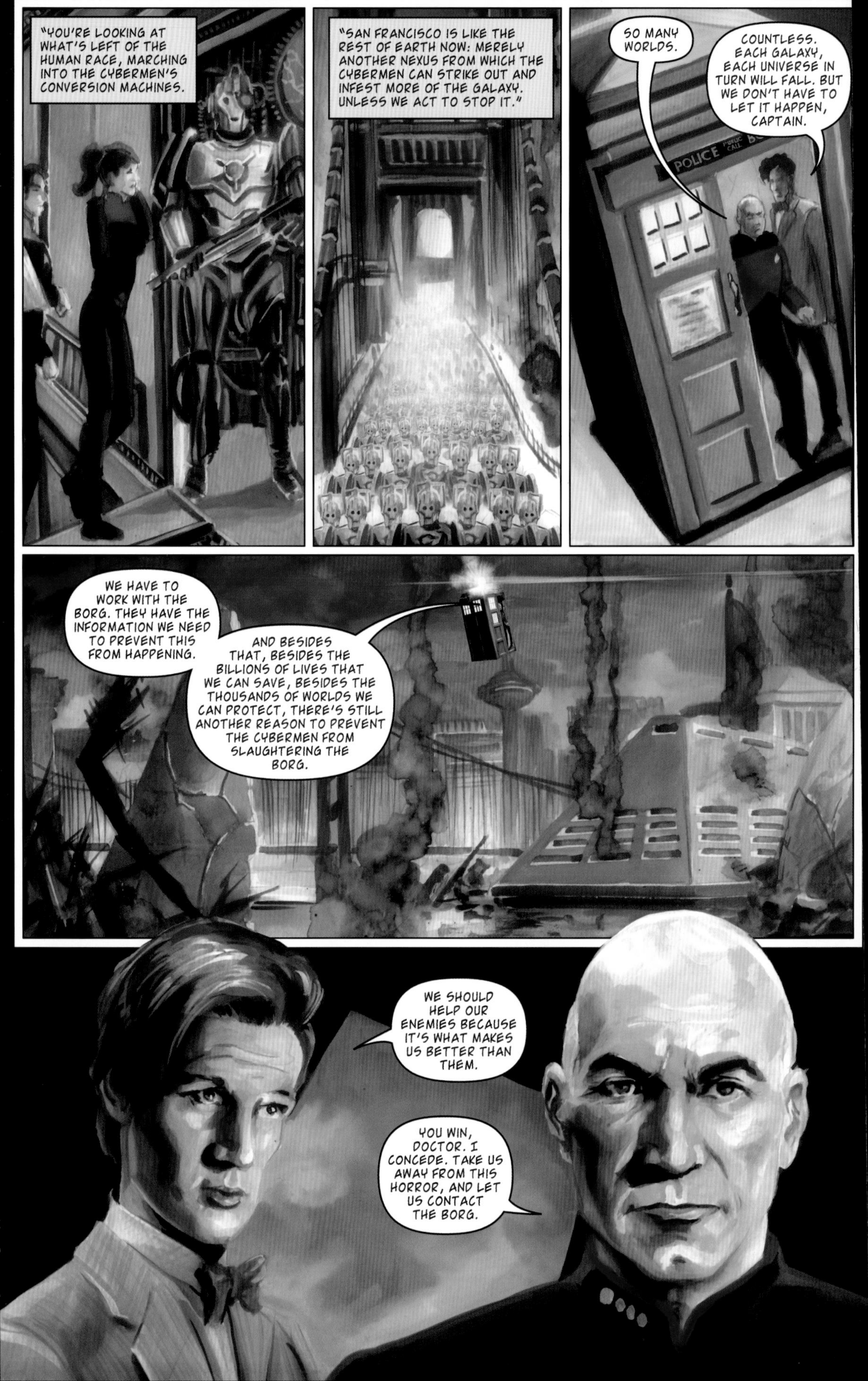
"YOU'RE LOOKING AT WHAT'S LEFT OF THE HUMAN RACE, MARCHING INTO THE CYBERMEN'S CONVERSION MACHINES.
"SAN FRANCISCO IS LIKE THE REST OF EARTH NOW: MERELY ANOTHER NEXUS FROM WHICH THE CYBERMEN CAN STRIKE OUT AND INFEST MORE OF THE GALAXY. UNLESS WE ACT TO STOP IT."
SO MANY WORLDS.
COUNTLESS. EACH GALAXY, EACH UNIVERSE IN TURN WILL FALL. BUT WE DON'T HAVE TO LET IT HAPPEN, CAPTAIN.
POLICE
WE HAVE TO WORK WITH THE BORG. THEY HAVE THE INFORMATION WE NEED TO PREVENT THIS FROM HAPPENING.
AND BESIDES THAT, BESIDES THE BILLIONS OF LIVES THAT WE CAN SAVE, BESIDES THE THOUSANDS OF WORLDS WE CAN PROTECT, THERE'S STILL ANOTHER REASON TO PREVENT THE CYBERMEN FROM SLAUGHTERING THE BORG.
WE SHOULD HELP OUR ENEMIES BECAUSE IT'S WHAT MAKES US BETTER THAN THEM.
YOU WIN, DOCTOR. I CONCEDE. TAKE US AWAY FROM THIS HORROR, AND LET US CONTACT THE BORG.

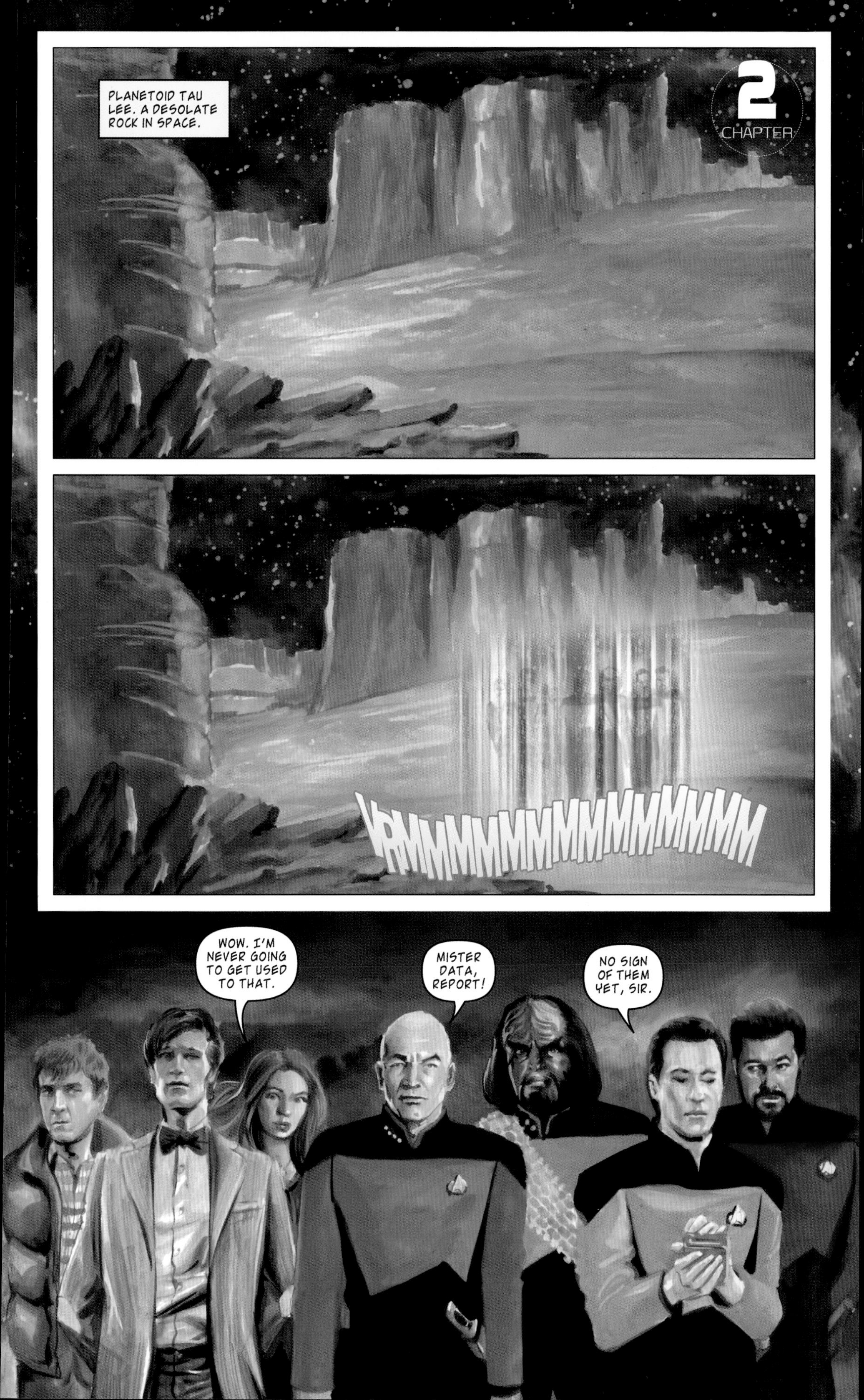
2
CHAPTER
PLANETOID TAU LEE. A DESOLATE ROCK IN SPACE.
VRMMMMMMMMMMMMMMM
WOW. I'M NEVER GOING TO GET USED TO THAT.
MISTER DATA, REPORT!
NO SIGN OF THEM YET, SIR.

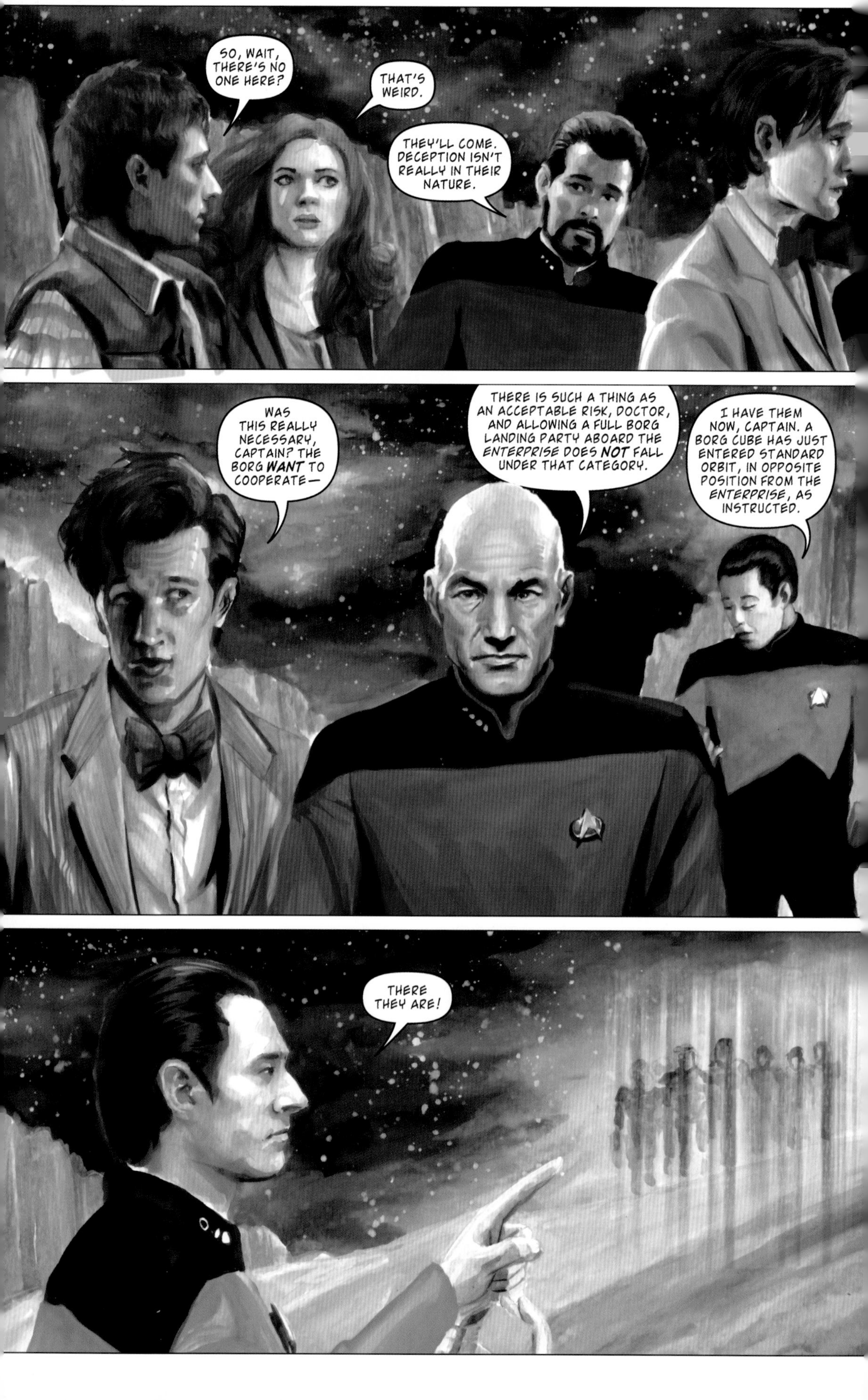
SO, WAIT, THERE'S NO ONE HERE?
THAT'S WEIRD.
THEY'LL COME. DECEPTION ISN'T REALLY IN THEIR NATURE.
WAS THIS REALLY NECESSARY, CAPTAIN? THE BORG WANT TO COOPERATE—
THERE IS SUCH A THING AS AN ACCEPTABLE RISK, DOCTOR, AND ALLOWING A FULL BORG LANDING PARTY ABOARD THE ENTERPRISE DOES NOT FALL UNDER THAT CATEGORY.
I HAVE THEM NOW, CAPTAIN. A BORG CUBE HAS JUST ENTERED STANDARD ORBIT, IN OPPOSITE POSITION FROM THE ENTERPRISE, AS INSTRUCTED.
THERE THEY ARE!

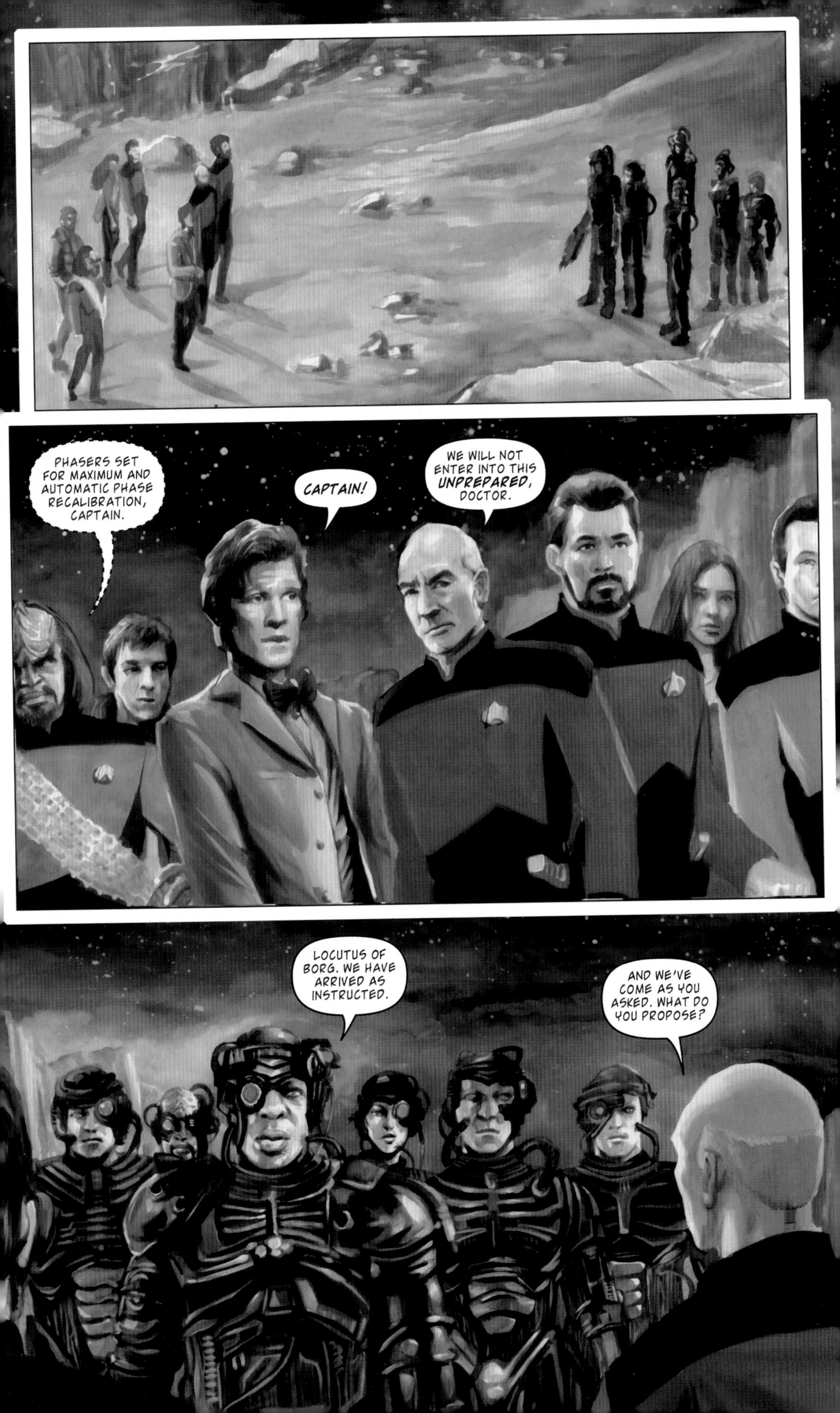
PHASERS SET FOR MAXIMUM AND AUTOMATIC PHASE RECALIBRATION, CAPTAIN.
CAPTAIN!
WE WILL NOT ENTER INTO THIS UNPREPARED, DOCTOR.
LOCUTUS OF BORG. WE HAVE ARRIVED AS INSTRUCTED.
AND WE'VE COME AS YOU ASKED. WHAT DO YOU PROPOSE?

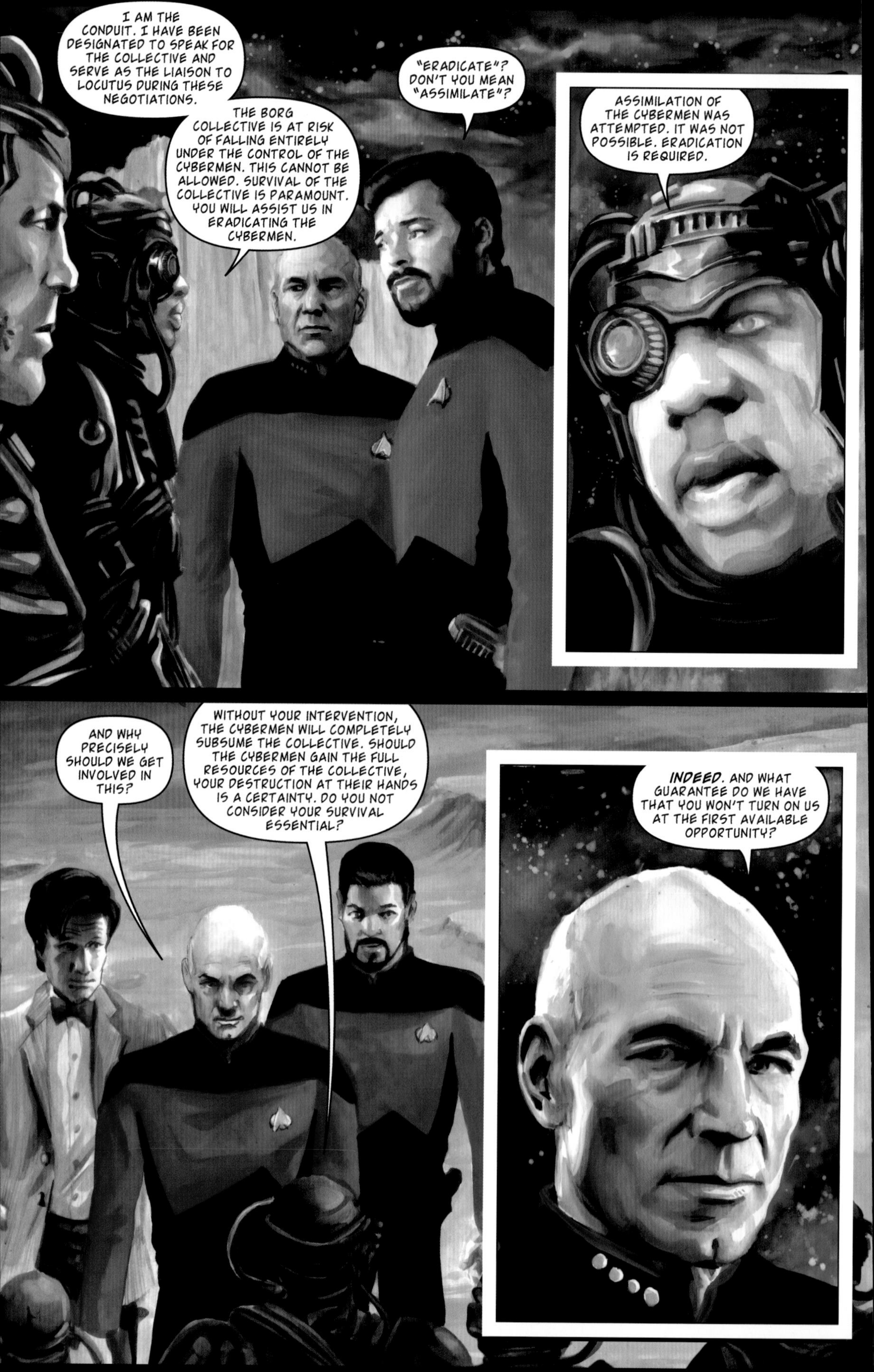
I AM THE CONDUIT. I HAVE BEEN DESIGNATED TO SPEAK FOR THE COLLECTIVE AND SERVE AS THE LIAISON TO LOCUTUS DURING THESE NEGOTIATIONS.
THE BORG COLLECTIVE IS AT RISK OF FALLING ENTIRELY UNDER THE CONTROL OF THE CYBERMEN. THIS CANNOT BE ALLOWED. SURVIVAL OF THE COLLECTIVE IS PARAMOUNT. YOU WILL ASSIST US IN ERADICATING THE CYBERMEN.
"ERADICATE"? DON'T YOU MEAN "ASSIMILATE"?
ASSIMILATION OF THE CYBERMEN WAS ATTEMPTED. IT WAS NOT POSSIBLE. ERADICATION IS REQUIRED.
AND WHY PRECISELY SHOULD WE GET INVOLVED IN THIS?
WITHOUT YOUR INTERVENTION, THE CYBERMEN WILL COMPLETELY SUBSUME THE COLLECTIVE. SHOULD THE CYBERMEN GAIN THE FULL RESOURCES OF THE COLLECTIVE, YOUR DESTRUCTION AT THEIR HANDS IS A CERTAINTY. DO YOU NOT CONSIDER YOUR SURVIVAL ESSENTIAL?
INDEED. AND WHAT GUARANTEE DO WE HAVE THAT YOU WON'T TURN ON US AT THE FIRST AVAILABLE OPPORTUNITY?

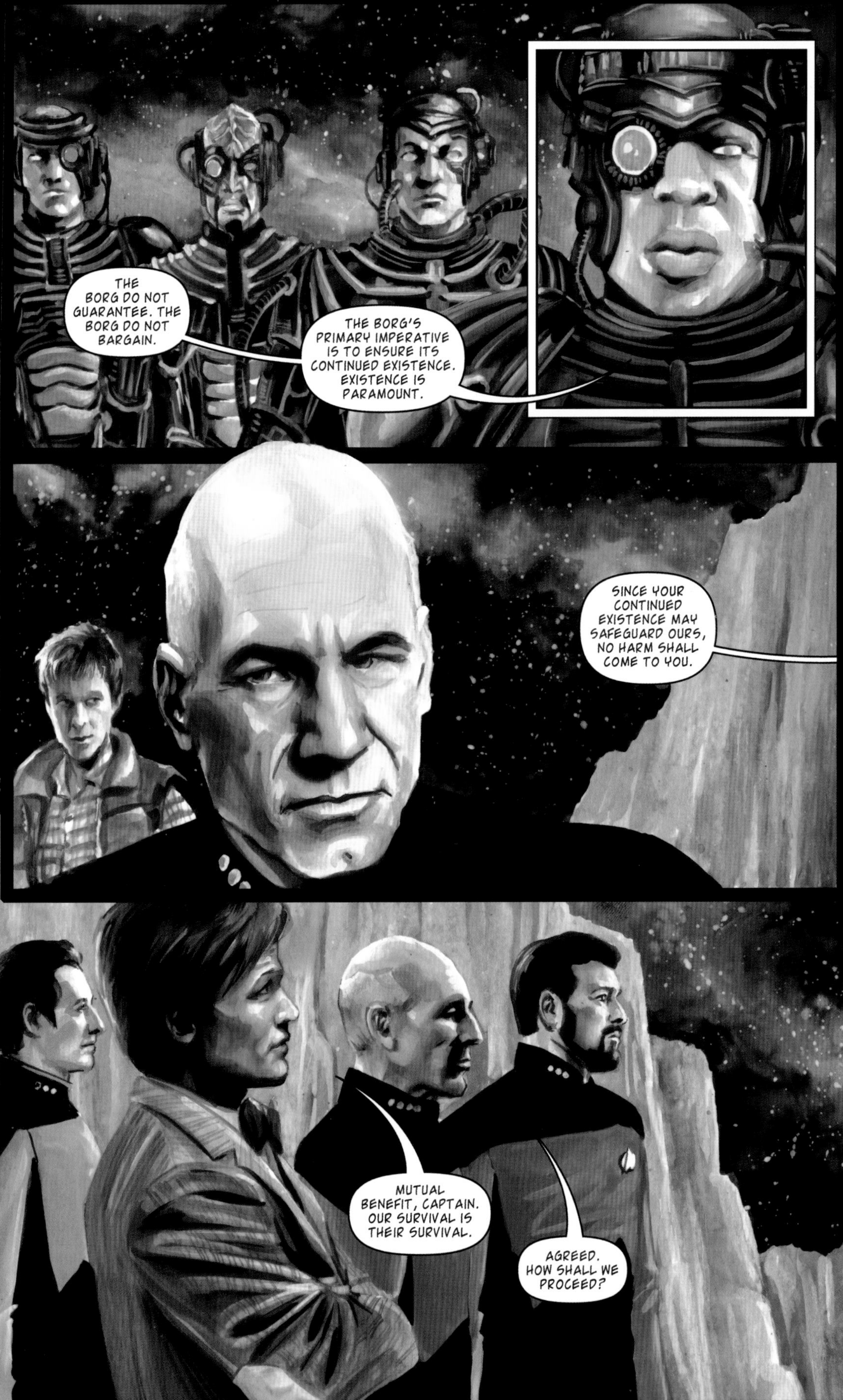

THE BORG DO NOT GUARANTEE. THE BORG DO NOT BARGAIN.
THE BORG'S PRIMARY IMPERATIVE IS TO ENSURE ITS CONTINUED EXISTENCE. EXISTENCE IS PARAMOUNT.
SINCE YOUR CONTINUED EXISTENCE MAY SAFEGUARD OURS, NO HARM SHALL COME TO YOU.
MUTUAL BENEFIT, CAPTAIN. OUR SURVIVAL IS THEIR SURVIVAL.
AGREED. HOW SHALL WE PROCEED?

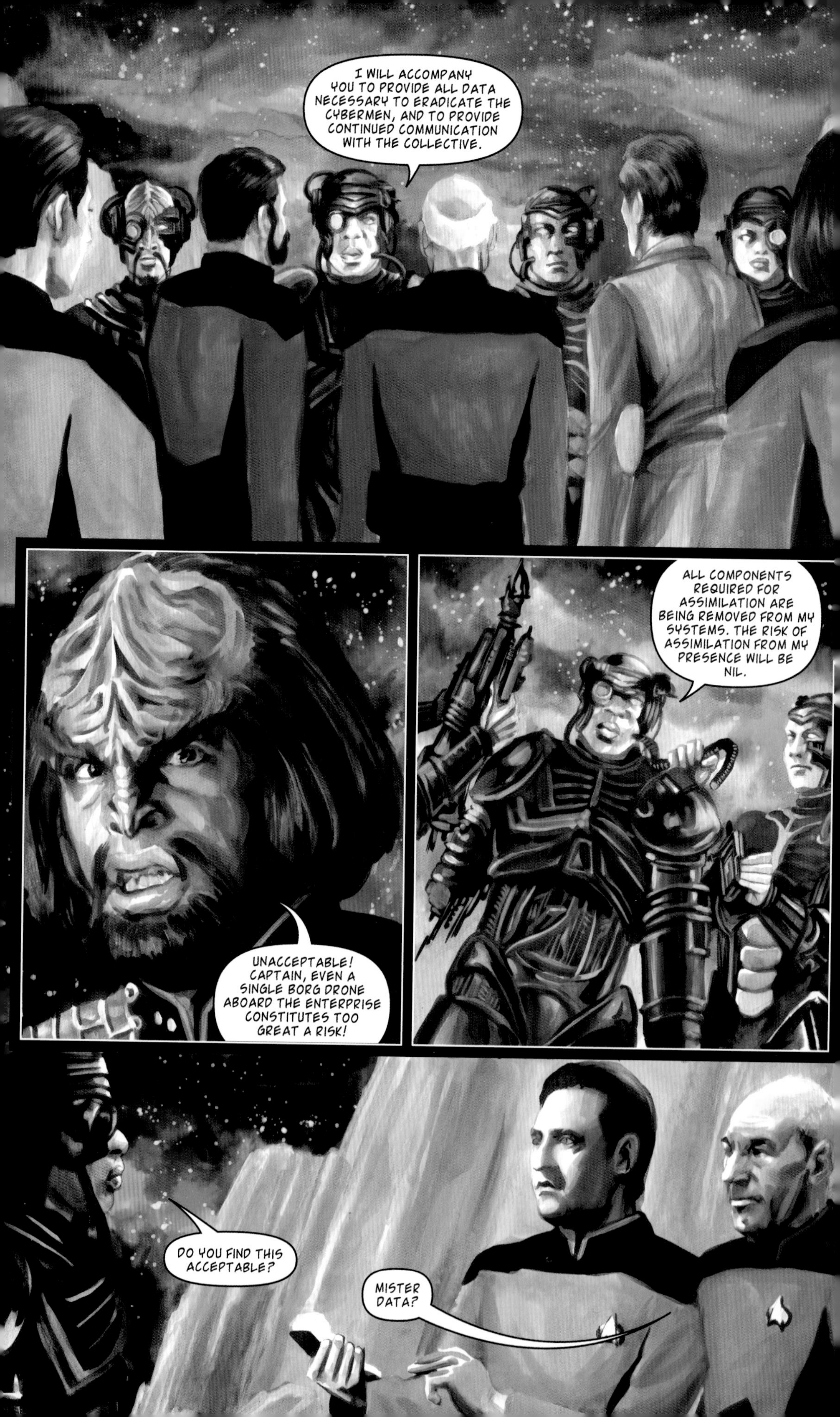
I WILL ACCOMPANY YOU TO PROVIDE ALL DATA NECESSARY TO ERADICATE THE CYBERMEN, AND TO PROVIDE CONTINUED COMMUNICATION WITH THE COLLECTIVE.
UNACCEPTABLE! CAPTAIN, EVEN A SINGLE BORG DRONE ABOARD THE ENTERPRISE CONSTITUTES TOO GREAT A RISK!
ALL COMPONENTS REQUIRED FOR ASSIMILATION ARE BEING REMOVED FROM MY SYSTEMS. THE RISK OF ASSIMILATION FROM MY PRESENCE WILL BE NIL.
DO YOU FIND THIS ACCEPTABLE?
MISTER DATA?

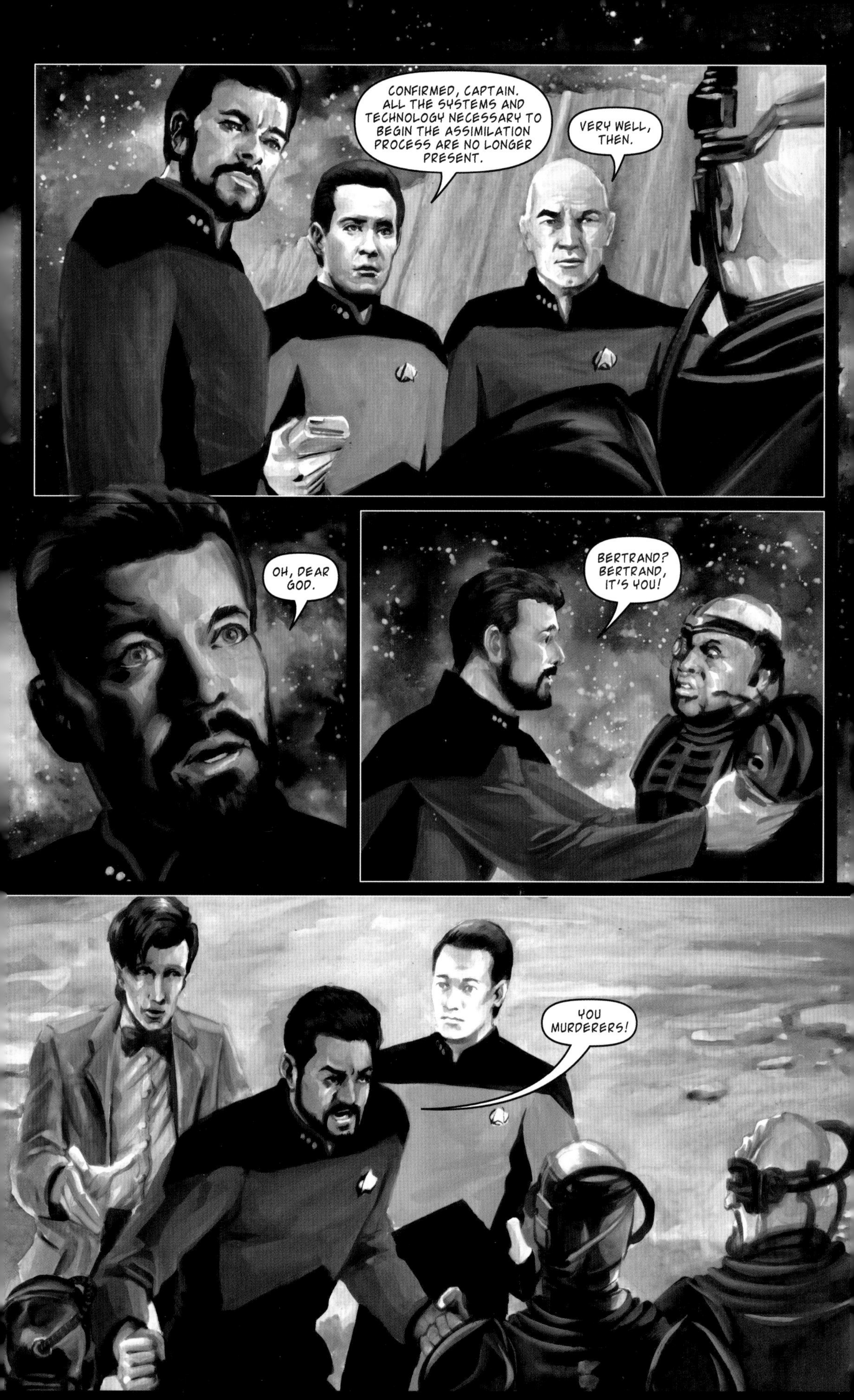
CONFIRMED, CAPTAIN. ALL THE SYSTEMS AND TECHNOLOGY NECESSARY TO BEGIN THE ASSIMILATION PROCESS ARE NO LONGER PRESENT.
VERY WELL, THEN.
OH, DEAR GOD.
BERTRAND? BERTRAND, IT'S YOU!
YOU MURDERERS!

IT'S MARCUS BERTRAND, CAPTAIN OF THE *POTEMKIN!* THAT MAN WAS MY FRIEND! YOU HAD TO RUB OUR NOSES IN IT, DIDN'T YOU?

COME, COMMANDER. THIS WON'T SOLVE ANYTHING.

BERTRAND WAS ASSIMILATED WHEN HIS SHIP WAS TAKEN AT DELTA IV. IT WAS BELIEVED THAT UTILIZING ONE YOU WERE FAMILIAR WITH WOULD MORE EASILY FACILITATE OUR PARTNERSHIP. ARE YOU READY TO DEPART?

YES. LET US.

PICARD TO ENTERPRISE. EIGHT TO BEAM UP.

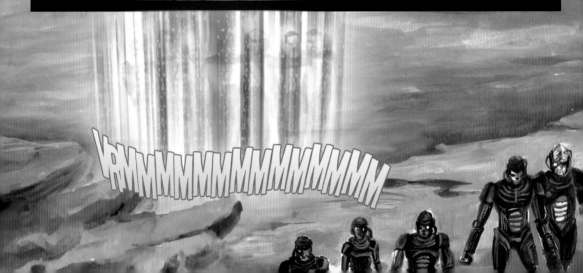

VRMMMMMMMMMMMMMM

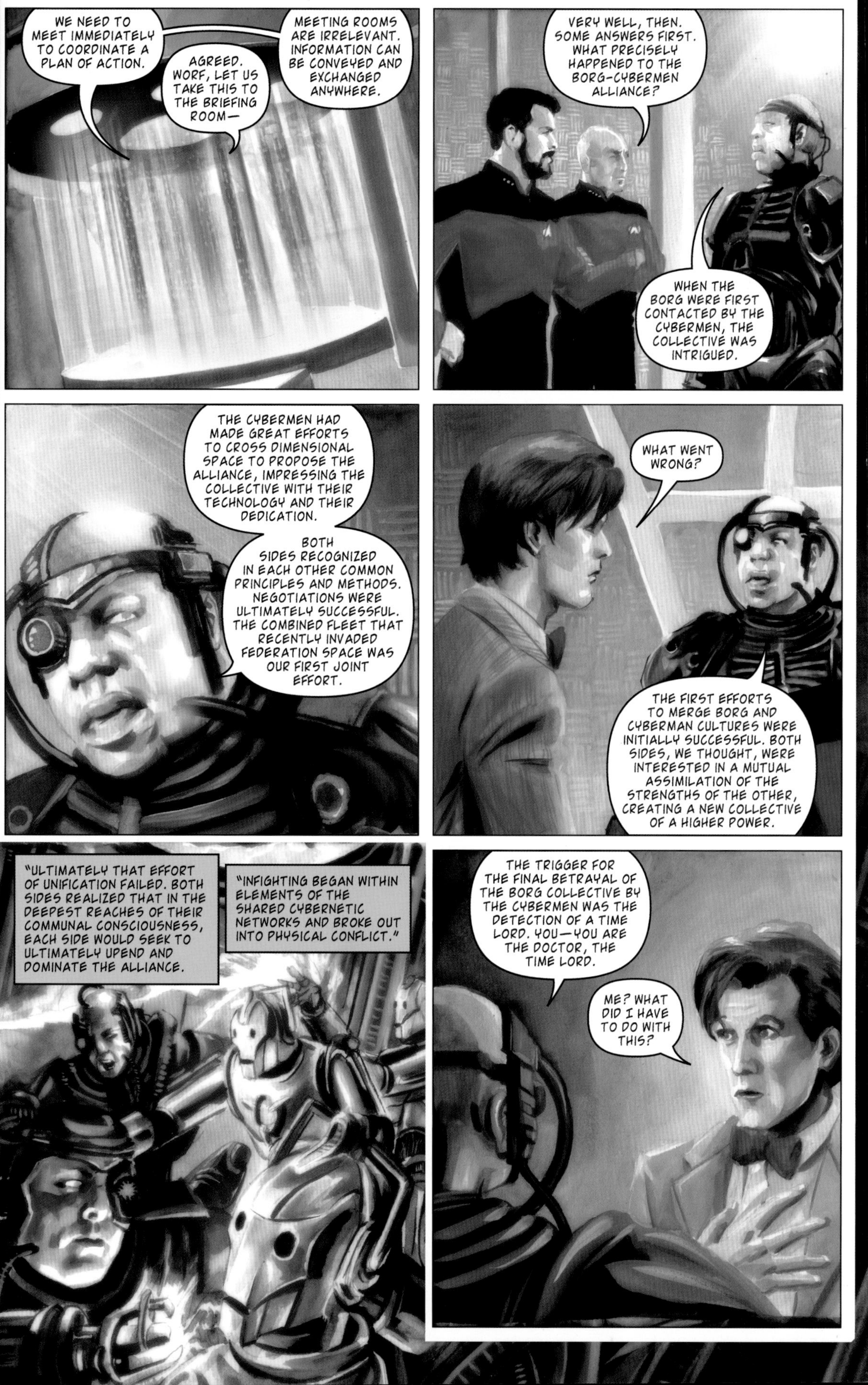
WE NEED TO MEET IMMEDIATELY TO COORDINATE A PLAN OF ACTION.
AGREED. WORF, LET US TAKE THIS TO THE BRIEFING ROOM—
MEETING ROOMS ARE IRRELEVANT. INFORMATION CAN BE CONVEYED AND EXCHANGED ANYWHERE.
VERY WELL, THEN. SOME ANSWERS FIRST. WHAT PRECISELY HAPPENED TO THE BORG-CYBERMEN ALLIANCE?
WHEN THE BORG WERE FIRST CONTACTED BY THE CYBERMEN, THE COLLECTIVE WAS INTRIGUED.
THE CYBERMEN HAD MADE GREAT EFFORTS TO CROSS DIMENSIONAL SPACE TO PROPOSE THE ALLIANCE, IMPRESSING THE COLLECTIVE WITH THEIR TECHNOLOGY AND THEIR DEDICATION.
BOTH SIDES RECOGNIZED IN EACH OTHER COMMON PRINCIPLES AND METHODS. NEGOTIATIONS WERE ULTIMATELY SUCCESSFUL. THE COMBINED FLEET THAT RECENTLY INVADED FEDERATION SPACE WAS OUR FIRST JOINT EFFORT.
WHAT WENT WRONG?
THE FIRST EFFORTS TO MERGE BORG AND CYBERMAN CULTURES WERE INITIALLY SUCCESSFUL. BOTH SIDES, WE THOUGHT, WERE INTERESTED IN A MUTUAL ASSIMILATION OF THE STRENGTHS OF THE OTHER, CREATING A NEW COLLECTIVE OF A HIGHER POWER.
"ULTIMATELY THAT EFFORT OF UNIFICATION FAILED. BOTH SIDES REALIZED THAT IN THE DEEPEST REACHES OF THEIR COMMUNAL CONSCIOUSNESS, EACH SIDE WOULD SEEK TO ULTIMATELY UPEND AND DOMINATE THE ALLIANCE.
"INFIGHTING BEGAN WITHIN ELEMENTS OF THE SHARED CYBERNETIC NETWORKS AND BROKE OUT INTO PHYSICAL CONFLICT."
THE TRIGGER FOR THE FINAL BETRAYAL OF THE BORG COLLECTIVE BY THE CYBERMEN WAS THE DETECTION OF A TIME LORD. YOU—YOU ARE THE DOCTOR, THE TIME LORD.
ME? WHAT DID I HAVE TO DO WITH THIS?

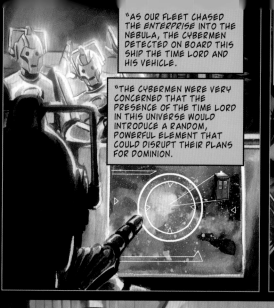

"AS OUR FLEET CHASED THE ENTERPRISE INTO THE NEBULA, THE CYBERMEN DETECTED ON BOARD THIS SHIP THE TIME LORD AND HIS VEHICLE.

"THE CYBERMEN WERE VERY CONCERNED THAT THE PRESENCE OF THE TIME LORD IN THIS UNIVERSE WOULD INTRODUCE A RANDOM, POWERFUL ELEMENT THAT COULD DISRUPT THEIR PLANS FOR DOMINION.

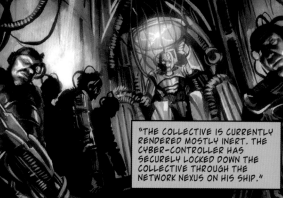

"JUST AS TENSIONS WITHIN THE ALLIANCE WERE REACHING A CLIMAX, THE CYBERMEN FOUND A WEAKNESS IN THE BORG COLLECTIVE. THE CYBERMEN THEN GAINED ACCESS TO AND OVERWROTE THE EXECUTIVE LIBRARY ROUTINES IN THE COLLECTIVE'S CORE MEMORY. AS A RESULT, THE BORG HAVE BEEN STRIPPED OF MOST HIGHER FUNCTIONS AND ALL DECISION-MAKING FUNCTIONALITY.

"THE COLLECTIVE IS CURRENTLY RENDERED MOSTLY INERT. THE CYBER-CONTROLLER HAS SECURELY LOCKED DOWN THE COLLECTIVE THROUGH THE NETWORK NEXUS ON HIS SHIP."

HOW *DEVIOUS.* JUST LIKE THE CYBERMEN TO DO SOMETHING LIKE THAT.

NOW THE CYBERMEN RACE TOWARD THE BORG HOMEWORLD TO PERMANENTLY CONVERT THE COLLECTIVE TO THEIR WILL. FROM THE HOMEWORLD, THE CYBER-CONTROLLER WILL BE ABLE TO COMPLETELY FINALIZE THE CONVERSION OF THE RESOURCES, NETWORKS, AND DRONE POPULATION OF THE ENTIRE COLLECTIVE.

THE BORG WILL CEASE TO EXIST, AND THE CYBERMEN WILL BE TRIUMPHANT.

THE CYBERMEN WERE CONVINCED THAT IF THEY CAN COMPLETE THIS TASK BEFORE THE TIME LORD REALIZES WHAT THEY HAVE IN MIND, THERE WILL BE NO STOPPING THEM.

THEY MAY WELL BE RIGHT ABOUT THAT. THEY'VE MASKED THEIR STEPS SO WELL THAT I HAVE BEEN ALL ALONG A STEP BEHIND THEM.

AND THE CYBERMEN WITH THE FULL RESOURCES OF THE BORG COLLECTIVE MAY WELL BE INSURMOUNTABLE.

A QUESTION, CONDUIT. HOW ARE YOU YOURSELF FUNCTIONING WITHOUT THOSE EXECUTIVE ROUTINES?

I OPERATE AS THE CONDUIT ONLY AS A FINAL DESPERATE EFFORT ON THE PART OF A SPLINTER GROUP FROM THE COLLECTIVE, UNDETECTED BY THE CYBERMEN, TO PIECE TOGETHER AND ROUTE SOME SPARE DECISION-MAKING AND INITIATIVE ROUTINES FROM NON-ESSENTIAL PARTS OF THE COLLECTIVE'S NETWORK.

THESE RESOURCES ARE DWINDLING, HOWEVER, AND MY TIME REMAINING FOR INDEPENDENT ACTION AND INITIATIVE IS CERTAINLY LIMITED.

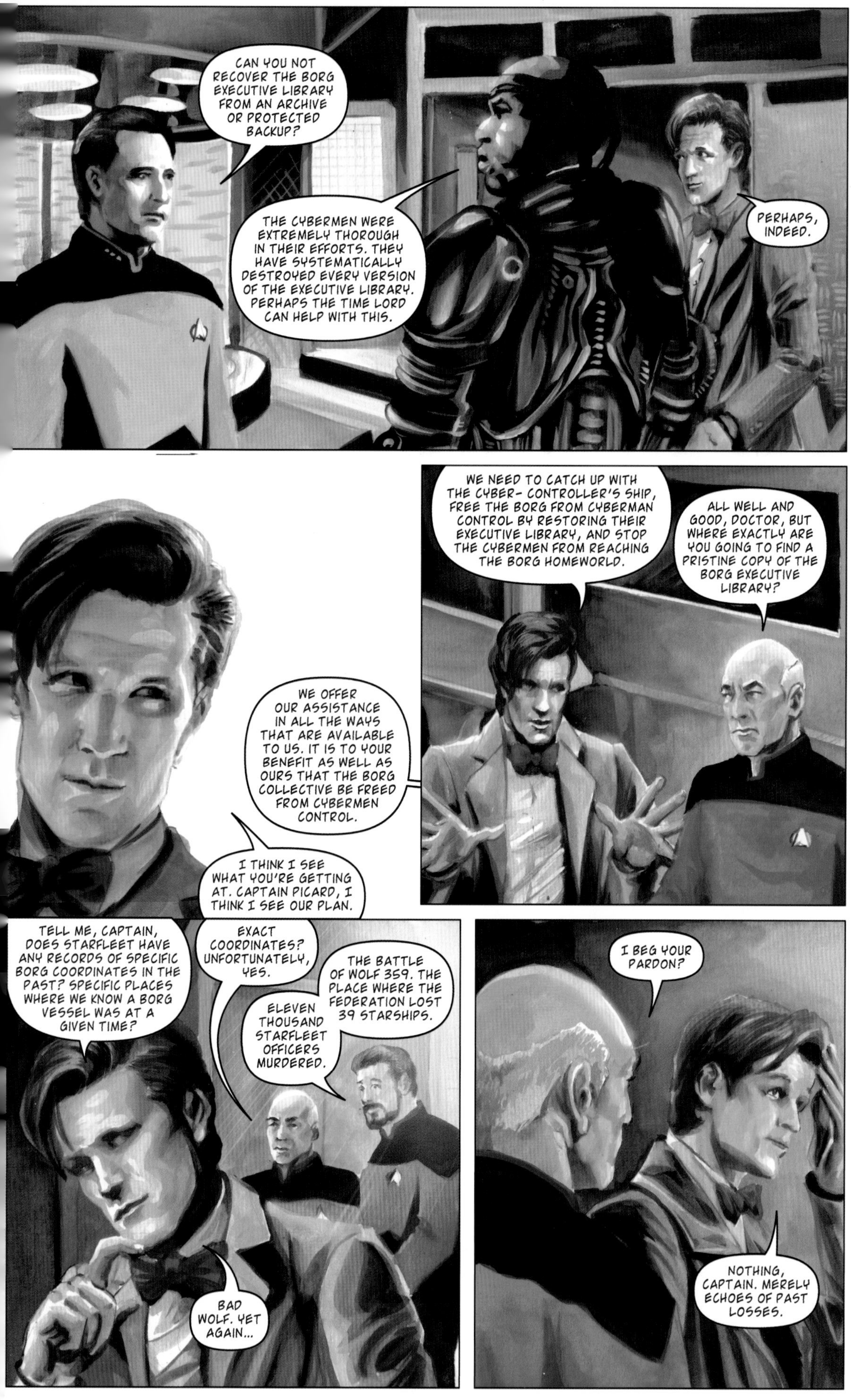
CAN YOU NOT RECOVER THE BORG EXECUTIVE LIBRARY FROM AN ARCHIVE OR PROTECTED BACKUP?
THE CYBERMEN WERE EXTREMELY THOROUGH IN THEIR EFFORTS. THEY HAVE SYSTEMATICALLY DESTROYED EVERY VERSION OF THE EXECUTIVE LIBRARY. PERHAPS THE TIME LORD CAN HELP WITH THIS.
PERHAPS, INDEED.
WE NEED TO CATCH UP WITH THE CYBER- CONTROLLER'S SHIP, FREE THE BORG FROM CYBERMAN CONTROL BY RESTORING THEIR EXECUTIVE LIBRARY, AND STOP THE CYBERMEN FROM REACHING THE BORG HOMEWORLD.
ALL WELL AND GOOD, DOCTOR, BUT WHERE EXACTLY ARE YOU GOING TO FIND A PRISTINE COPY OF THE BORG EXECUTIVE LIBRARY?
WE OFFER OUR ASSISTANCE IN ALL THE WAYS THAT ARE AVAILABLE TO US. IT IS TO YOUR BENEFIT AS WELL AS OURS THAT THE BORG COLLECTIVE BE FREED FROM CYBERMEN CONTROL.
I THINK I SEE WHAT YOU'RE GETTING AT. CAPTAIN PICARD, I THINK I SEE OUR PLAN.
TELL ME, CAPTAIN, DOES STARFLEET HAVE ANY RECORDS OF SPECIFIC BORG COORDINATES IN THE PAST? SPECIFIC PLACES WHERE WE KNOW A BORG VESSEL WAS AT A GIVEN TIME?
EXACT COORDINATES? UNFORTUNATELY, YES.
THE BATTLE OF WOLF 359. THE PLACE WHERE THE FEDERATION LOST 39 STARSHIPS.
ELEVEN THOUSAND STARFLEET OFFICERS MURDERED.
BAD WOLF. YET AGAIN...
I BEG YOUR PARDON?
NOTHING, CAPTAIN. MERELY ECHOES OF PAST LOSSES.

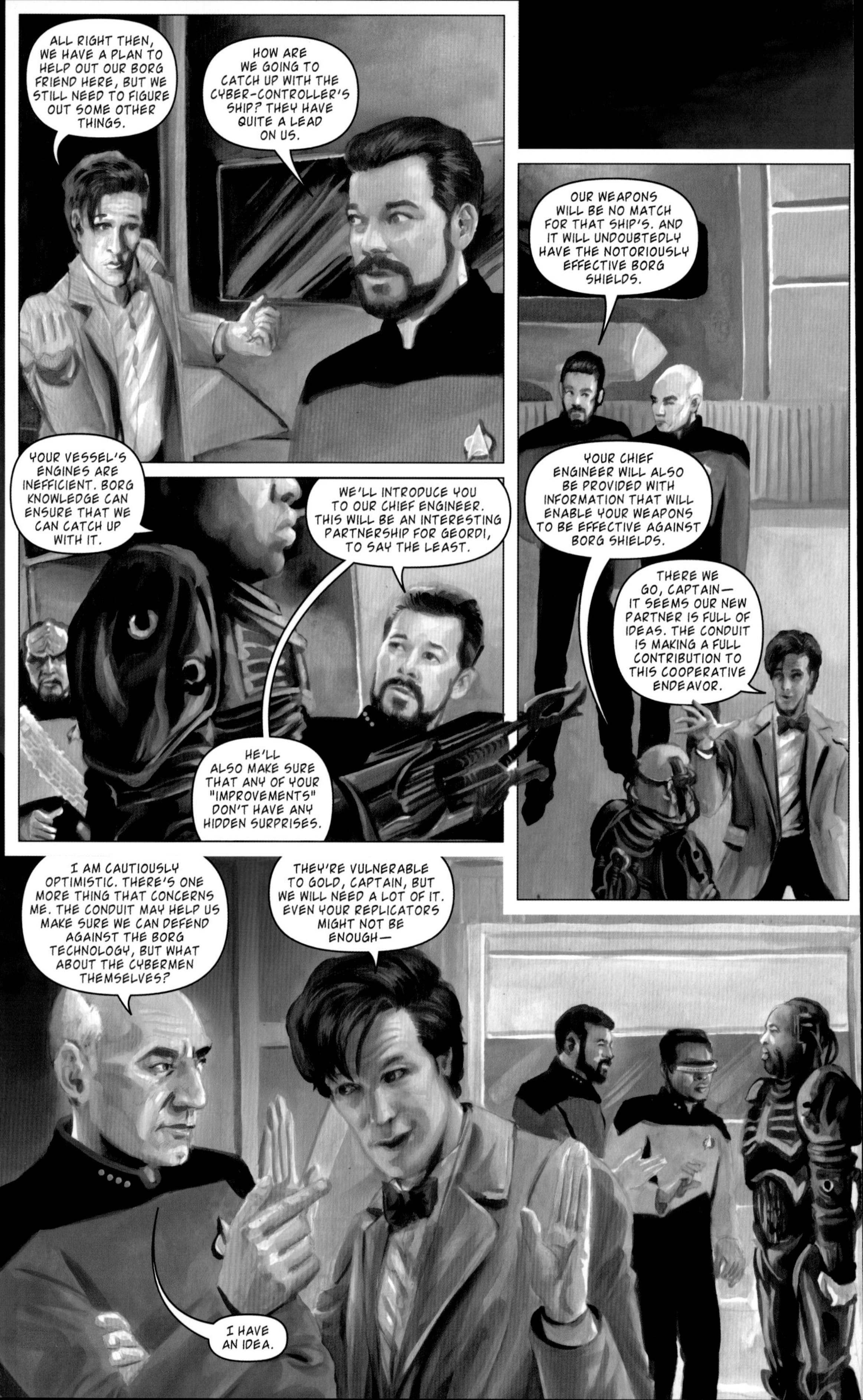
ALL RIGHT THEN, WE HAVE A PLAN TO HELP OUT OUR BORG FRIEND HERE, BUT WE STILL NEED TO FIGURE OUT SOME OTHER THINGS.
HOW ARE WE GOING TO CATCH UP WITH THE CYBER-CONTROLLER'S SHIP? THEY HAVE QUITE A LEAD ON US.
YOUR VESSEL'S ENGINES ARE INEFFICIENT. BORG KNOWLEDGE CAN ENSURE THAT WE CAN CATCH UP WITH IT.
WE'LL INTRODUCE YOU TO OUR CHIEF ENGINEER. THIS WILL BE AN INTERESTING PARTNERSHIP FOR GEORDI, TO SAY THE LEAST.
HE'LL ALSO MAKE SURE THAT ANY OF YOUR "IMPROVEMENTS" DON'T HAVE ANY HIDDEN SURPRISES.
OUR WEAPONS WILL BE NO MATCH FOR THAT SHIP'S. AND IT WILL UNDOUBTEDLY HAVE THE NOTORIOUSLY EFFECTIVE BORG SHIELDS.
YOUR CHIEF ENGINEER WILL ALSO BE PROVIDED WITH INFORMATION THAT WILL ENABLE YOUR WEAPONS TO BE EFFECTIVE AGAINST BORG SHIELDS.
THERE WE GO, CAPTAIN— IT SEEMS OUR NEW PARTNER IS FULL OF IDEAS. THE CONDUIT IS MAKING A FULL CONTRIBUTION TO THIS COOPERATIVE ENDEAVOR.
I AM CAUTIOUSLY OPTIMISTIC. THERE'S ONE MORE THING THAT CONCERNS ME. THE CONDUIT MAY HELP US MAKE SURE WE CAN DEFEND AGAINST THE BORG TECHNOLOGY, BUT WHAT ABOUT THE CYBERMEN THEMSELVES?
I HAVE AN IDEA.
THEY'RE VULNERABLE TO GOLD, CAPTAIN, BUT WE WILL NEED A LOT OF IT. EVEN YOUR REPLICATORS MIGHT NOT BE ENOUGH—

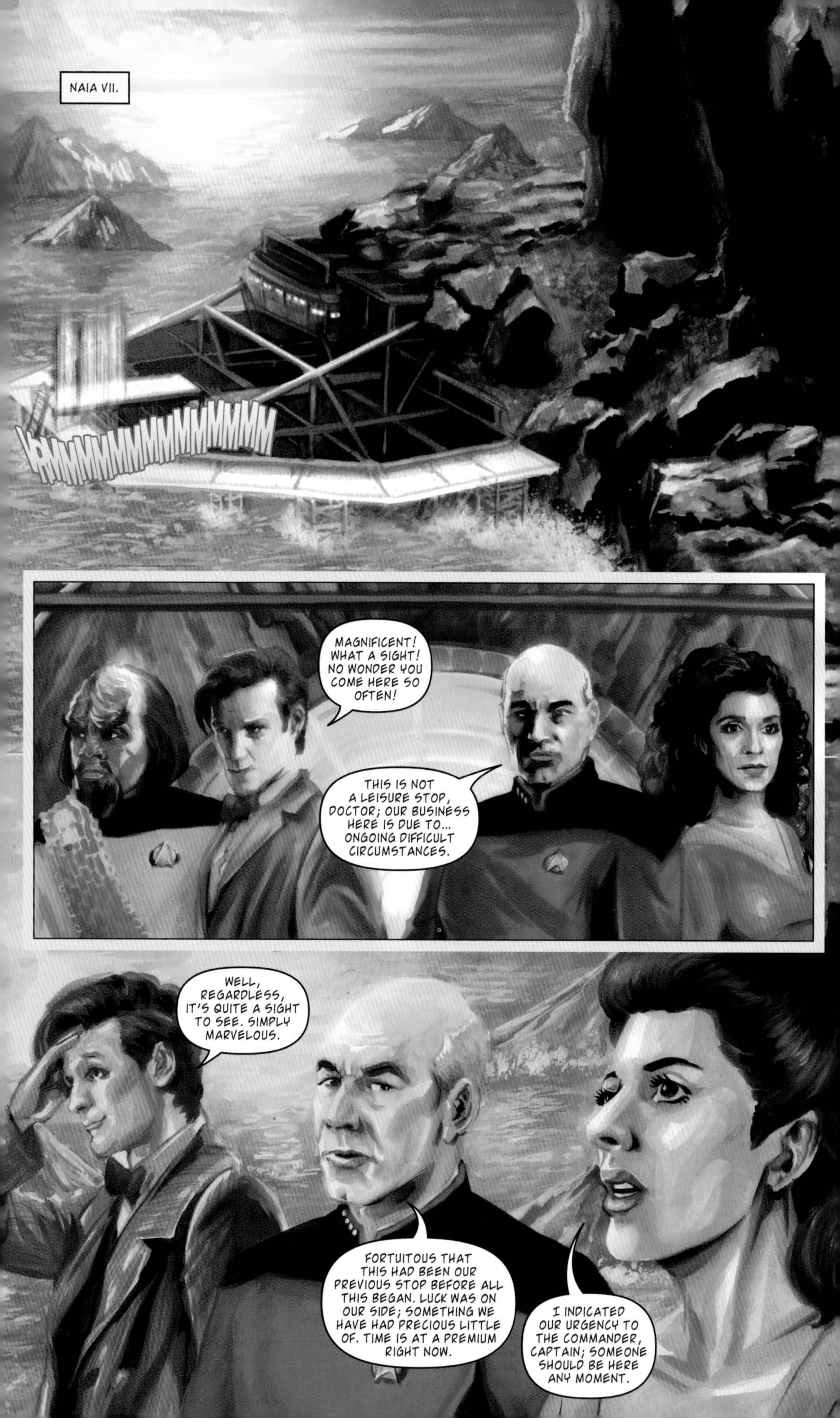

NAIA VII.
VRMMMMMMMMMMMMMM
MAGNIFICENT! WHAT A SIGHT! NO WONDER YOU COME HERE SO OFTEN!
THIS IS NOT A LEISURE STOP, DOCTOR; OUR BUSINESS HERE IS DUE TO... ONGOING DIFFICULT CIRCUMSTANCES.
WELL, REGARDLESS, IT'S QUITE A SIGHT TO SEE. SIMPLY MARVELOUS.
FORTUITOUS THAT THIS HAD BEEN OUR PREVIOUS STOP BEFORE ALL THIS BEGAN. LUCK WAS ON OUR SIDE; SOMETHING WE HAVE HAD PRECIOUS LITTLE OF. TIME IS AT A PREMIUM RIGHT NOW.
I INDICATED OUR URGENCY TO THE COMMANDER, CAPTAIN; SOMEONE SHOULD BE HERE ANY MOMENT.

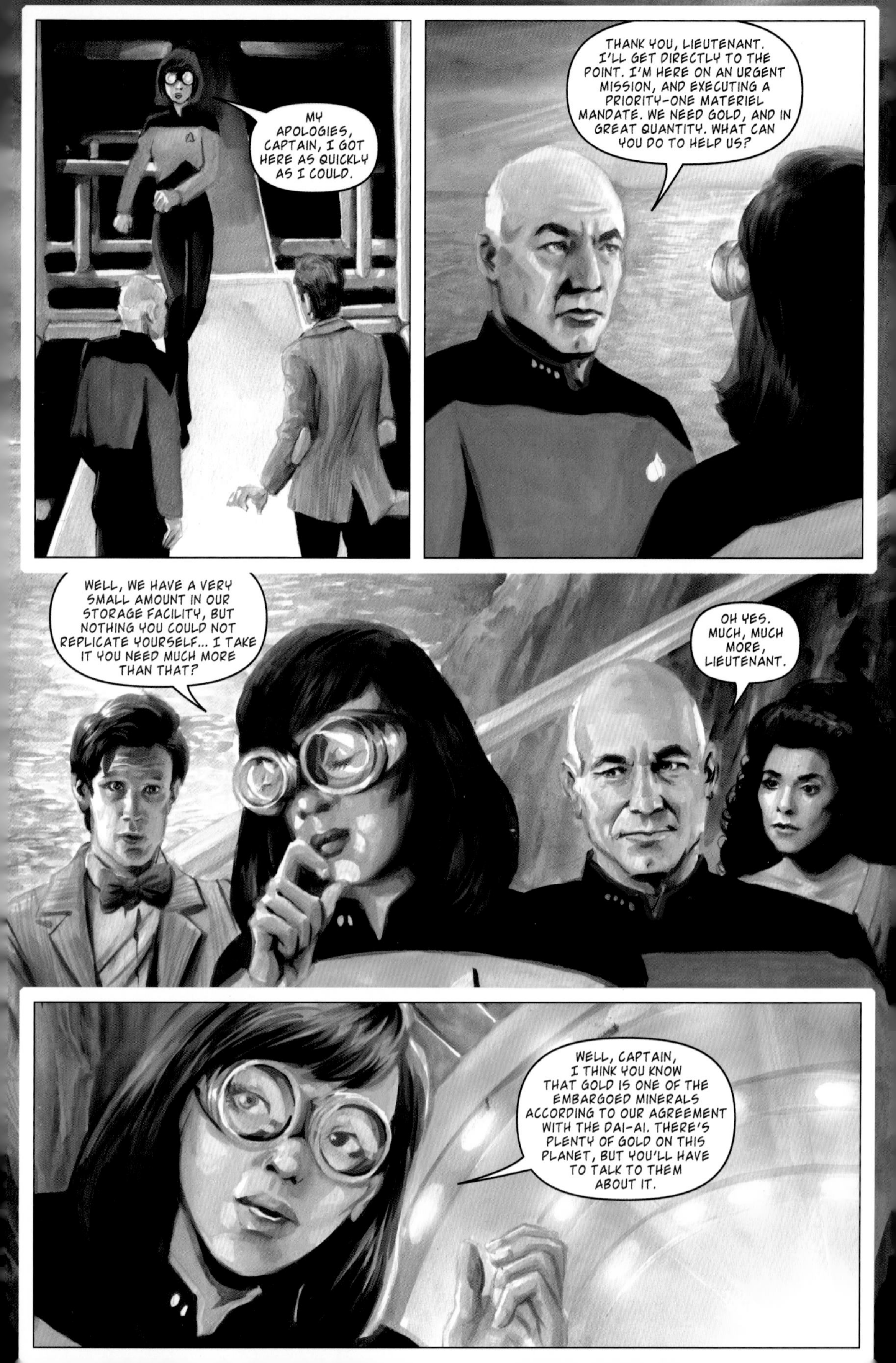
MY APOLOGIES, CAPTAIN, I GOT HERE AS QUICKLY AS I COULD.
THANK YOU, LIEUTENANT. I'LL GET DIRECTLY TO THE POINT. I'M HERE ON AN URGENT MISSION, AND EXECUTING A PRIORITY-ONE MATERIEL MANDATE. WE NEED GOLD, AND IN GREAT QUANTITY. WHAT CAN YOU DO TO HELP US?
WELL, WE HAVE A VERY SMALL AMOUNT IN OUR STORAGE FACILITY, BUT NOTHING YOU COULD NOT REPLICATE YOURSELF... I TAKE IT YOU NEED MUCH MORE THAN THAT?
OH YES. MUCH, MUCH MORE, LIEUTENANT.
WELL, CAPTAIN, I THINK YOU KNOW THAT GOLD IS ONE OF THE EMBARGOED MINERALS ACCORDING TO OUR AGREEMENT WITH THE DAI-AI. THERE'S PLENTY OF GOLD ON THIS PLANET, BUT YOU'LL HAVE TO TALK TO THEM ABOUT IT.

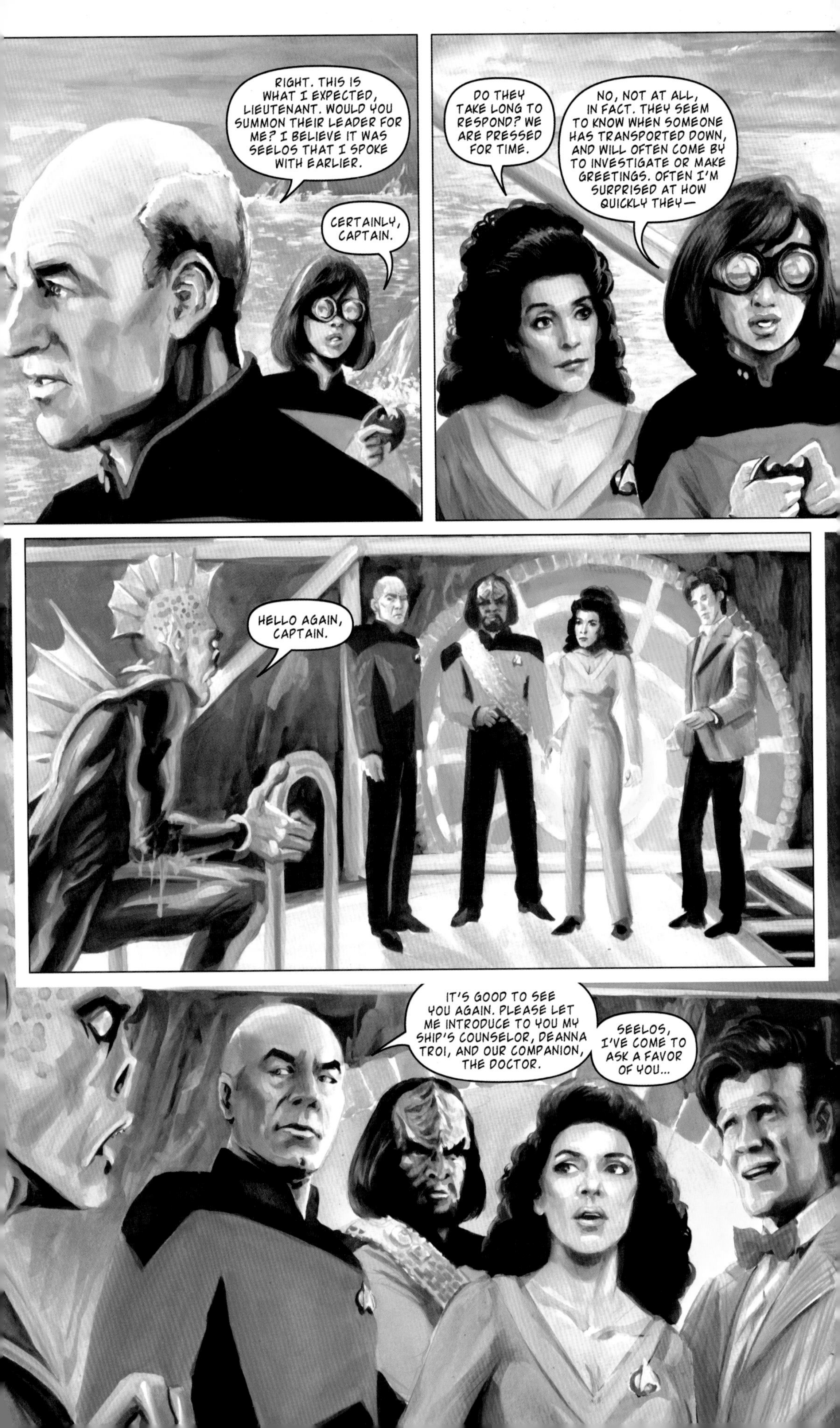
RIGHT. THIS IS WHAT I EXPECTED, LIEUTENANT. WOULD YOU SUMMON THEIR LEADER FOR ME? I BELIEVE IT WAS SEELOS THAT I SPOKE WITH EARLIER.
CERTAINLY, CAPTAIN.
DO THEY TAKE LONG TO RESPOND? WE ARE PRESSED FOR TIME.
NO, NOT AT ALL, IN FACT. THEY SEEM TO KNOW WHEN SOMEONE HAS TRANSPORTED DOWN, AND WILL OFTEN COME BY TO INVESTIGATE OR MAKE GREETINGS. OFTEN I'M SURPRISED AT HOW QUICKLY THEY—
HELLO AGAIN, CAPTAIN.
IT'S GOOD TO SEE YOU AGAIN. PLEASE LET ME INTRODUCE TO YOU MY SHIP'S COUNSELOR, DEANNA TROI, AND OUR COMPANION, THE DOCTOR.
SEELOS, I'VE COME TO ASK A FAVOR OF YOU...

CAPTAIN, I CAN SCARCELY BELIEVE WHAT YOU'RE ASKING OF MY PEOPLE. YOU UNDERSTAND THAT THE MONETARY SYSTEM OF MY PEOPLE IS ENTIRELY LINKED TO A GOLD STANDARD, DO YOU NOT? DO YOU REALIZE THE *HARDSHIPS* THIS WOULD CREATE? THE POTENTIAL FOR ECONOMIC *CATASTROPHE*?

WE DO, SEELOS. WE WOULD NEVER ASK SOMETHING LIKE THIS IF THE CAUSE WERE NOT SO IMPORTANT. AND THE STAKES SO *HIGH.*

MY PEOPLE HAVE ALREADY PROVIDED THE FEDERATION WITH SO MANY RESOURCES FROM OUR PLANET, CAPTAIN. AND WHILE I VERY MUCH APPRECIATE THE POTENTIAL THREAT YOU HAVE DESCRIBED TO ME, I DON'T SEE HOW I CAN POSSIBLY ASK MY PEOPLE TO MAKE THIS SORT OF SACRIFICE.

SEELOS, WE WILL MAKE EVERY EFFORT TO COMPENSATE YOUR PEOPLE FOR—

SEELOS, I THINK I UNDERSTAND THE SITUATION YOU'RE IN HERE. YOURS IS A SMALL SOCIETY COMPARED TO THE FEDERATION, AND YOU DID NOT AGREE TO THIS INITIAL ALLIANCE LIGHTLY, IF I'M NOT MISTAKEN.

I COULD TELL YOU THAT YOU SHOULD HELP US FOR STRATEGIC ADVANTAGE. I COULD EXPLAIN TO YOU HOW HELPING US NOW WOULD GIVE YOU ENORMOUS LEVERAGE IN FUTURE NEGOTIATIONS WITH THE FEDERATION. AND THAT WOULD BE TRUE.

OR I COULD TELL YOU HOW HELPING US WOULD HELP YOU AND YOUR PEOPLE IN THE LONG RUN. I KNOW THAT YOUR PEOPLE FACED SOME HARD TIMES BEFORE THE FEDERATION CAME HERE, AND NOW YOU COULD EARN THE HEARTFELT GRATITUDE OF THOUSANDS OF WORLDS.

AND I COULD SUGGEST THAT YOU PERSONALLY COULD BENEFIT POLITICALLY FROM HELPING US, RAISING YOUR STATURE HERE AND ACROSS THE GALAXY. AND THAT WOULD BE TRUE.

OR I COULD TELL YOU THAT HELPING US WOULD ENSURE THE SAFETY OF BILLIONS ACROSS COUNTLESS WORLDS, BEINGS WHO OTHERWISE WOULD BE LOST OR ENSLAVED, CONVERTED INTO SOULLESS AUTOMATONS WITHOUT FREE WILL OR THE PROSPECT OF HAPPINESS.

AND THAT WOULD ALSO BE TRUE.

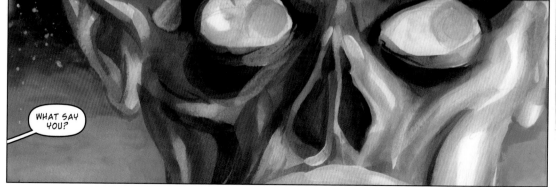

WHAT SAY YOU?

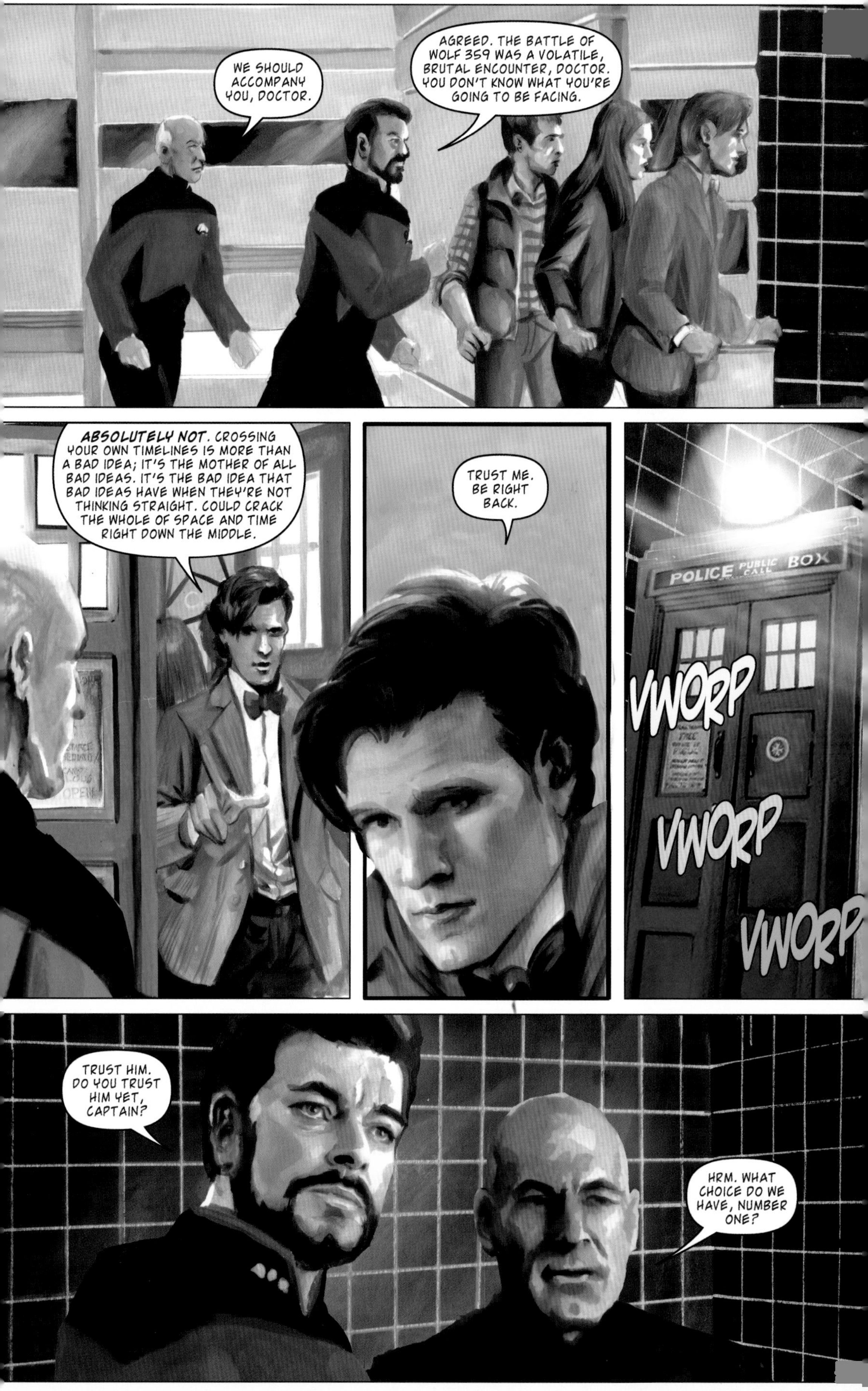
WE SHOULD ACCOMPANY YOU, DOCTOR.
AGREED. THE BATTLE OF WOLF 359 WAS A VOLATILE, BRUTAL ENCOUNTER, DOCTOR. YOU DON'T KNOW WHAT YOU'RE GOING TO BE FACING.
ABSOLUTELY NOT. CROSSING YOUR OWN TIMELINES IS MORE THAN A BAD IDEA; IT'S THE MOTHER OF ALL BAD IDEAS. IT'S THE BAD IDEA THAT BAD IDEAS HAVE WHEN THEY'RE NOT THINKING STRAIGHT. COULD CRACK THE WHOLE OF SPACE AND TIME RIGHT DOWN THE MIDDLE.
TRUST ME. BE RIGHT BACK.
POLICE PUBLIC CALL BOX
VWORP
VWORP
VWORP
TRUST HIM. DO YOU TRUST HIM YET, CAPTAIN?
HRM. WHAT CHOICE DO WE HAVE, NUMBER ONE?

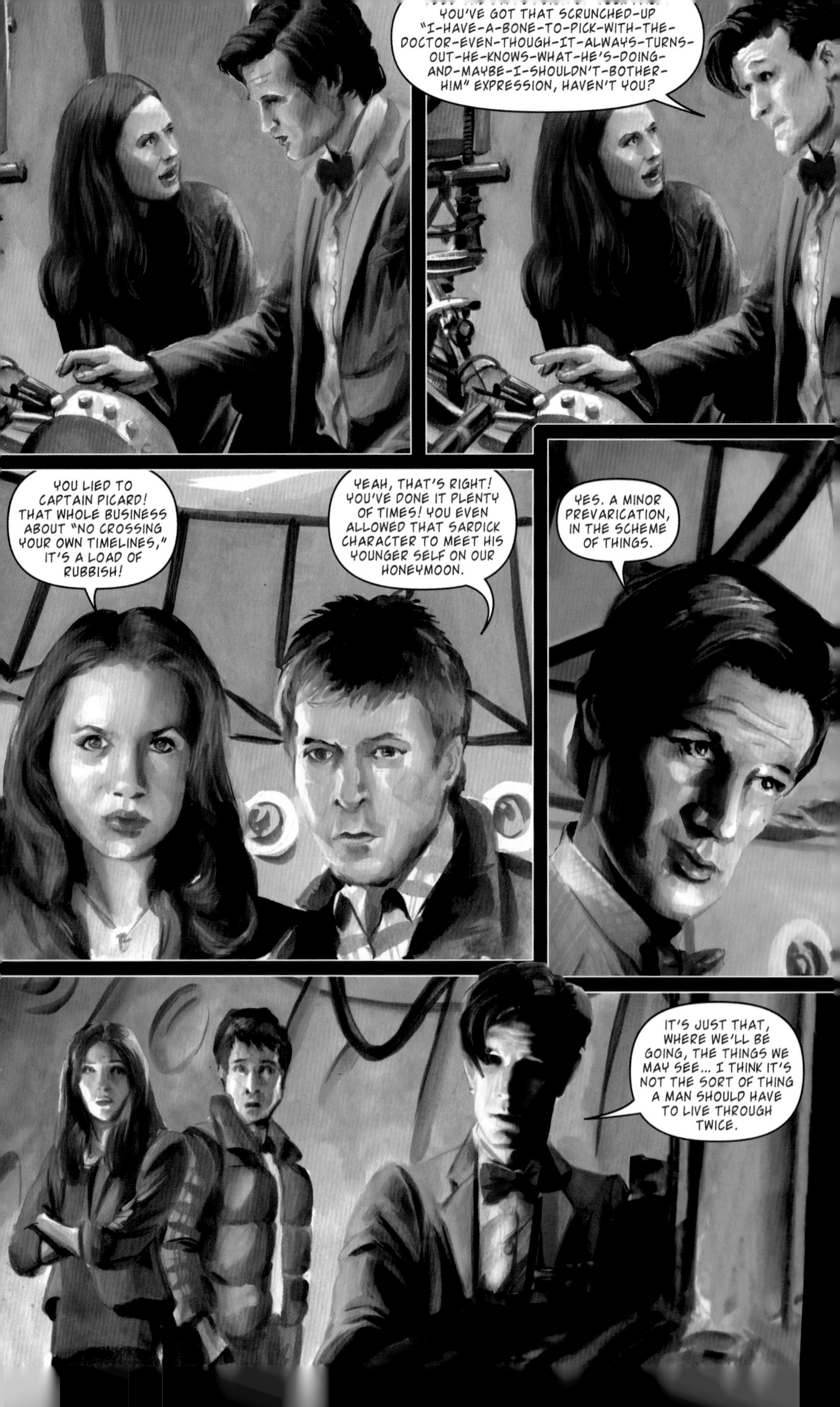
YOU'VE GOT THAT SCRUNCHED-UP "I-HAVE-A-BONE-TO-PICK-WITH-THE-DOCTOR-EVEN-THOUGH-IT-ALWAYS-TURNS-OUT-HE-KNOWS-WHAT-HE'S-DOING-AND-MAYBE-I-SHOULDN'T-BOTHER-HIM" EXPRESSION, HAVEN'T YOU?
YOU LIED TO CAPTAIN PICARD! THAT WHOLE BUSINESS ABOUT "NO CROSSING YOUR OWN TIMELINES," IT'S A LOAD OF RUBBISH!
YEAH, THAT'S RIGHT! YOU'VE DONE IT PLENTY OF TIMES! YOU EVEN ALLOWED THAT SARDICK CHARACTER TO MEET HIS YOUNGER SELF ON OUR HONEYMOON.
YES. A MINOR PREVARICATION, IN THE SCHEME OF THINGS.
IT'S JUST THAT, WHERE WE'LL BE GOING, THE THINGS WE MAY SEE... I THINK IT'S NOT THE SORT OF THING A MAN SHOULD HAVE TO LIVE THROUGH TWICE.

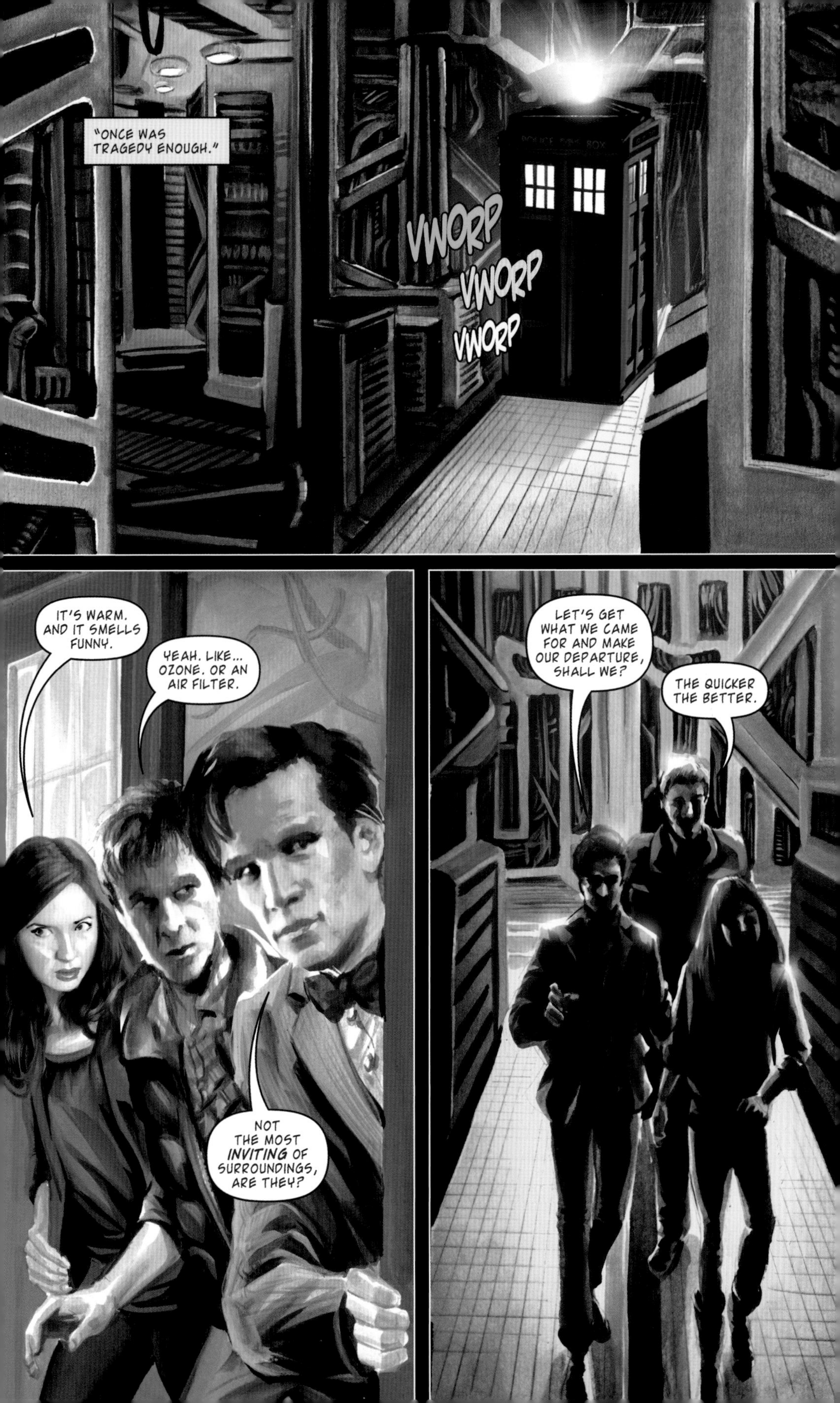
"ONCE WAS TRAGEDY ENOUGH."
VWORP
VWORP
VWORP
IT'S WARM. AND IT SMELLS FUNNY.
YEAH. LIKE... OZONE. OR AN AIR FILTER.
NOT THE MOST *INVITING* OF SURROUNDINGS, ARE THEY?
LET'S GET WHAT WE CAME FOR AND MAKE OUR DEPARTURE, SHALL WE?
THE QUICKER THE BETTER.

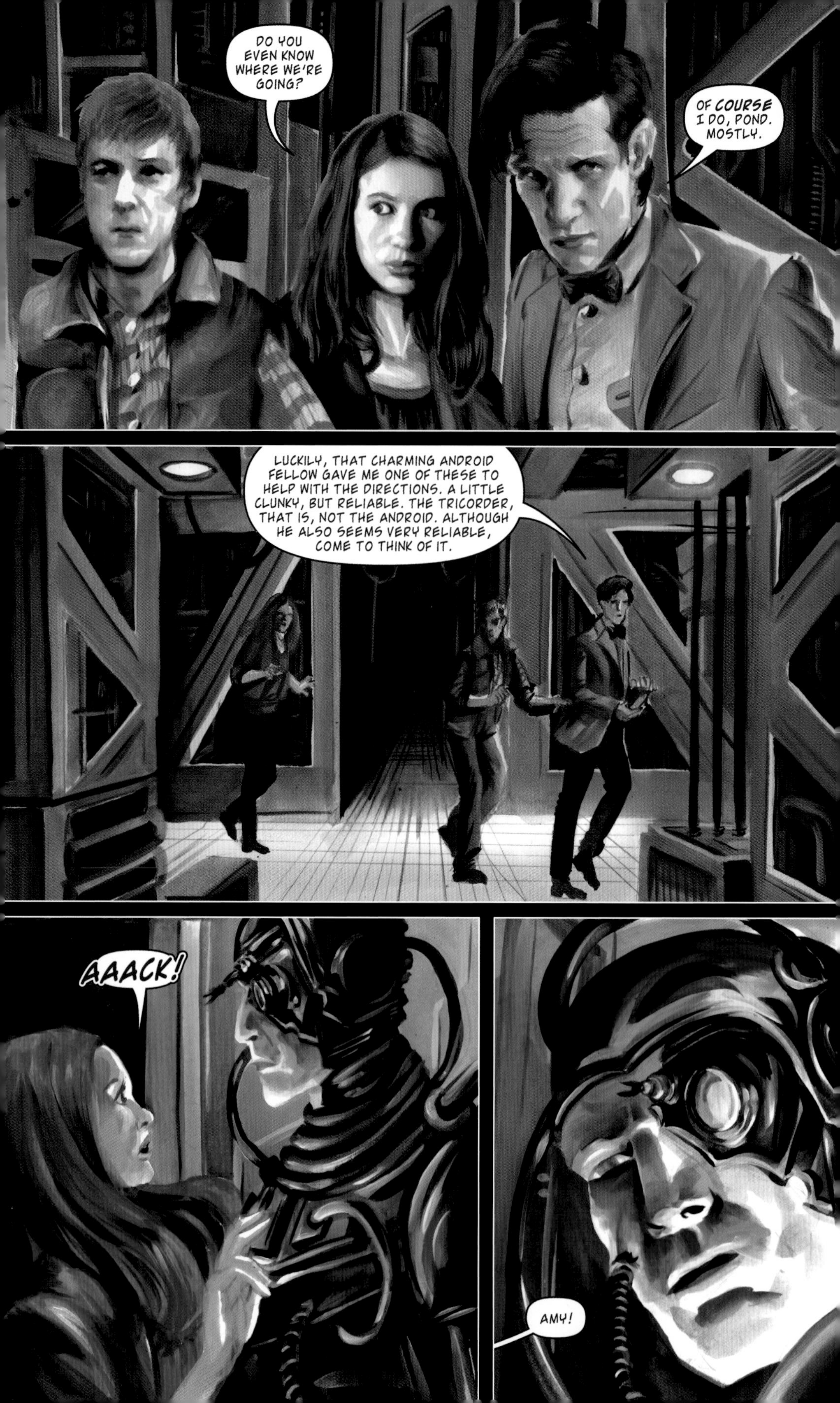
DO YOU EVEN KNOW WHERE WE'RE GOING?
OF COURSE I DO, POND. MOSTLY.
LUCKILY, THAT CHARMING ANDROID FELLOW GAVE ME ONE OF THESE TO HELP WITH THE DIRECTIONS. A LITTLE CLUNKY, BUT RELIABLE. THE TRICORDER, THAT IS, NOT THE ANDROID. ALTHOUGH HE ALSO SEEMS VERY RELIABLE, COME TO THINK OF IT.
AAACK!
AMY!

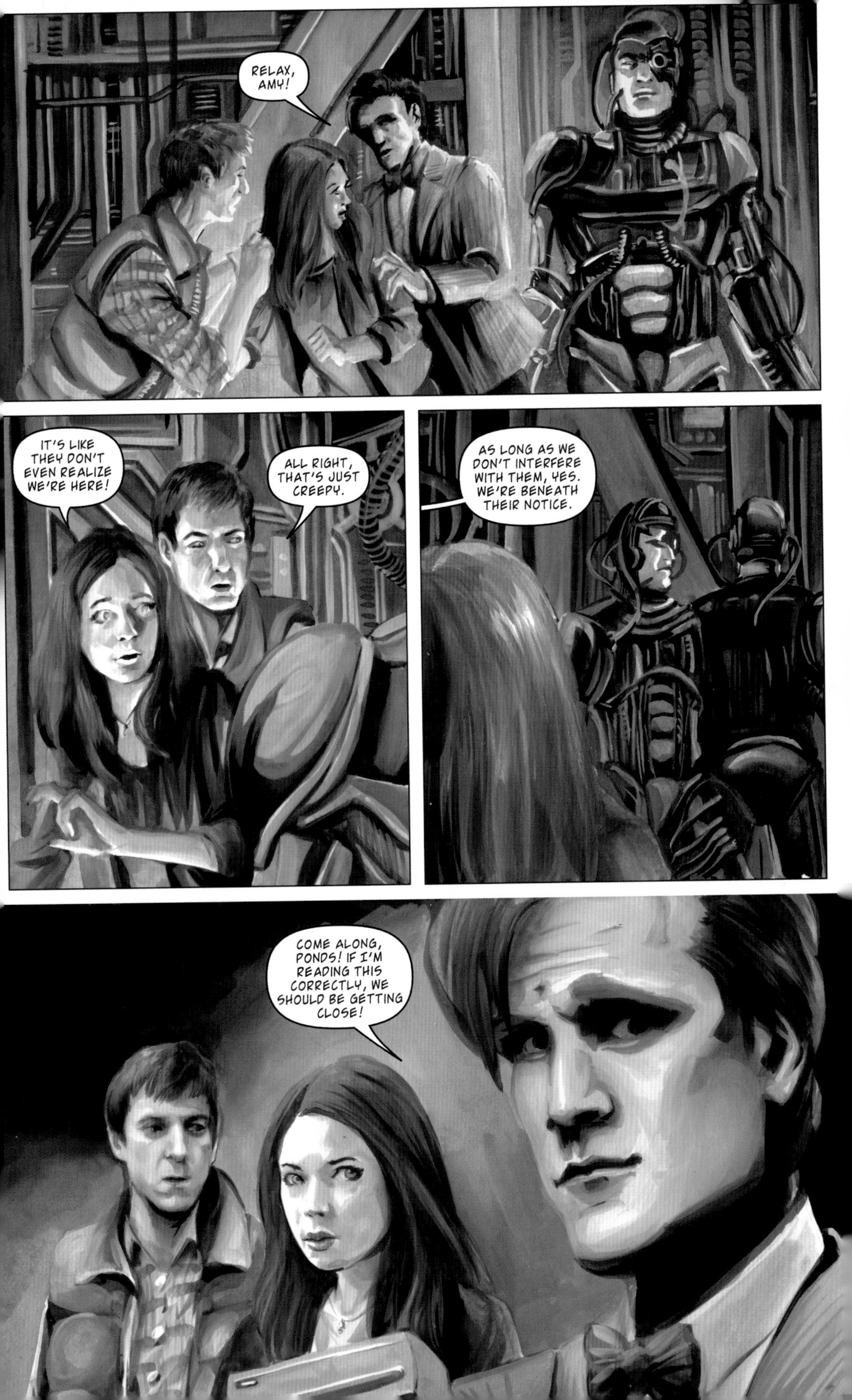
RELAX, AMY!
IT'S LIKE THEY DON'T EVEN REALIZE WE'RE HERE!
ALL RIGHT, THAT'S JUST CREEPY.
AS LONG AS WE DON'T INTERFERE WITH THEM, YES. WE'RE BENEATH THEIR NOTICE.
COME ALONG, PONDS! IF I'M READING THIS CORRECTLY, WE SHOULD BE GETTING CLOSE!

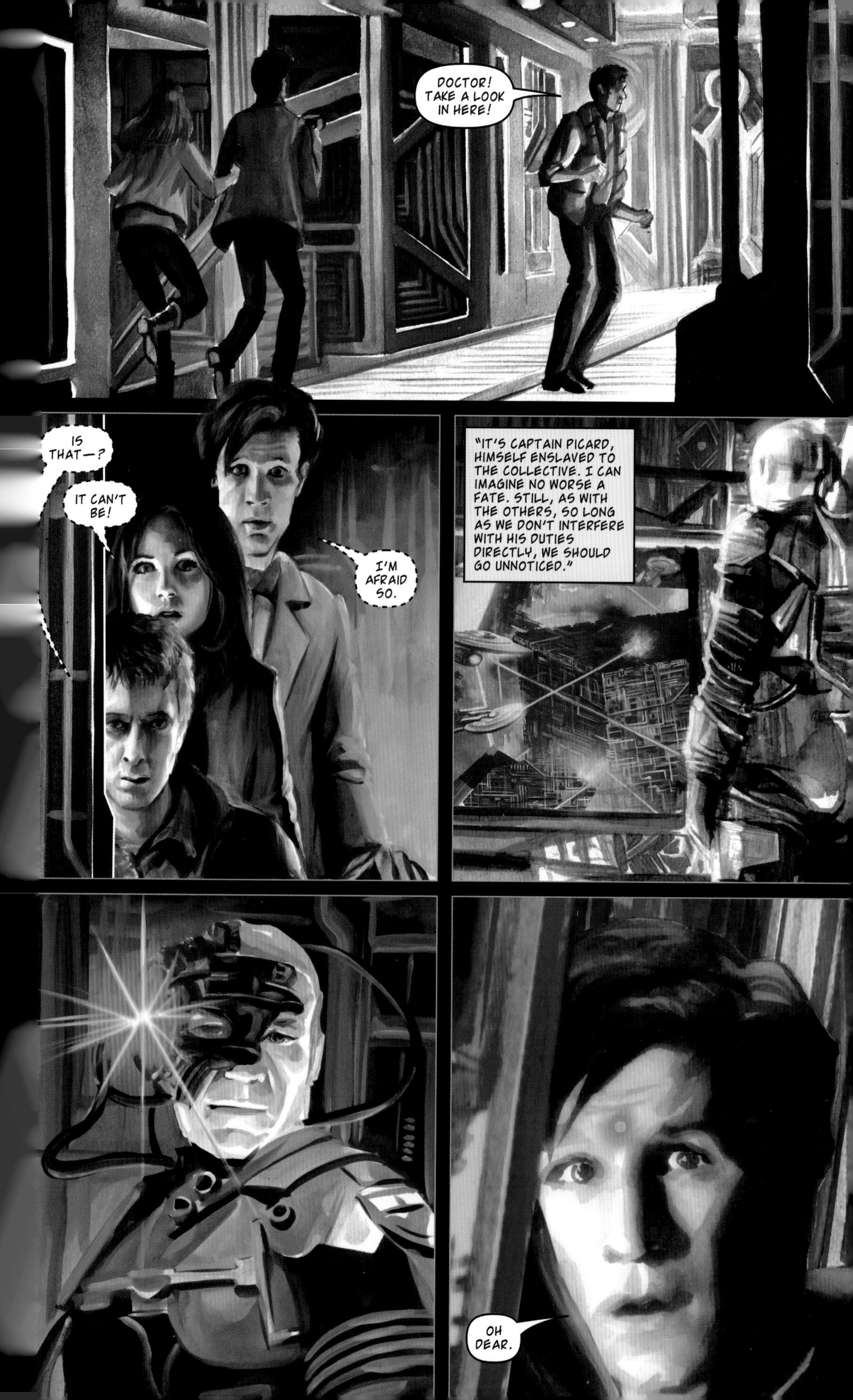
DOCTOR! TAKE A LOOK IN HERE!
IS THAT—?
IT CAN'T BE!
I'M AFRAID SO.
"IT'S CAPTAIN PICARD, HIMSELF ENSLAVED TO THE COLLECTIVE. I CAN IMAGINE NO WORSE A FATE. STILL, AS WITH THE OTHERS, SO LONG AS WE DON'T INTERFERE WITH HIS DUTIES DIRECTLY, WE SHOULD GO UNNOTICED."
OH DEAR.

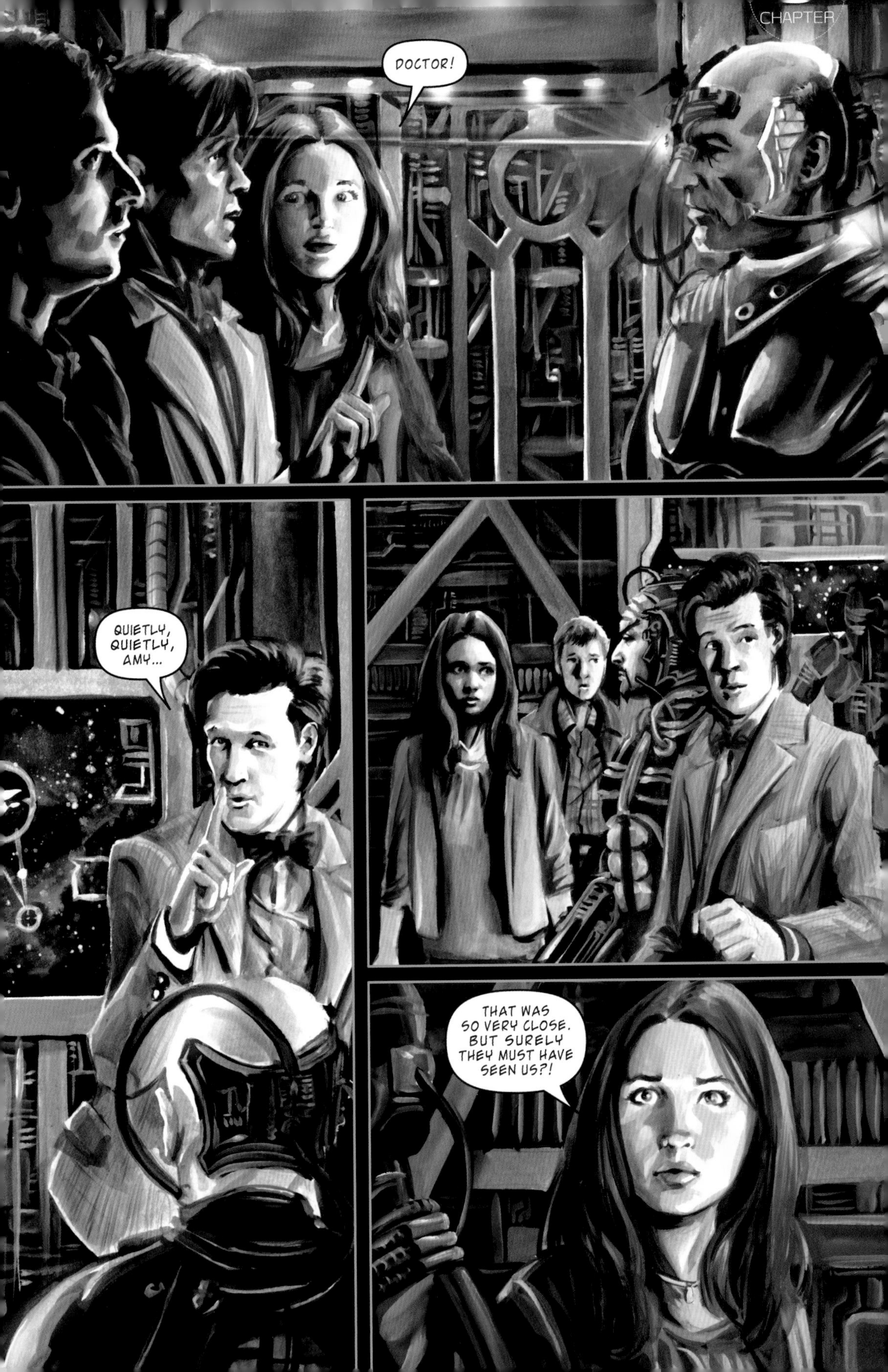
DOCTOR!
QUIETLY, QUIETLY, AMY...
THAT WAS SO VERY CLOSE. BUT SURELY THEY MUST HAVE SEEN US?!

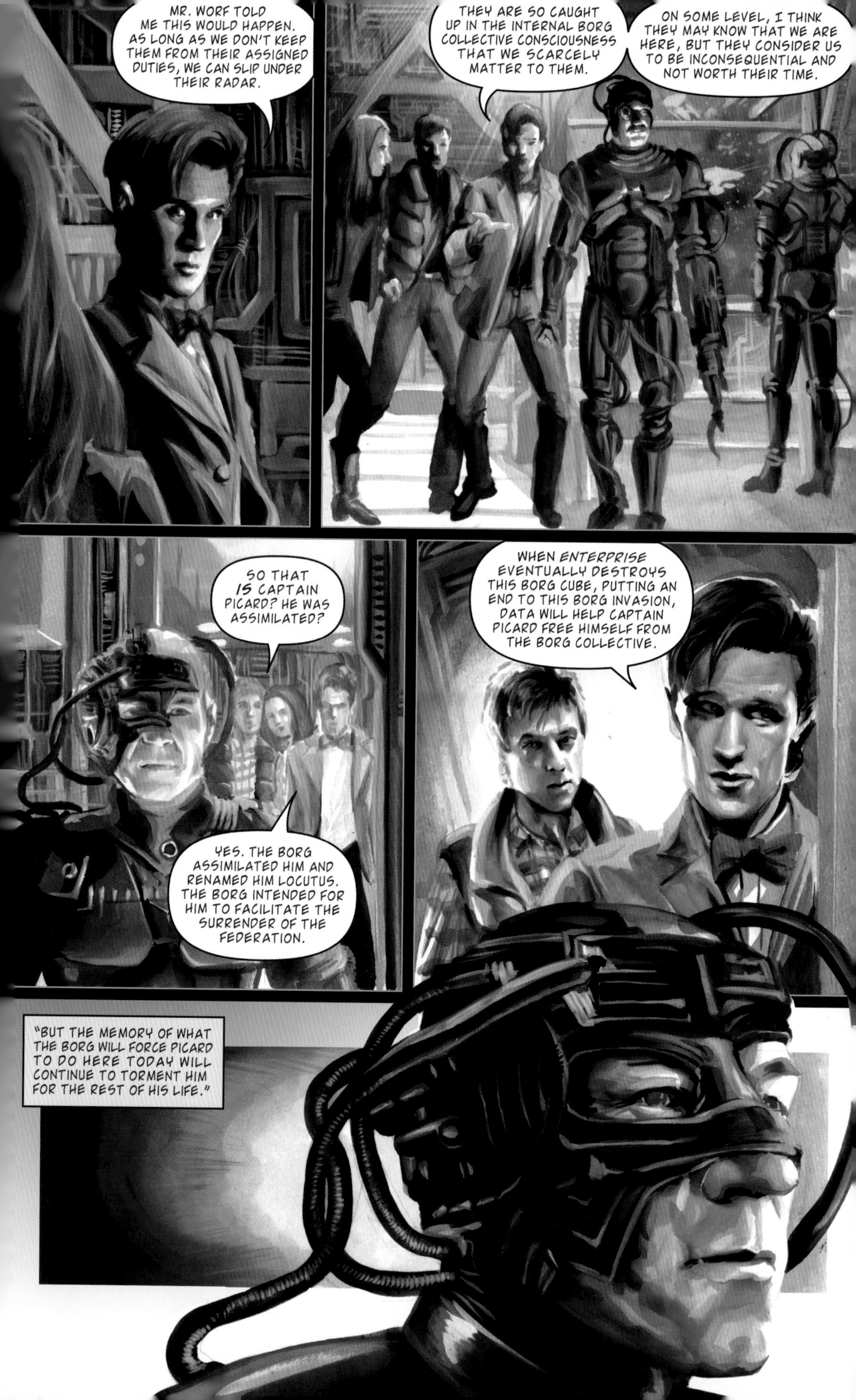
MR. WORF TOLD ME THIS WOULD HAPPEN. AS LONG AS WE DON'T KEEP THEM FROM THEIR ASSIGNED DUTIES, WE CAN SLIP UNDER THEIR RADAR.
THEY ARE SO CAUGHT UP IN THE INTERNAL BORG COLLECTIVE CONSCIOUSNESS THAT WE SCARCELY MATTER TO THEM.
ON SOME LEVEL, I THINK THEY MAY KNOW THAT WE ARE HERE, BUT THEY CONSIDER US TO BE INCONSEQUENTIAL AND NOT WORTH THEIR TIME.
SO THAT *IS* CAPTAIN PICARD? HE WAS ASSIMILATED?
YES. THE BORG ASSIMILATED HIM AND RENAMED HIM LOCUTUS. THE BORG INTENDED FOR HIM TO FACILITATE THE SURRENDER OF THE FEDERATION.
WHEN *ENTERPRISE* EVENTUALLY DESTROYS THIS BORG CUBE, PUTTING AN END TO THIS BORG INVASION, DATA WILL HELP CAPTAIN PICARD FREE HIMSELF FROM THE BORG COLLECTIVE.
"BUT THE MEMORY OF WHAT THE BORG WILL FORCE PICARD TO DO HERE TODAY WILL CONTINUE TO TORMENT HIM FOR THE REST OF HIS LIFE."

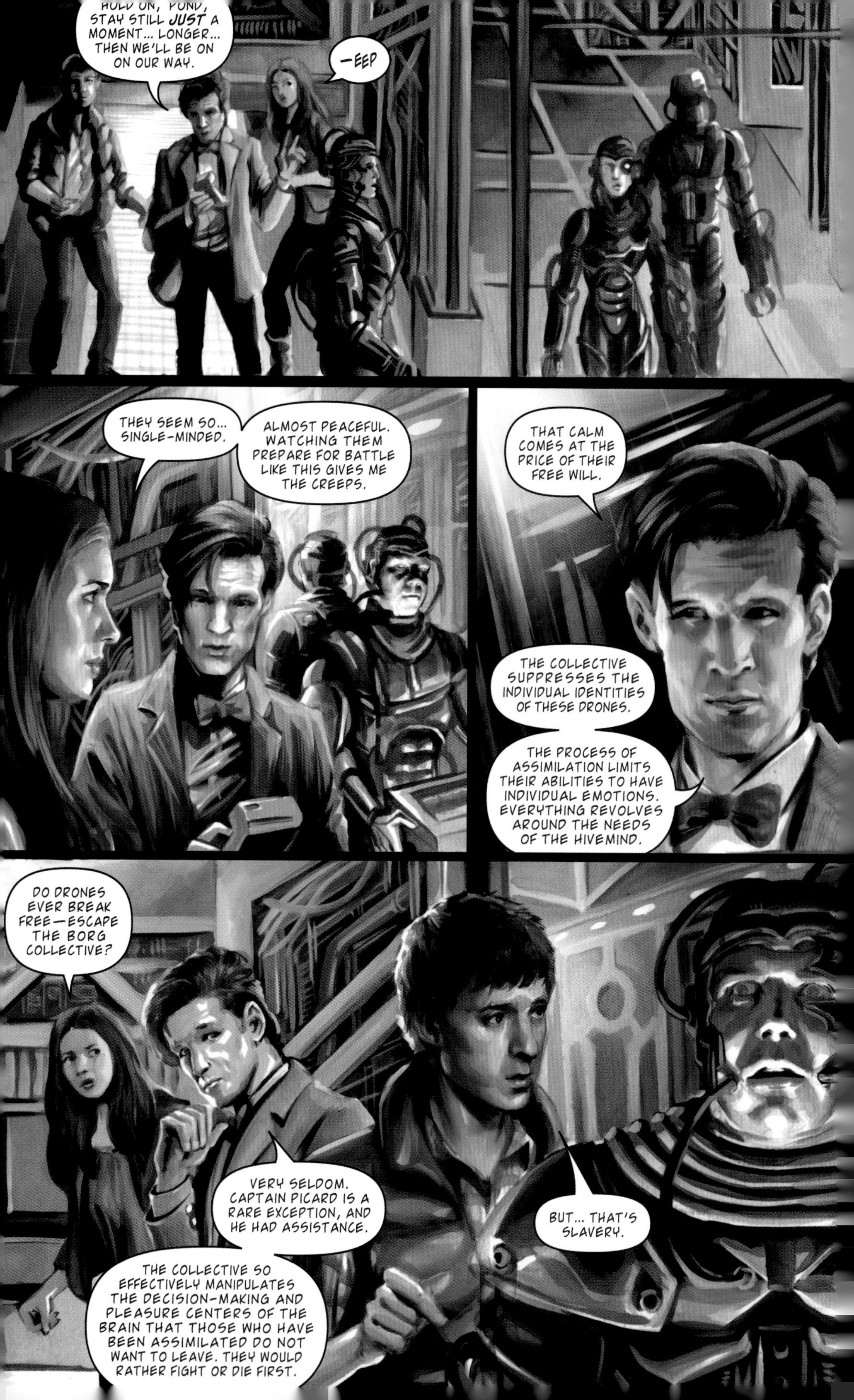
HOLD ON, POND, STAY STILL JUST A MOMENT... LONGER... THEN WE'LL BE ON ON OUR WAY.
—EEP
THEY SEEM SO... SINGLE-MINDED.
ALMOST PEACEFUL. WATCHING THEM PREPARE FOR BATTLE LIKE THIS GIVES ME THE CREEPS.
THAT CALM COMES AT THE PRICE OF THEIR FREE WILL.
THE COLLECTIVE SUPPRESSES THE INDIVIDUAL IDENTITIES OF THESE DRONES.
THE PROCESS OF ASSIMILATION LIMITS THEIR ABILITIES TO HAVE INDIVIDUAL EMOTIONS. EVERYTHING REVOLVES AROUND THE NEEDS OF THE HIVEMIND.
DO DRONES EVER BREAK FREE—ESCAPE THE BORG COLLECTIVE?
VERY SELDOM. CAPTAIN PICARD IS A RARE EXCEPTION, AND HE HAD ASSISTANCE.
THE COLLECTIVE SO EFFECTIVELY MANIPULATES THE DECISION-MAKING AND PLEASURE CENTERS OF THE BRAIN THAT THOSE WHO HAVE BEEN ASSIMILATED DO NOT WANT TO LEAVE. THEY WOULD RATHER FIGHT OR DIE FIRST.
BUT... THAT'S SLAVERY.

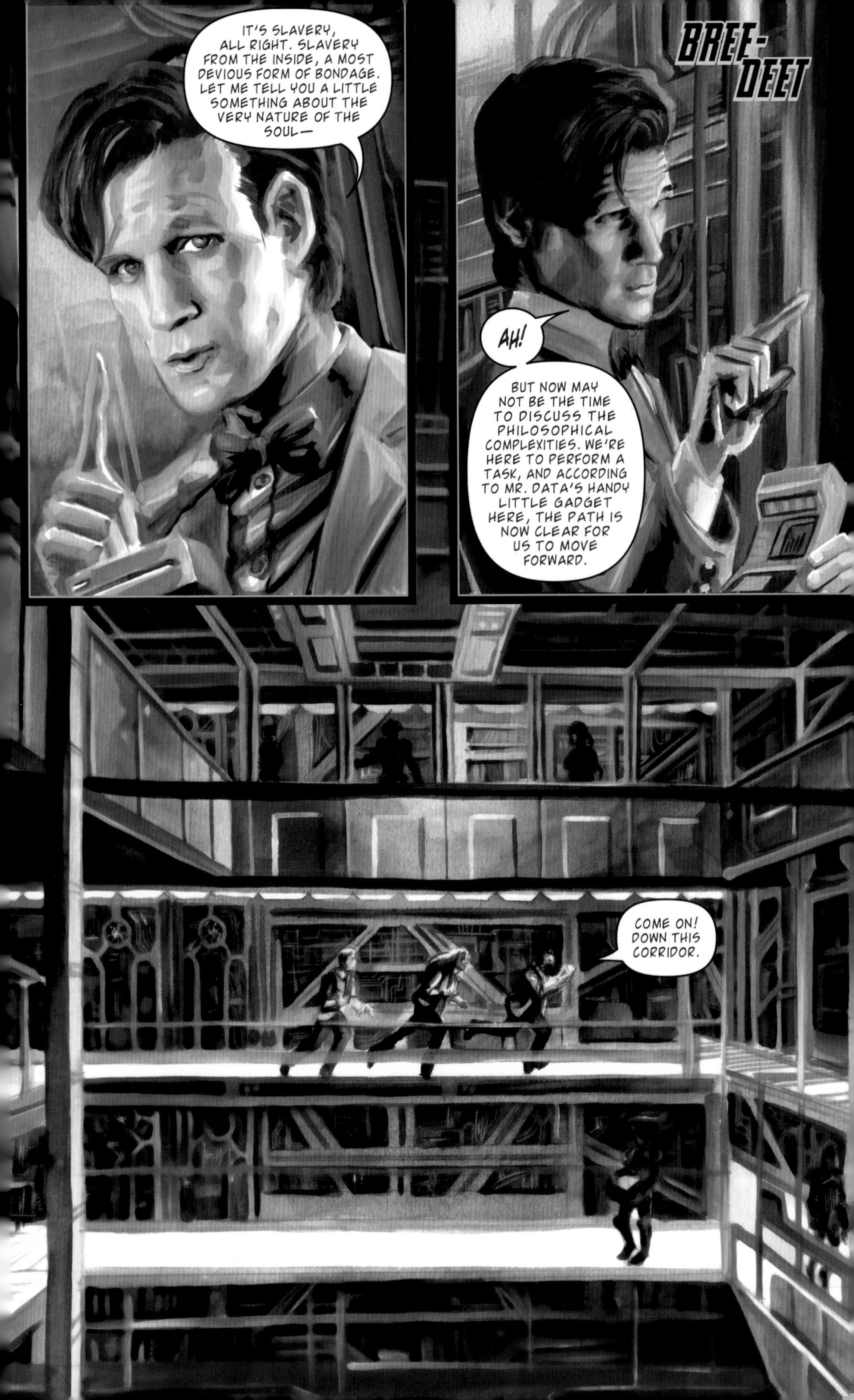
IT'S SLAVERY, ALL RIGHT. SLAVERY FROM THE INSIDE, A MOST DEVIOUS FORM OF BONDAGE. LET ME TELL YOU A LITTLE SOMETHING ABOUT THE VERY NATURE OF THE SOUL—
BREE-DEET
AH!
BUT NOW MAY NOT BE THE TIME TO DISCUSS THE PHILOSOPHICAL COMPLEXITIES. WE'RE HERE TO PERFORM A TASK, AND ACCORDING TO MR. DATA'S HANDY LITTLE GADGET HERE, THE PATH IS NOW CLEAR FOR US TO MOVE FORWARD.
COME ON! DOWN THIS CORRIDOR.

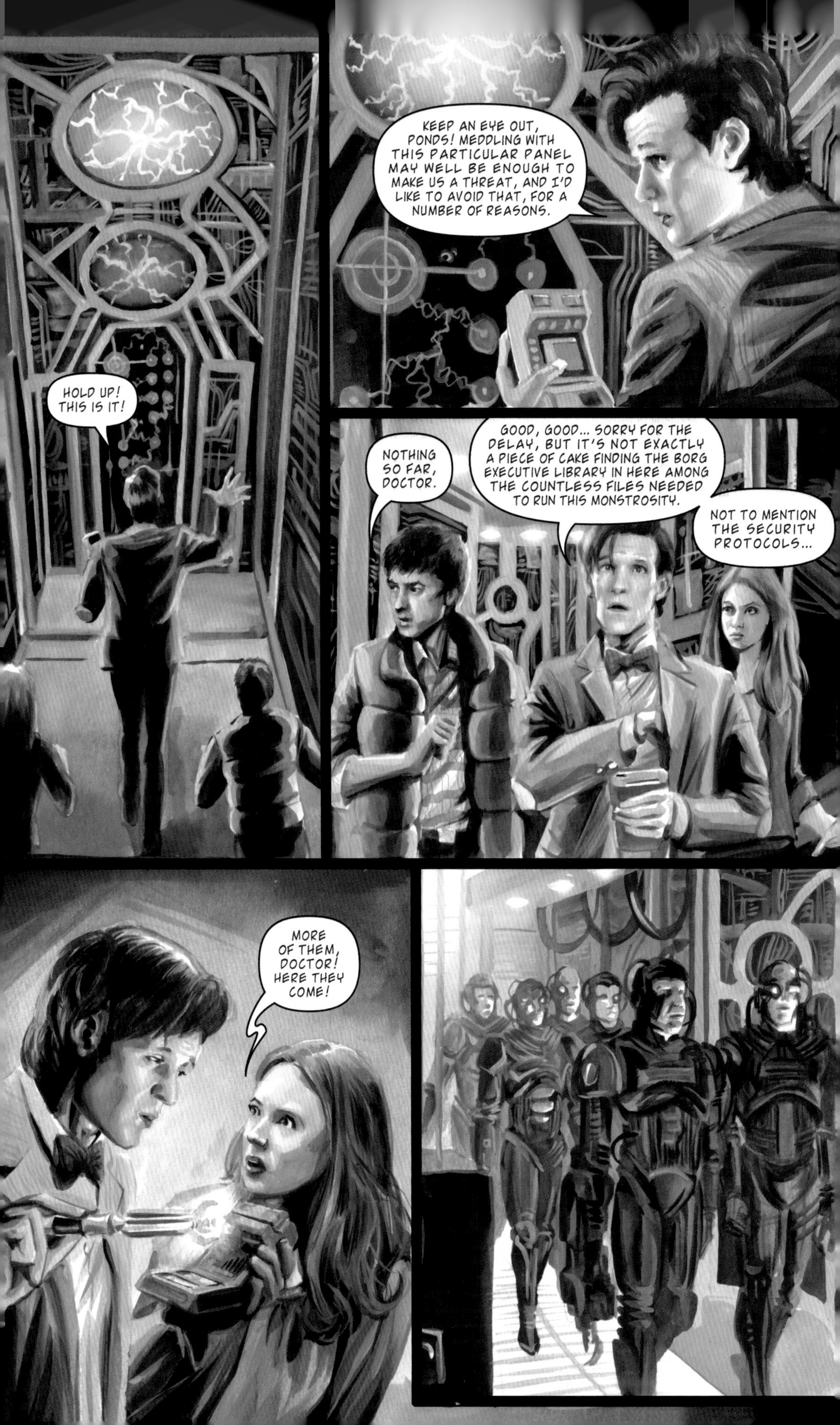
HOLD UP! THIS IS IT!
KEEP AN EYE OUT, PONDS! MEDDLING WITH THIS PARTICULAR PANEL MAY WELL BE ENOUGH TO MAKE US A THREAT, AND I'D LIKE TO AVOID THAT, FOR A NUMBER OF REASONS.
NOTHING SO FAR, DOCTOR.
GOOD, GOOD... SORRY FOR THE DELAY, BUT IT'S NOT EXACTLY A PIECE OF CAKE FINDING THE BORG EXECUTIVE LIBRARY IN HERE AMONG THE COUNTLESS FILES NEEDED TO RUN THIS MONSTROSITY.
NOT TO MENTION THE SECURITY PROTOCOLS...
MORE OF THEM, DOCTOR! HERE THEY COME!

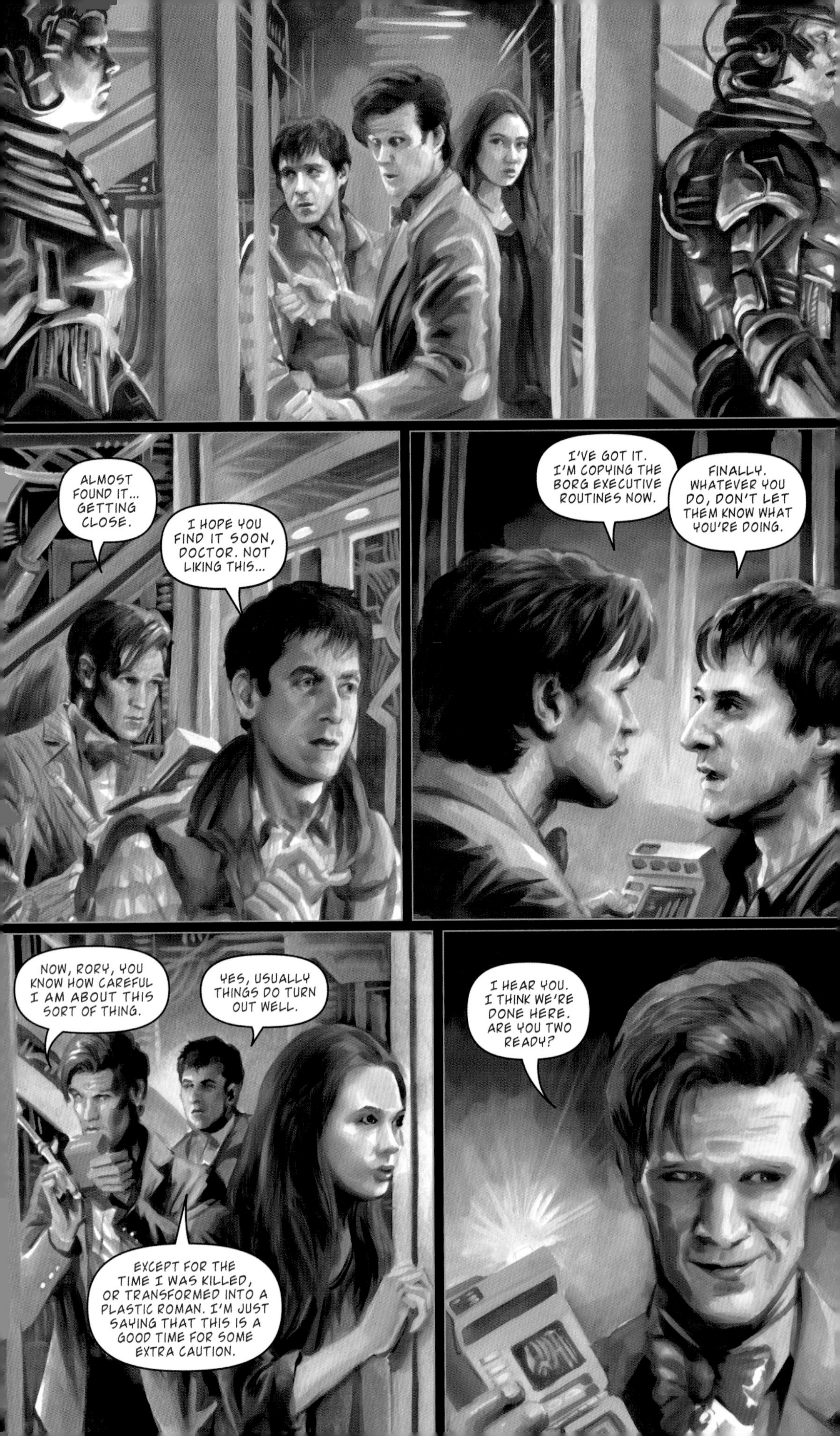
ALMOST FOUND IT... GETTING CLOSE.
I HOPE YOU FIND IT SOON, DOCTOR. NOT LIKING THIS...
I'VE GOT IT. I'M COPYING THE BORG EXECUTIVE ROUTINES NOW.
FINALLY. WHATEVER YOU DO, DON'T LET THEM KNOW WHAT YOU'RE DOING.
NOW, RORY, YOU KNOW HOW CAREFUL I AM ABOUT THIS SORT OF THING.
YES, USUALLY THINGS DO TURN OUT WELL.
EXCEPT FOR THE TIME I WAS KILLED, OR TRANSFORMED INTO A PLASTIC ROMAN. I'M JUST SAYING THAT THIS IS A GOOD TIME FOR SOME EXTRA CAUTION.
I HEAR YOU. I THINK WE'RE DONE HERE. ARE YOU TWO READY?

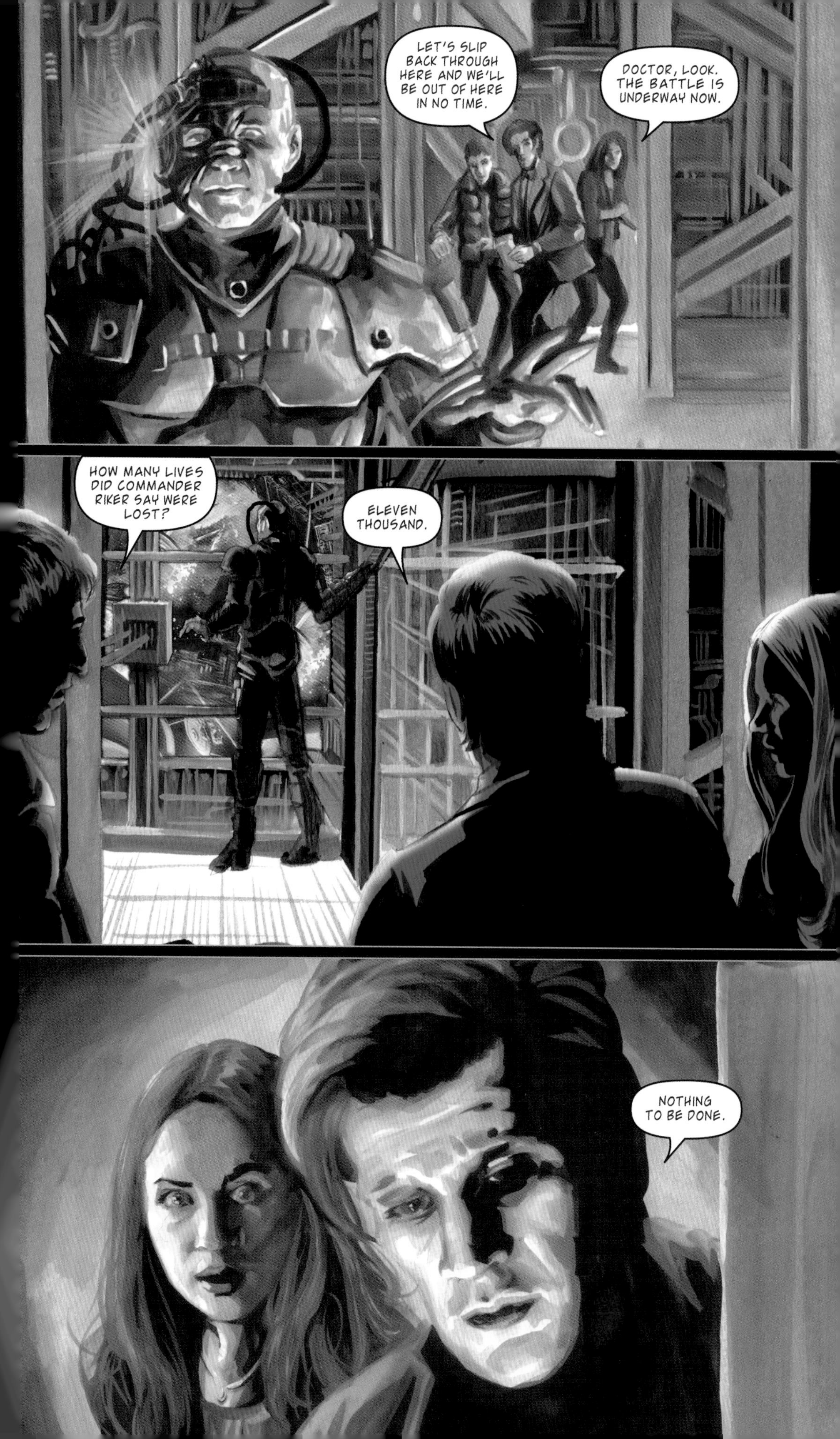

LET'S SLIP BACK THROUGH HERE AND WE'LL BE OUT OF HERE IN NO TIME.
DOCTOR, LOOK. THE BATTLE IS UNDERWAY NOW.
HOW MANY LIVES DID COMMANDER RIKER SAY WERE LOST?
ELEVEN THOUSAND.
NOTHING TO BE DONE.

TIME TO DEPART. EVERYBODY READY?

DOCTOR!

THOUSANDS OF PEOPLE ARE DYING OUT THERE. WHY CAN'T WE DO SOMETHING?

YOU HAVE TO LET IT GO, AMY. THE PAST IS THE PAST.

YOU COULD DO SOMETHING IF YOU WANTED!

THIS BATTLE IS A FIXED POINT IN TIME, AMY. IT CAN'T BE CHANGED.

SECONDLY, EVEN IF I COULD SOMEHOW INTERVENE AND PREVENT THAT BATTLE, HOW CAN I POSSIBLY KNOW WHAT THE POSSIBLE OUTCOME OF THAT INTERVENTION WOULD BE? ARE YOU SURE THAT THINGS WOULD COME OUT BETTER?

WE HAVE OUR OWN CATASTROPHE TO PREVENT, AND I CAN'T LET ANYTHING GET IN THE WAY OF THAT. WITH LUCK, WHAT WE HAVE HERE WILL RESTORE THE BORG AND STOP THE PLANS OF THE CYBERMEN.

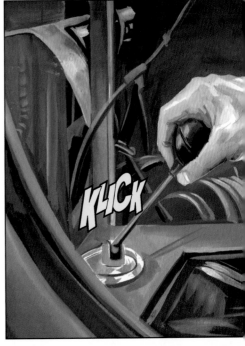

KLICK

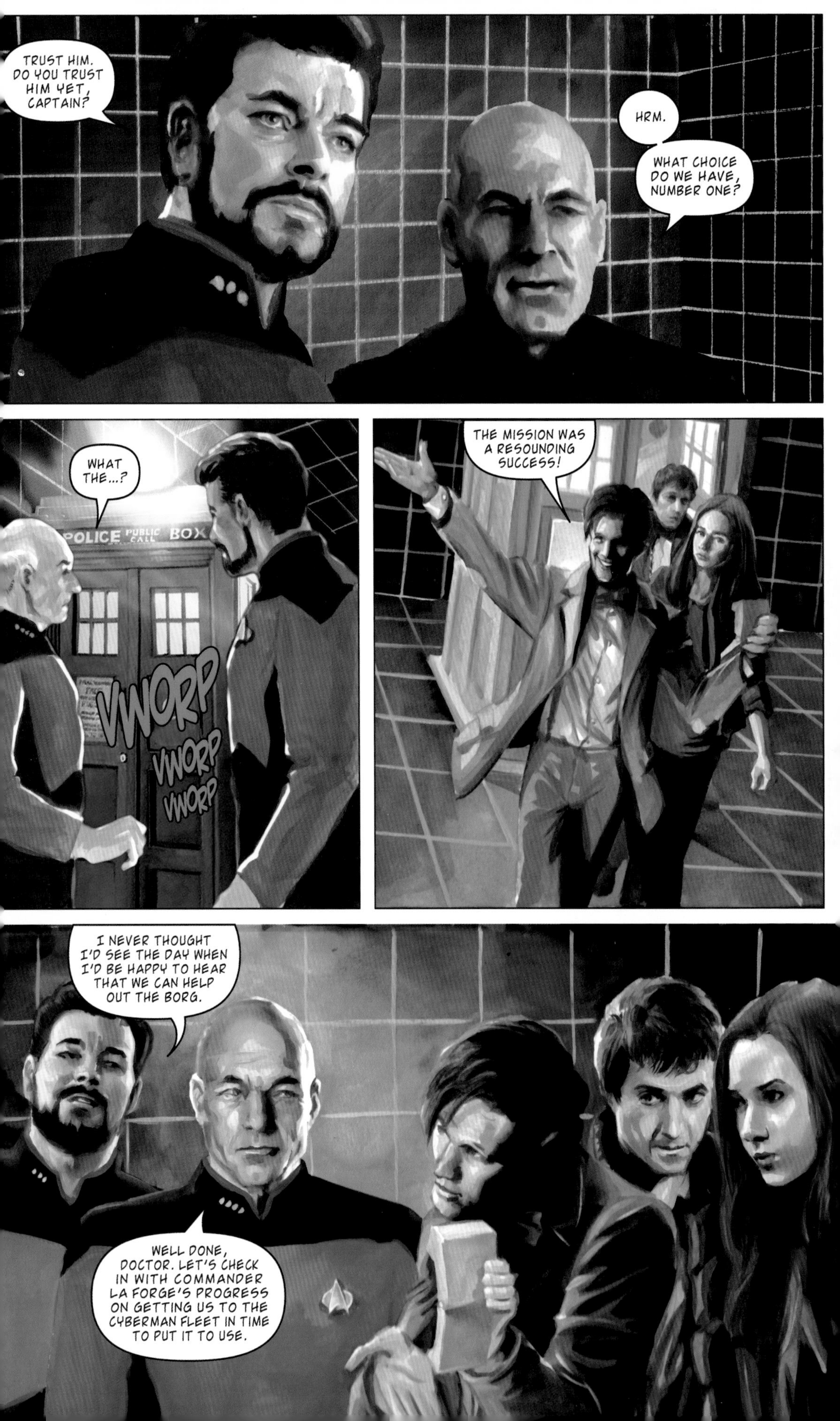
TRUST HIM. DO YOU TRUST HIM YET, CAPTAIN?
HRM.
WHAT CHOICE DO WE HAVE, NUMBER ONE?
WHAT THE...?
POLICE PUBLIC CALL BOX
VWORP
VWORP
VWORP
THE MISSION WAS A RESOUNDING SUCCESS!
I NEVER THOUGHT I'D SEE THE DAY WHEN I'D BE HAPPY TO HEAR THAT WE CAN HELP OUT THE BORG.
WELL DONE, DOCTOR. LET'S CHECK IN WITH COMMANDER LA FORGE'S PROGRESS ON GETTING US TO THE CYBERMAN FLEET IN TIME TO PUT IT TO USE.

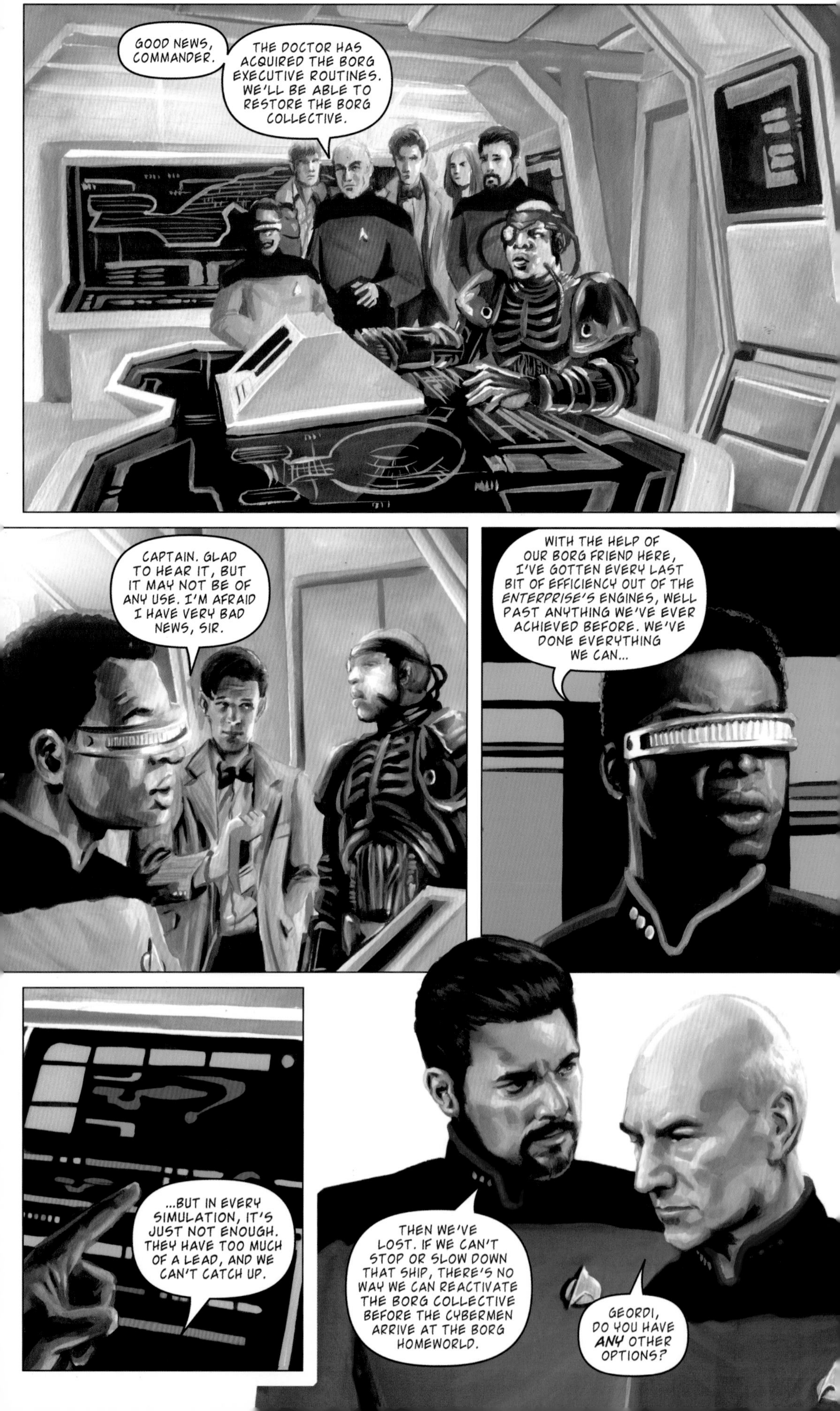
GOOD NEWS, COMMANDER.
THE DOCTOR HAS ACQUIRED THE BORG EXECUTIVE ROUTINES. WE'LL BE ABLE TO RESTORE THE BORG COLLECTIVE.
CAPTAIN. GLAD TO HEAR IT, BUT IT MAY NOT BE OF ANY USE. I'M AFRAID I HAVE VERY BAD NEWS, SIR.
WITH THE HELP OF OUR BORG FRIEND HERE, I'VE GOTTEN EVERY LAST BIT OF EFFICIENCY OUT OF THE *ENTERPRISE'S* ENGINES, WELL PAST ANYTHING WE'VE EVER ACHIEVED BEFORE. WE'VE DONE EVERYTHING WE CAN...
...BUT IN EVERY SIMULATION, IT'S JUST NOT ENOUGH. THEY HAVE TOO MUCH OF A LEAD, AND WE CAN'T CATCH UP.
THEN WE'VE LOST. IF WE CAN'T STOP OR SLOW DOWN THAT SHIP, THERE'S NO WAY WE CAN REACTIVATE THE BORG COLLECTIVE BEFORE THE CYBERMEN ARRIVE AT THE BORG HOMEWORLD.
GEORDI, DO YOU HAVE ***ANY*** OTHER OPTIONS?

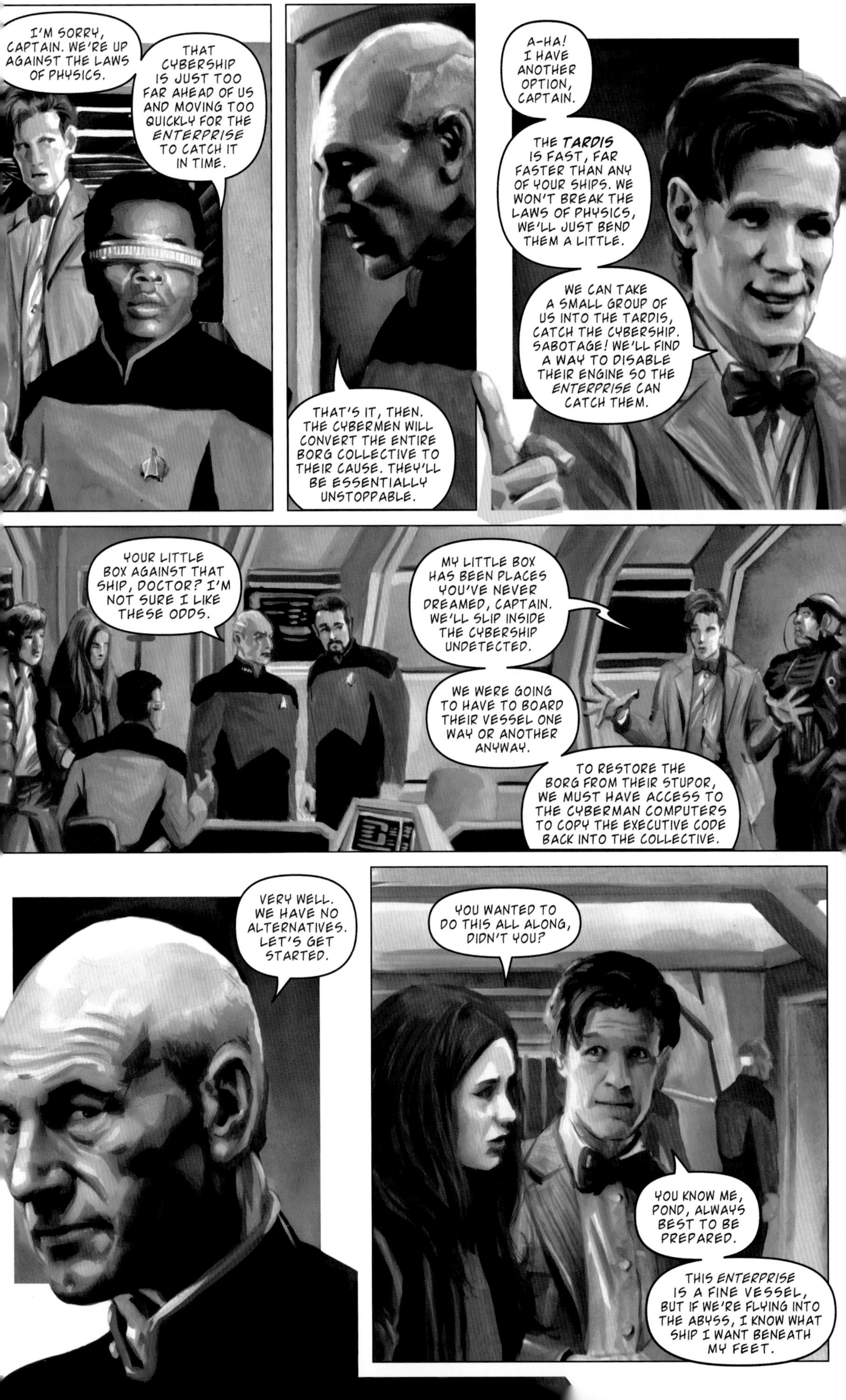

I'M SORRY, CAPTAIN. WE'RE UP AGAINST THE LAWS OF PHYSICS.
THAT CYBERSHIP IS JUST TOO FAR AHEAD OF US AND MOVING TOO QUICKLY FOR THE *ENTERPRISE* TO CATCH IT IN TIME.
THAT'S IT, THEN. THE CYBERMEN WILL CONVERT THE ENTIRE BORG COLLECTIVE TO THEIR CAUSE. THEY'LL BE ESSENTIALLY UNSTOPPABLE.
A-HA! I HAVE ANOTHER OPTION, CAPTAIN.
THE ***TARDIS*** IS FAST, FAR FASTER THAN ANY OF YOUR SHIPS. WE WON'T BREAK THE LAWS OF PHYSICS, WE'LL JUST BEND THEM A LITTLE.
WE CAN TAKE A SMALL GROUP OF US INTO THE TARDIS, CATCH THE CYBERSHIP. SABOTAGE! WE'LL FIND A WAY TO DISABLE THEIR ENGINE SO THE *ENTERPRISE* CAN CATCH THEM.
YOUR LITTLE BOX AGAINST THAT SHIP, DOCTOR? I'M NOT SURE I LIKE THESE ODDS.
MY LITTLE BOX HAS BEEN PLACES YOU'VE NEVER DREAMED, CAPTAIN. WE'LL SLIP INSIDE THE CYBERSHIP UNDETECTED.
WE WERE GOING TO HAVE TO BOARD THEIR VESSEL ONE WAY OR ANOTHER ANYWAY.
TO RESTORE THE BORG FROM THEIR STUPOR, WE MUST HAVE ACCESS TO THE CYBERMAN COMPUTERS TO COPY THE EXECUTIVE CODE BACK INTO THE COLLECTIVE.
VERY WELL. WE HAVE NO ALTERNATIVES. LET'S GET STARTED.
YOU WANTED TO DO THIS ALL ALONG, DIDN'T YOU?
YOU KNOW ME, POND, ALWAYS BEST TO BE PREPARED.
THIS *ENTERPRISE* IS A FINE VESSEL, BUT IF WE'RE FLYING INTO THE ABYSS, I KNOW WHAT SHIP I WANT BENEATH MY FEET.

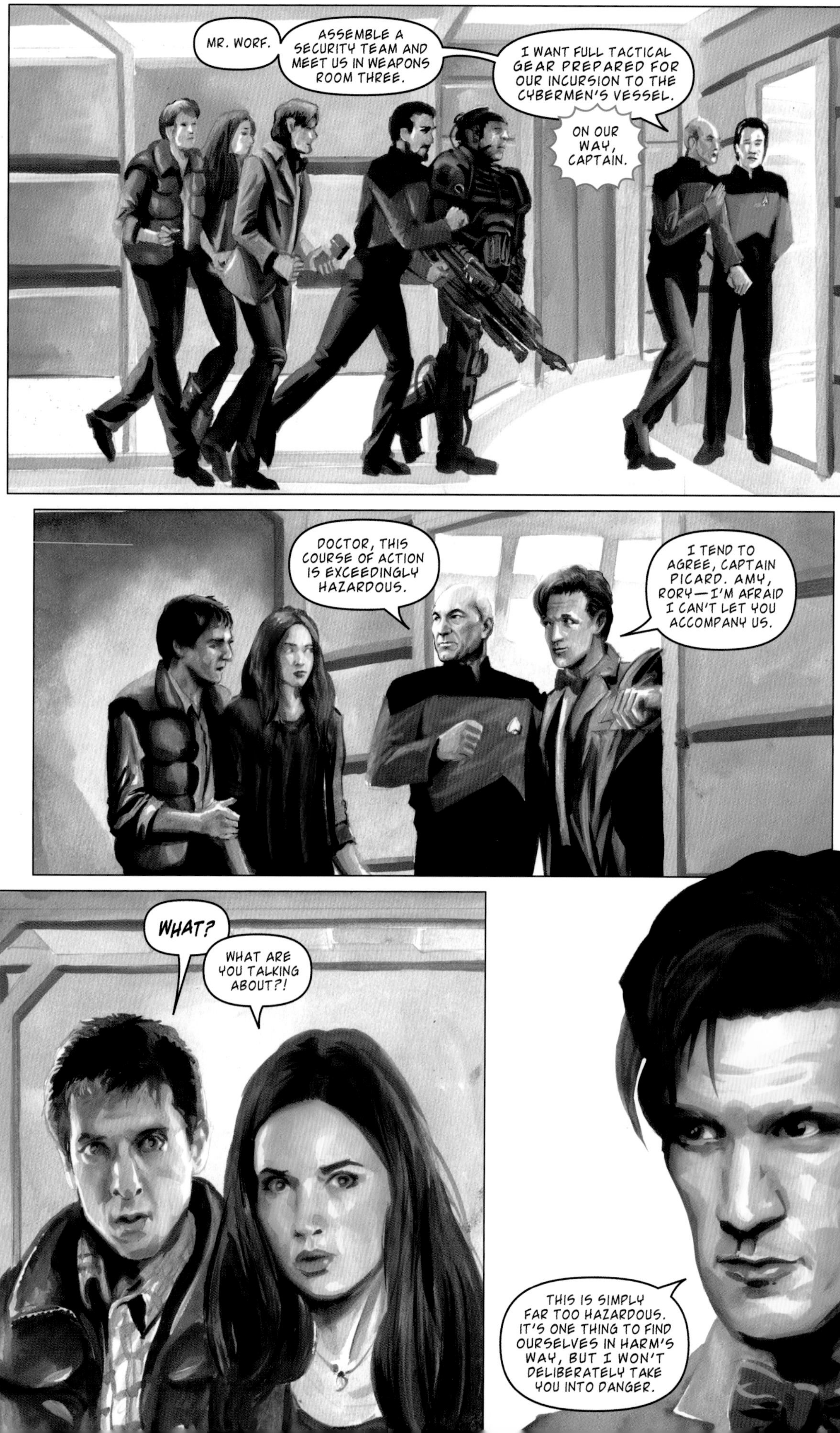

MR. WORF.
ASSEMBLE A SECURITY TEAM AND MEET US IN WEAPONS ROOM THREE.
I WANT FULL TACTICAL GEAR PREPARED FOR OUR INCURSION TO THE CYBERMEN'S VESSEL.
ON OUR WAY, CAPTAIN.
DOCTOR, THIS COURSE OF ACTION IS EXCEEDINGLY HAZARDOUS.
I TEND TO AGREE, CAPTAIN PICARD. AMY, RORY—I'M AFRAID I CAN'T LET YOU ACCOMPANY US.
WHAT?
WHAT ARE YOU TALKING ABOUT?!
THIS IS SIMPLY FAR TOO HAZARDOUS. IT'S ONE THING TO FIND OURSELVES IN HARM'S WAY, BUT I WON'T DELIBERATELY TAKE YOU INTO DANGER.

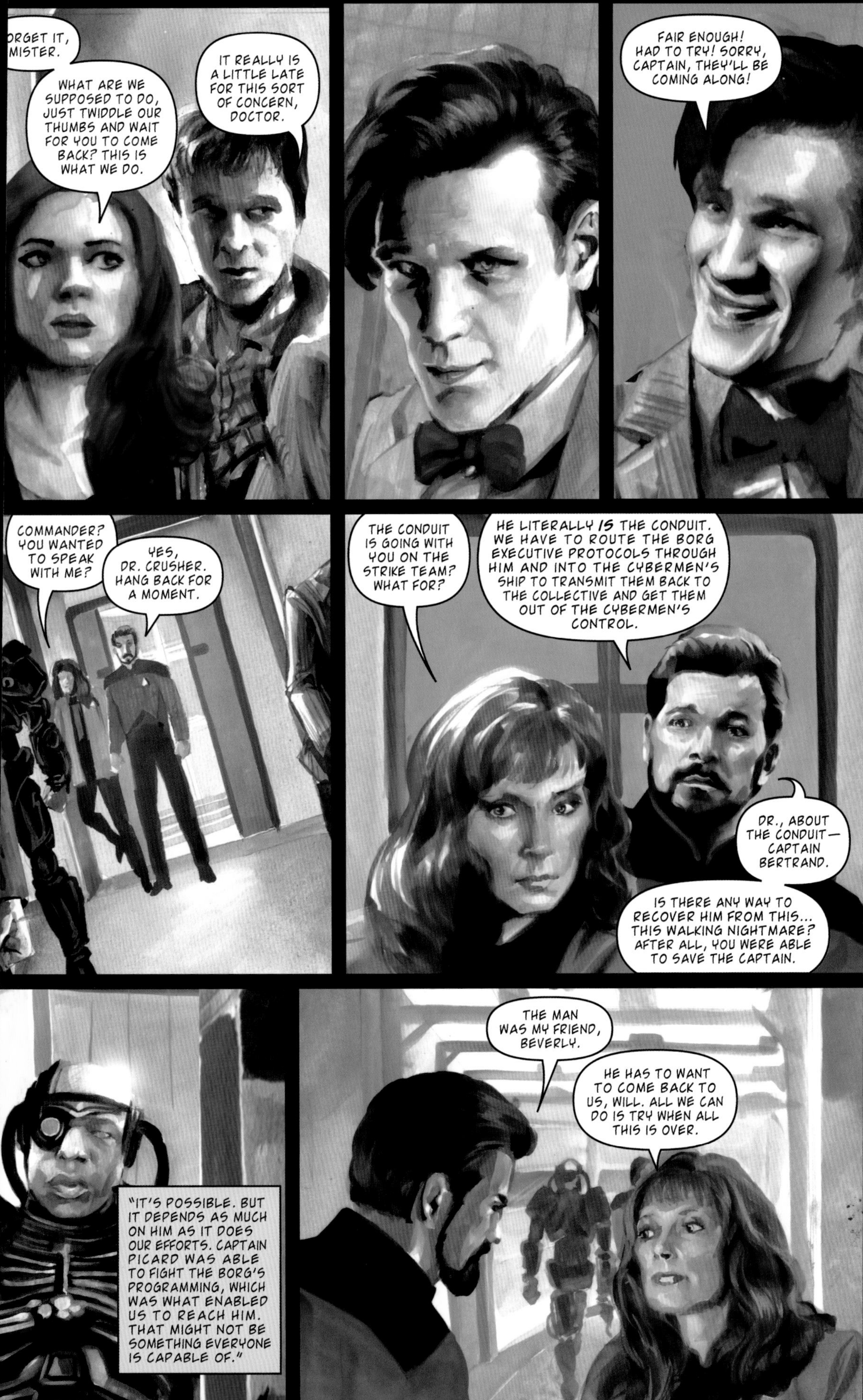
ORGET IT, MISTER.
WHAT ARE WE SUPPOSED TO DO, JUST TWIDDLE OUR THUMBS AND WAIT FOR YOU TO COME BACK? THIS IS WHAT WE DO.
IT REALLY IS A LITTLE LATE FOR THIS SORT OF CONCERN, DOCTOR.
FAIR ENOUGH! HAD TO TRY! SORRY, CAPTAIN, THEY'LL BE COMING ALONG!
COMMANDER? YOU WANTED TO SPEAK WITH ME?
YES, DR. CRUSHER. HANG BACK FOR A MOMENT.
THE CONDUIT IS GOING WITH YOU ON THE STRIKE TEAM? WHAT FOR?
HE LITERALLY *IS* THE CONDUIT. WE HAVE TO ROUTE THE BORG EXECUTIVE PROTOCOLS THROUGH HIM AND INTO THE CYBERMEN'S SHIP TO TRANSMIT THEM BACK TO THE COLLECTIVE AND GET THEM OUT OF THE CYBERMEN'S CONTROL.
DR., ABOUT THE CONDUIT— CAPTAIN BERTRAND.
IS THERE ANY WAY TO RECOVER HIM FROM THIS... THIS WALKING NIGHTMARE? AFTER ALL, YOU WERE ABLE TO SAVE THE CAPTAIN.
"IT'S POSSIBLE. BUT IT DEPENDS AS MUCH ON HIM AS IT DOES OUR EFFORTS. CAPTAIN PICARD WAS ABLE TO FIGHT THE BORG'S PROGRAMMING, WHICH WAS WHAT ENABLED US TO REACH HIM. THAT MIGHT NOT BE SOMETHING EVERYONE IS CAPABLE OF."
THE MAN WAS MY FRIEND, BEVERLY.
HE HAS TO WANT TO COME BACK TO US, WILL. ALL WE CAN DO IS TRY WHEN ALL THIS IS OVER.

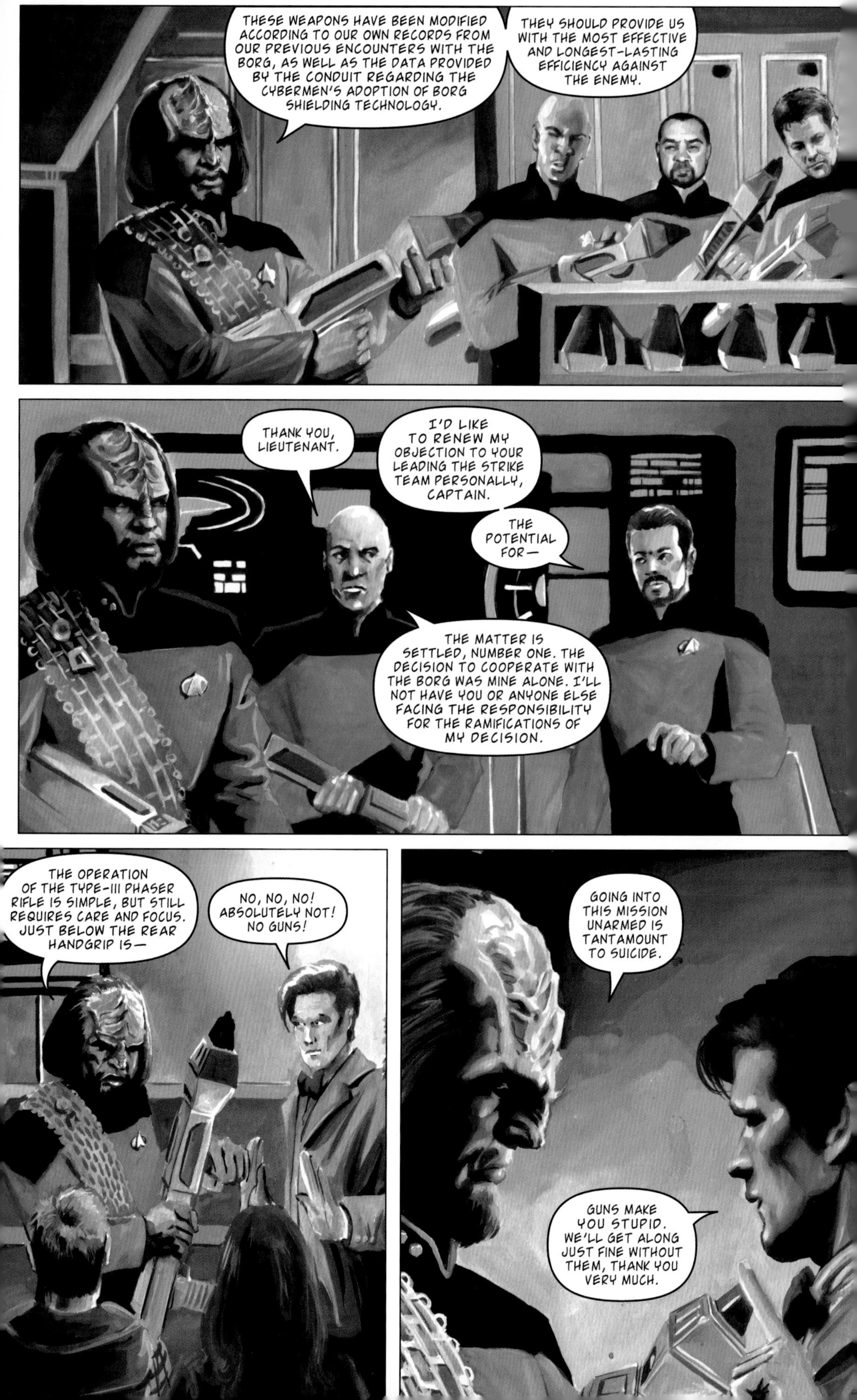

THESE WEAPONS HAVE BEEN MODIFIED ACCORDING TO OUR OWN RECORDS FROM OUR PREVIOUS ENCOUNTERS WITH THE BORG, AS WELL AS THE DATA PROVIDED BY THE CONDUIT REGARDING THE CYBERMEN'S ADOPTION OF BORG SHIELDING TECHNOLOGY.
THEY SHOULD PROVIDE US WITH THE MOST EFFECTIVE AND LONGEST-LASTING EFFICIENCY AGAINST THE ENEMY.
THANK YOU, LIEUTENANT.
I'D LIKE TO RENEW MY OBJECTION TO YOUR LEADING THE STRIKE TEAM PERSONALLY, CAPTAIN.
THE POTENTIAL FOR—
THE MATTER IS SETTLED, NUMBER ONE. THE DECISION TO COOPERATE WITH THE BORG WAS MINE ALONE. I'LL NOT HAVE YOU OR ANYONE ELSE FACING THE RESPONSIBILITY FOR THE RAMIFICATIONS OF MY DECISION.
THE OPERATION OF THE TYPE-III PHASER RIFLE IS SIMPLE, BUT STILL REQUIRES CARE AND FOCUS. JUST BELOW THE REAR HANDGRIP IS—
NO, NO, NO! ABSOLUTELY NOT! NO GUNS!
GOING INTO THIS MISSION UNARMED IS TANTAMOUNT TO SUICIDE.
GUNS MAKE YOU STUPID. WE'LL GET ALONG JUST FINE WITHOUT THEM, THANK YOU VERY MUCH.

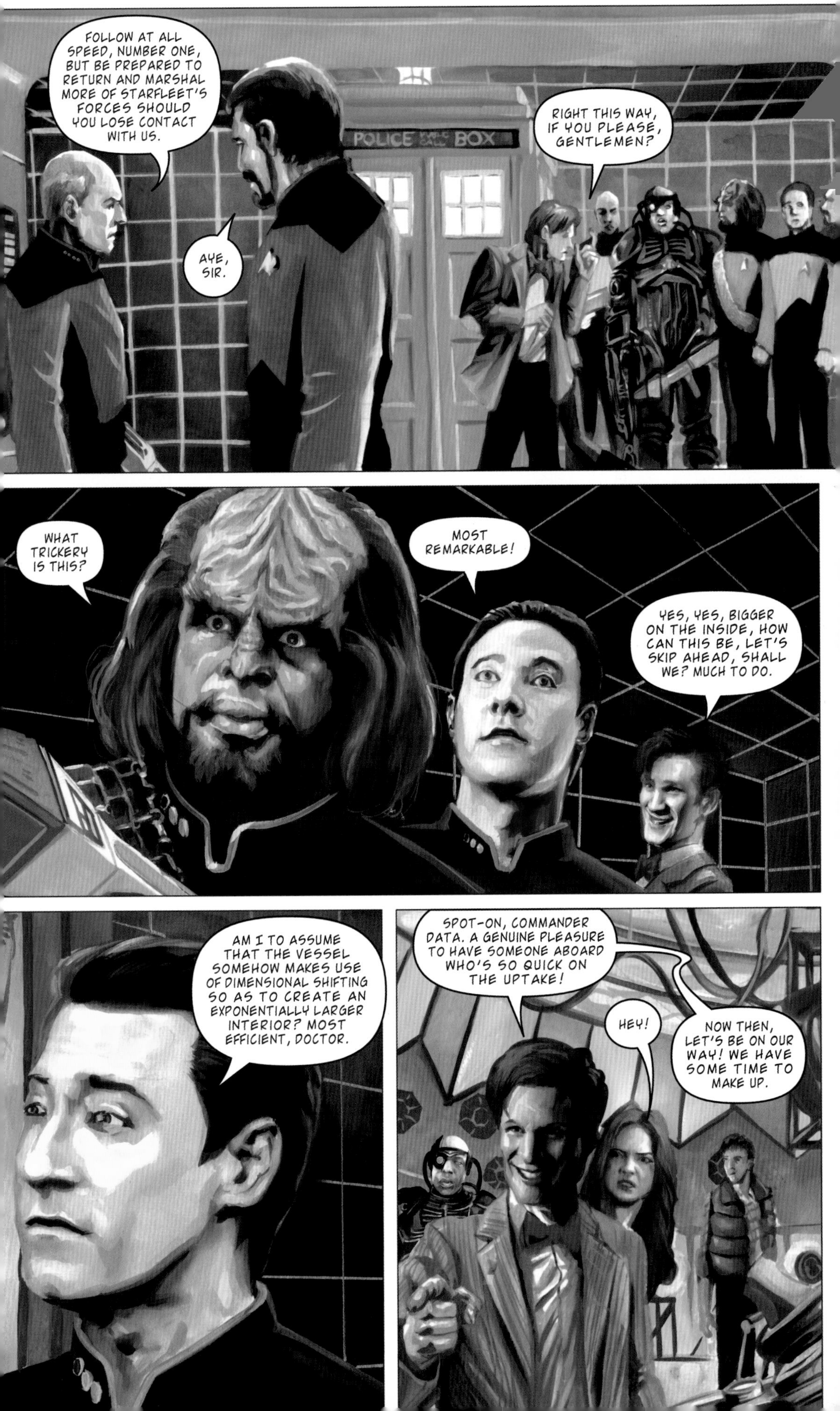
FOLLOW AT ALL SPEED, NUMBER ONE, BUT BE PREPARED TO RETURN AND MARSHAL MORE OF STARFLEET'S FORCES SHOULD YOU LOSE CONTACT WITH US.
AYE, SIR.
POLICE BOX
RIGHT THIS WAY, IF YOU PLEASE, GENTLEMEN?
WHAT TRICKERY IS THIS?
MOST REMARKABLE!
YES, YES, BIGGER ON THE INSIDE, HOW CAN THIS BE, LET'S SKIP AHEAD, SHALL WE? MUCH TO DO.
AM I TO ASSUME THAT THE VESSEL SOMEHOW MAKES USE OF DIMENSIONAL SHIFTING SO AS TO CREATE AN EXPONENTIALLY LARGER INTERIOR? MOST EFFICIENT, DOCTOR.
SPOT-ON, COMMANDER DATA. A GENUINE PLEASURE TO HAVE SOMEONE ABOARD WHO'S SO QUICK ON THE UPTAKE!
NOW THEN, LET'S BE ON OUR WAY! WE HAVE SOME TIME TO MAKE UP.
HEY!

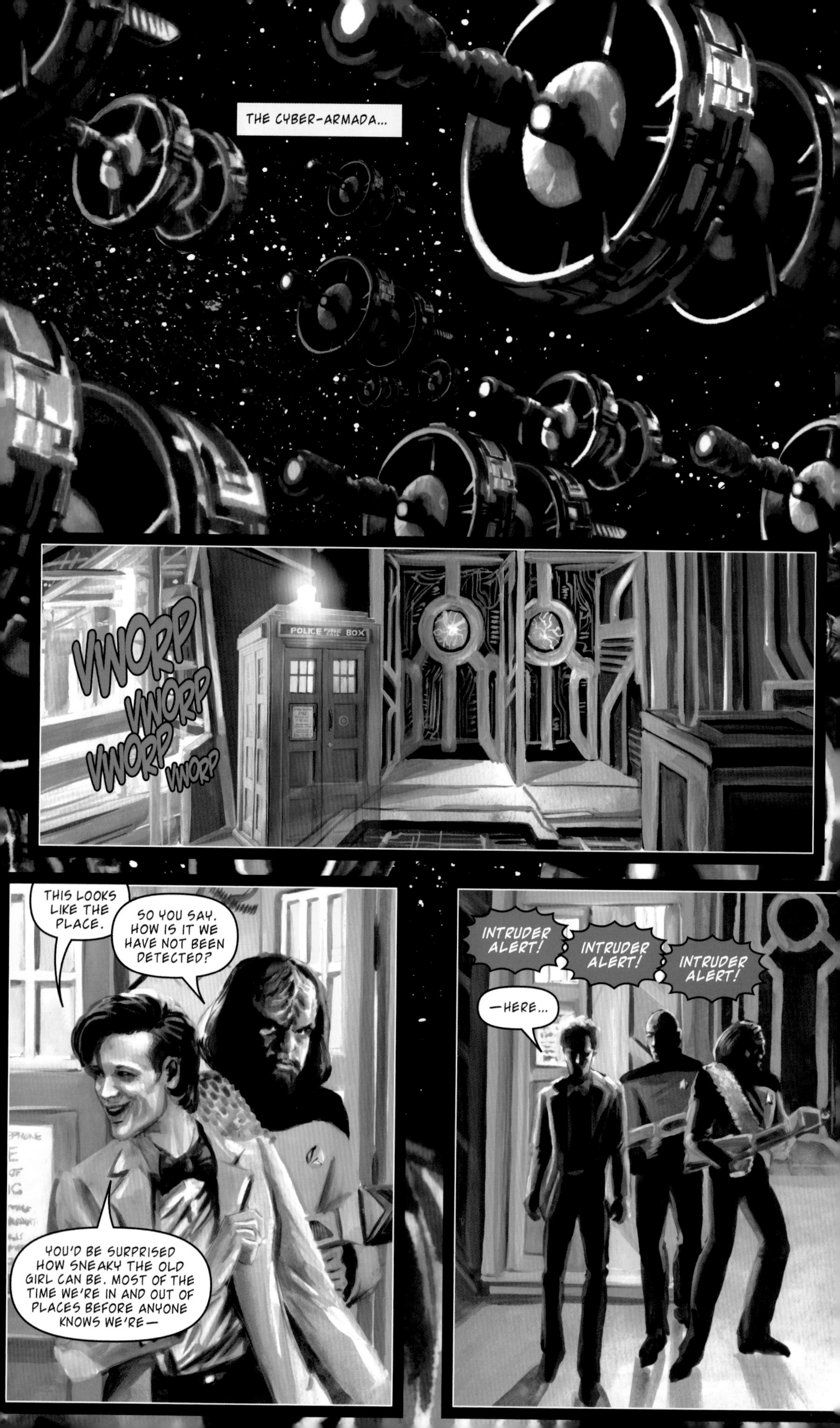
THE CYBER-ARMADA...
VWORP
VWORP
VWORP
VWORP
POLICE PUBLIC CALL BOX
THIS LOOKS LIKE THE PLACE.
SO YOU SAY. HOW IS IT WE HAVE NOT BEEN DETECTED?
YOU'D BE SURPRISED HOW SNEAKY THE OLD GIRL CAN BE. MOST OF THE TIME WE'RE IN AND OUT OF PLACES BEFORE ANYONE KNOWS WE'RE—
INTRUDER ALERT!
INTRUDER ALERT!
INTRUDER ALERT!
—HERE...

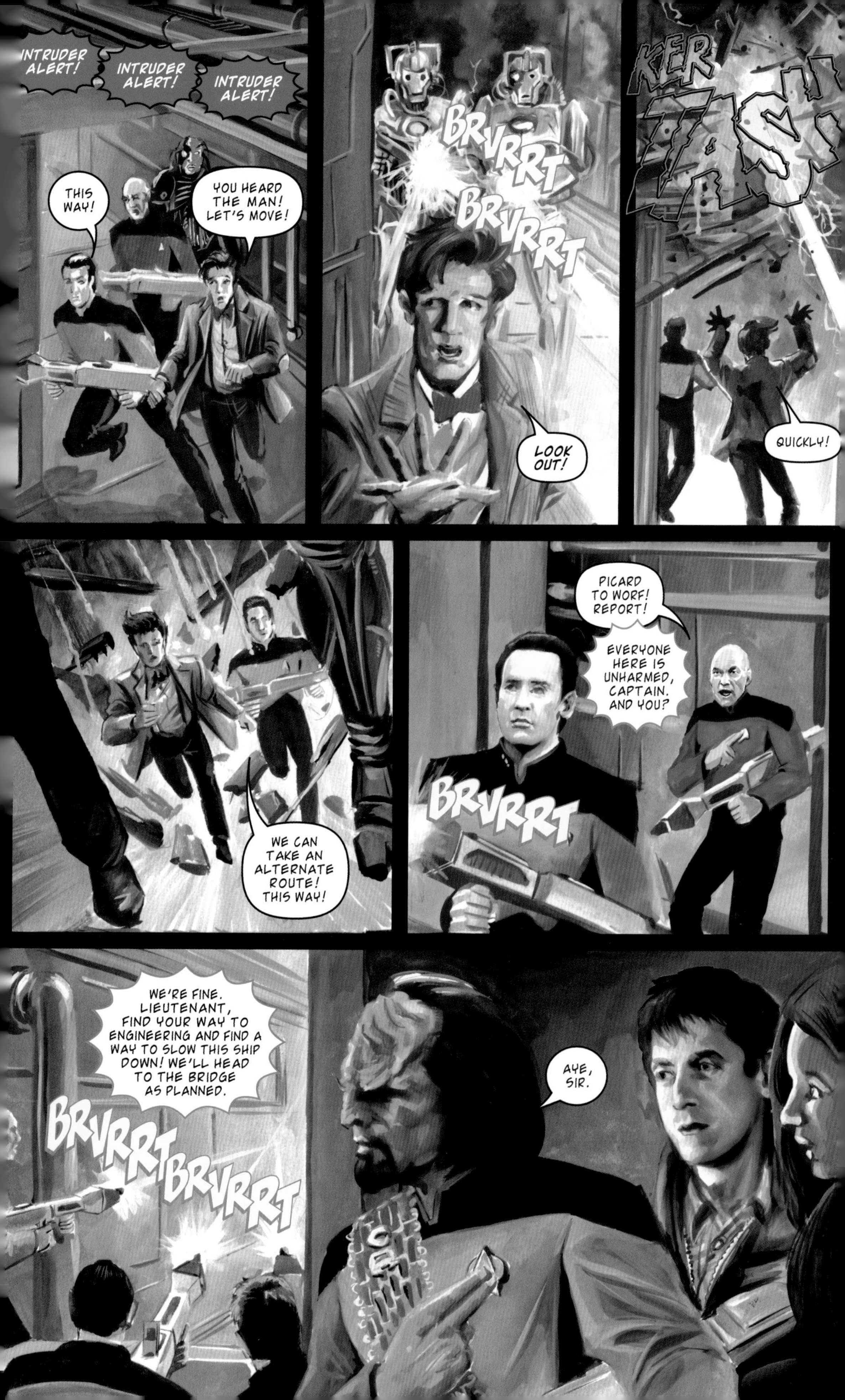

INTRUDER ALERT!
INTRUDER ALERT!
INTRUDER ALERT!
THIS WAY!
YOU HEARD THE MAN! LET'S MOVE!
BRVRRRT
BRVRRRT
LOOK OUT!
KER ZAS!
QUICKLY!
WE CAN TAKE AN ALTERNATE ROUTE! THIS WAY!
PICARD TO WORF! REPORT!
EVERYONE HERE IS UNHARMED, CAPTAIN. AND YOU?
BRVRRT
WE'RE FINE. LIEUTENANT, FIND YOUR WAY TO ENGINEERING AND FIND A WAY TO SLOW THIS SHIP DOWN! WE'LL HEAD TO THE BRIDGE AS PLANNED.
AYE, SIR.
BRVRRT BRVRRRT

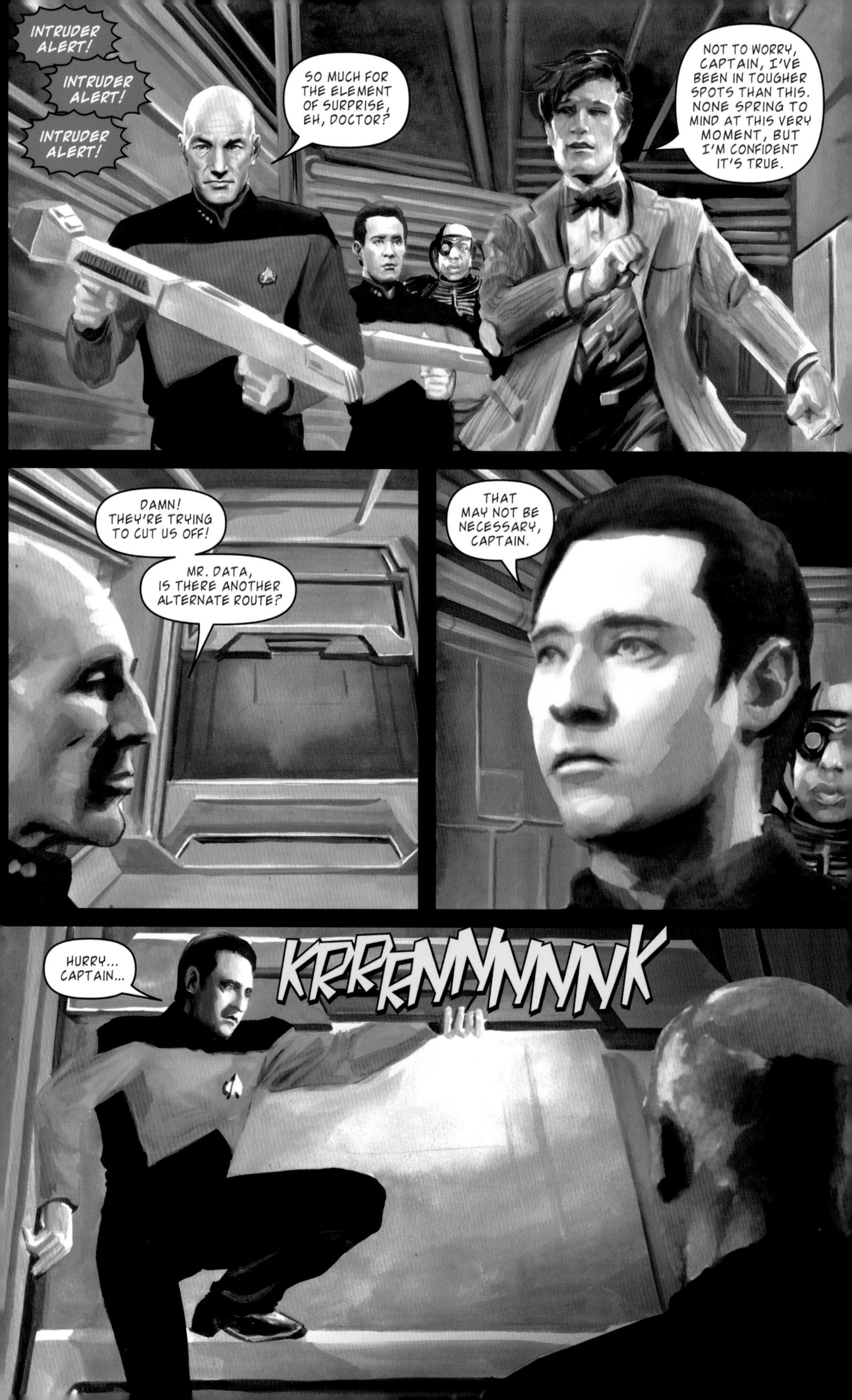
INTRUDER ALERT!
INTRUDER ALERT!
INTRUDER ALERT!
SO MUCH FOR THE ELEMENT OF SURPRISE, EH, DOCTOR?
NOT TO WORRY, CAPTAIN, I'VE BEEN IN TOUGHER SPOTS THAN THIS. NONE SPRING TO MIND AT THIS VERY MOMENT, BUT I'M CONFIDENT IT'S TRUE.
DAMN! THEY'RE TRYING TO CUT US OFF!
MR. DATA, IS THERE ANOTHER ALTERNATE ROUTE?
THAT MAY NOT BE NECESSARY, CAPTAIN.
HURRY... CAPTAIN...
KRRRNNNNNNK

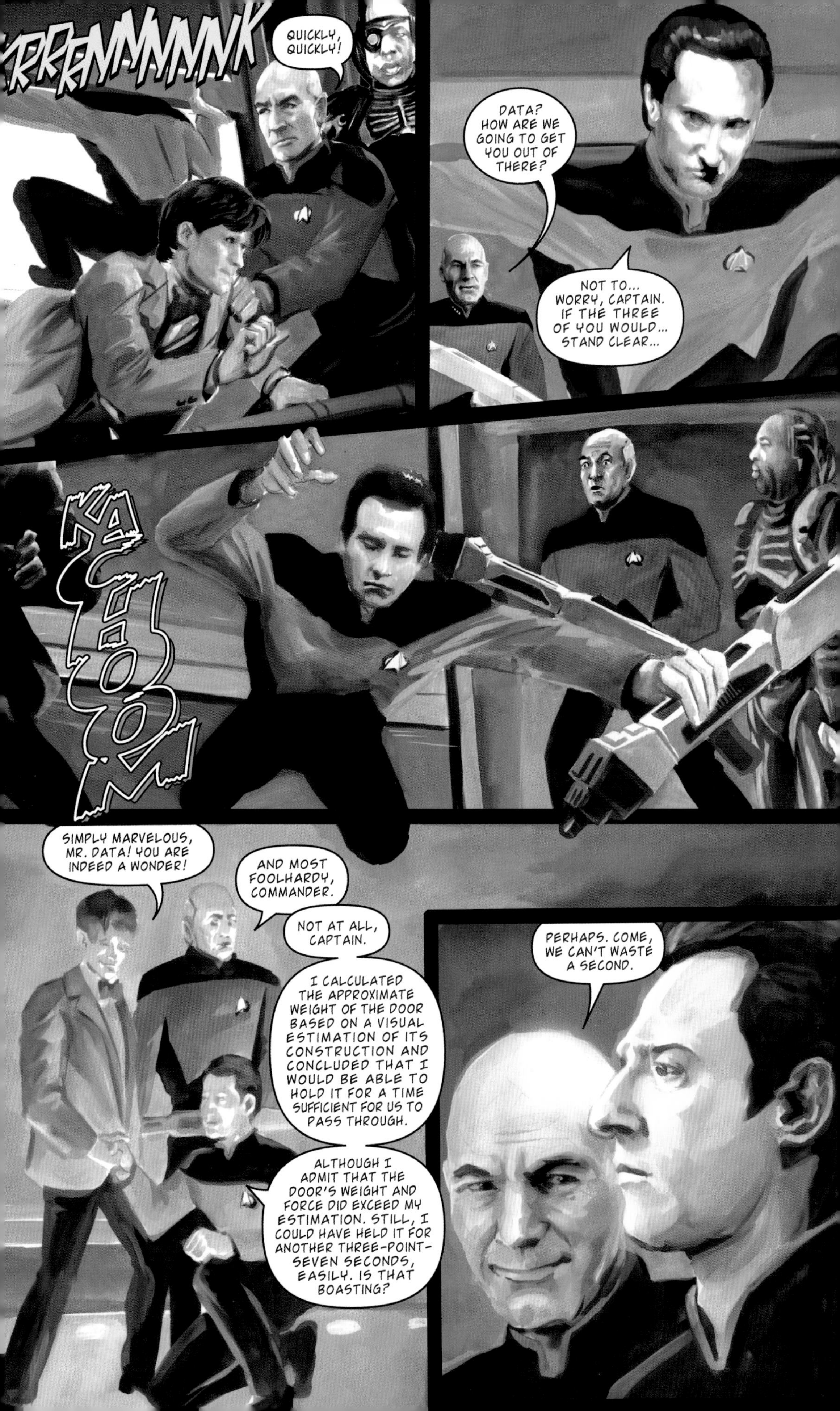
KRRRENNNNNNK
QUICKLY, QUICKLY!
DATA? HOW ARE WE GOING TO GET YOU OUT OF THERE?
NOT TO... WORRY, CAPTAIN. IF THE THREE OF YOU WOULD... STAND CLEAR...
KA-THOOOM
SIMPLY MARVELOUS, MR. DATA! YOU ARE INDEED A WONDER!
AND MOST FOOLHARDY, COMMANDER.
NOT AT ALL, CAPTAIN.
I CALCULATED THE APPROXIMATE WEIGHT OF THE DOOR BASED ON A VISUAL ESTIMATION OF ITS CONSTRUCTION AND CONCLUDED THAT I WOULD BE ABLE TO HOLD IT FOR A TIME SUFFICIENT FOR US TO PASS THROUGH.
ALTHOUGH I ADMIT THAT THE DOOR'S WEIGHT AND FORCE DID EXCEED MY ESTIMATION. STILL, I COULD HAVE HELD IT FOR ANOTHER THREE-POINT-SEVEN SECONDS, EASILY. IS THAT BOASTING?
PERHAPS. COME, WE CAN'T WASTE A SECOND.

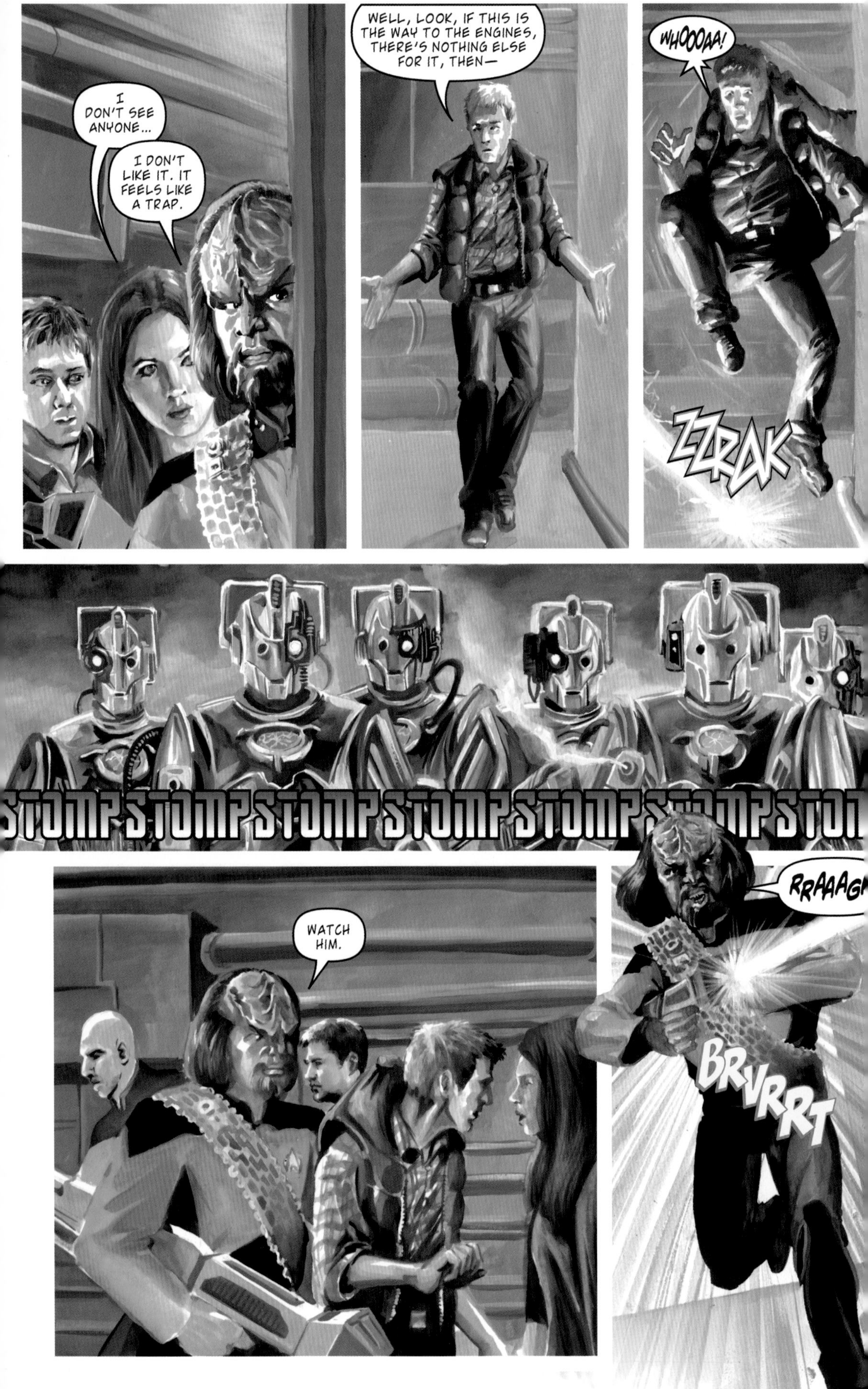
I DON'T SEE ANYONE...
I DON'T LIKE IT. IT FEELS LIKE A TRAP.
WELL, LOOK, IF THIS IS THE WAY TO THE ENGINES, THERE'S NOTHING ELSE FOR IT, THEN—
WHOOOAA!
ZZRAK
STOMP STOMP STOMP STOMP STOMP STOMP STOMP STOM
WATCH HIM.
RRAAAGH
BRVRRT

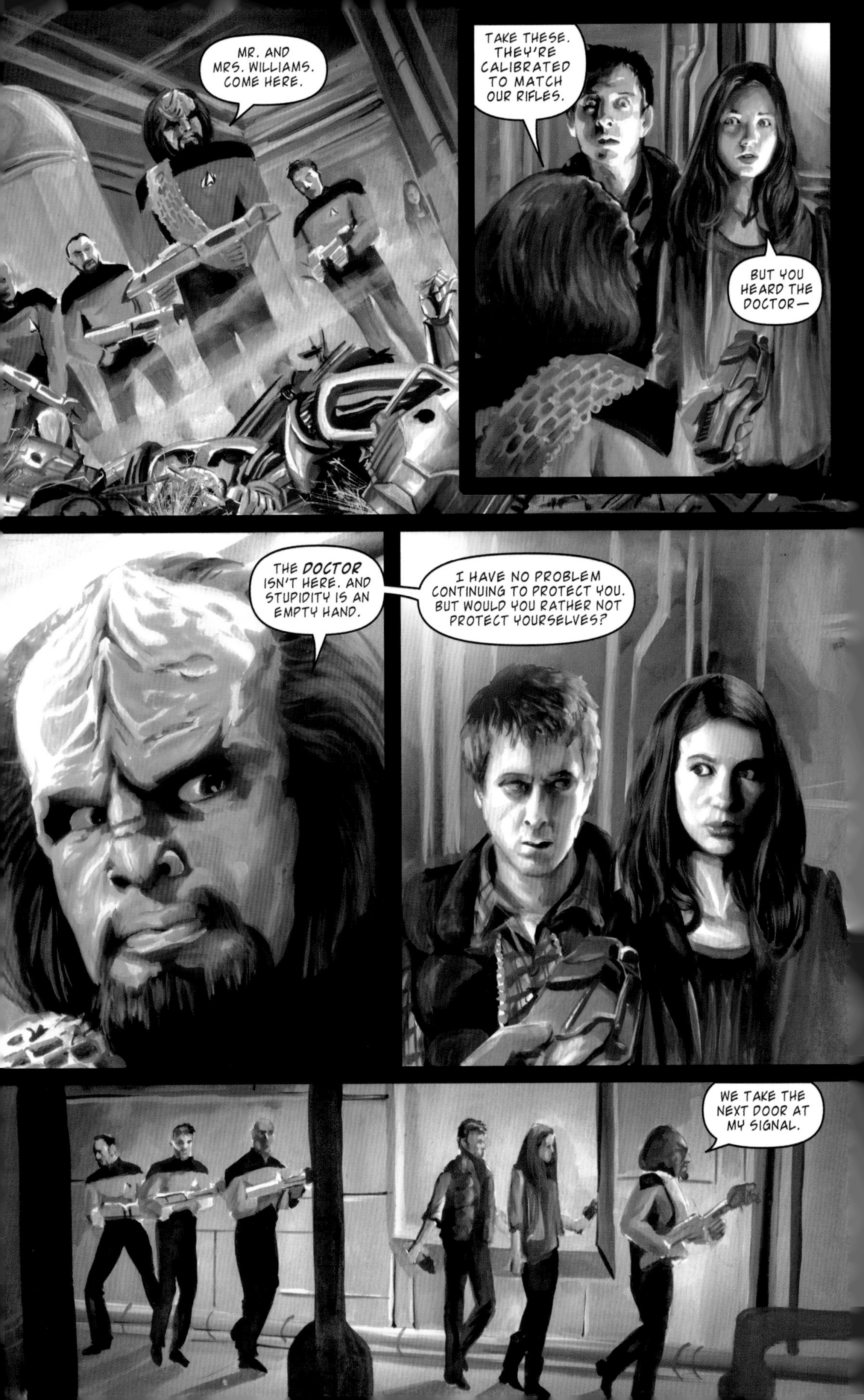
MR. AND MRS. WILLIAMS. COME HERE.
TAKE THESE. THEY'RE CALIBRATED TO MATCH OUR RIFLES.
BUT YOU HEARD THE DOCTOR—
THE *DOCTOR* ISN'T HERE. AND STUPIDITY IS AN EMPTY HAND.
I HAVE NO PROBLEM CONTINUING TO PROTECT YOU. BUT WOULD YOU RATHER NOT PROTECT YOURSELVES?
WE TAKE THE NEXT DOOR AT MY SIGNAL.

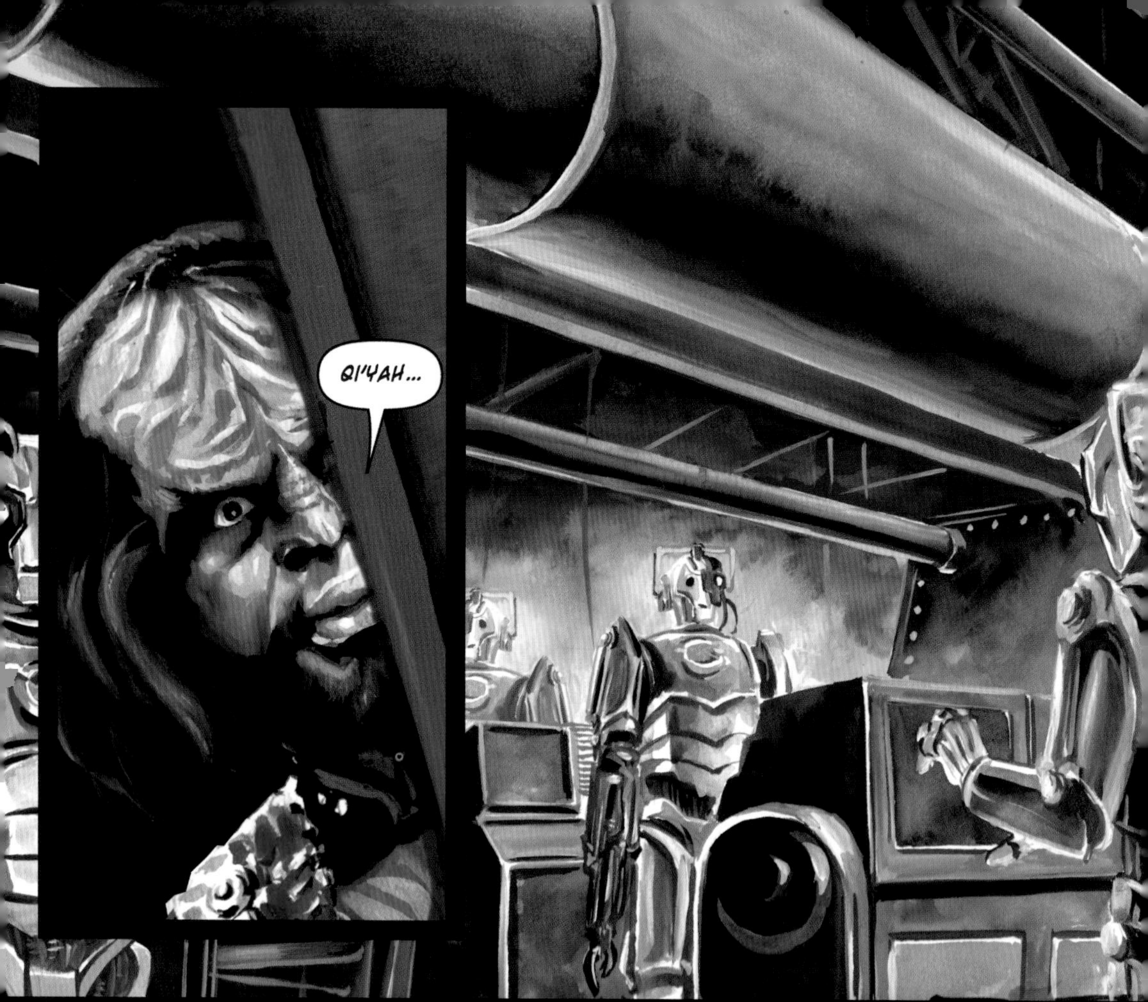
QI'YAH...
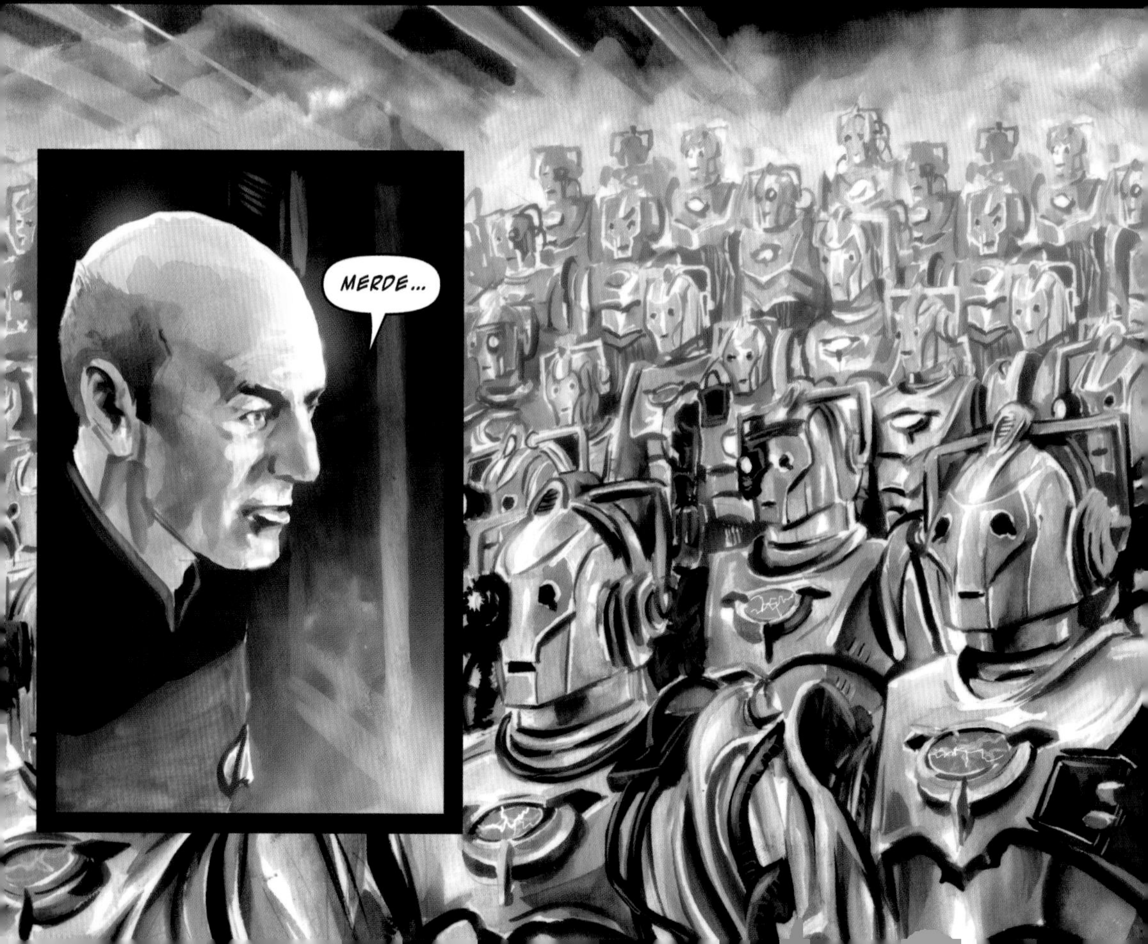
MERDE...

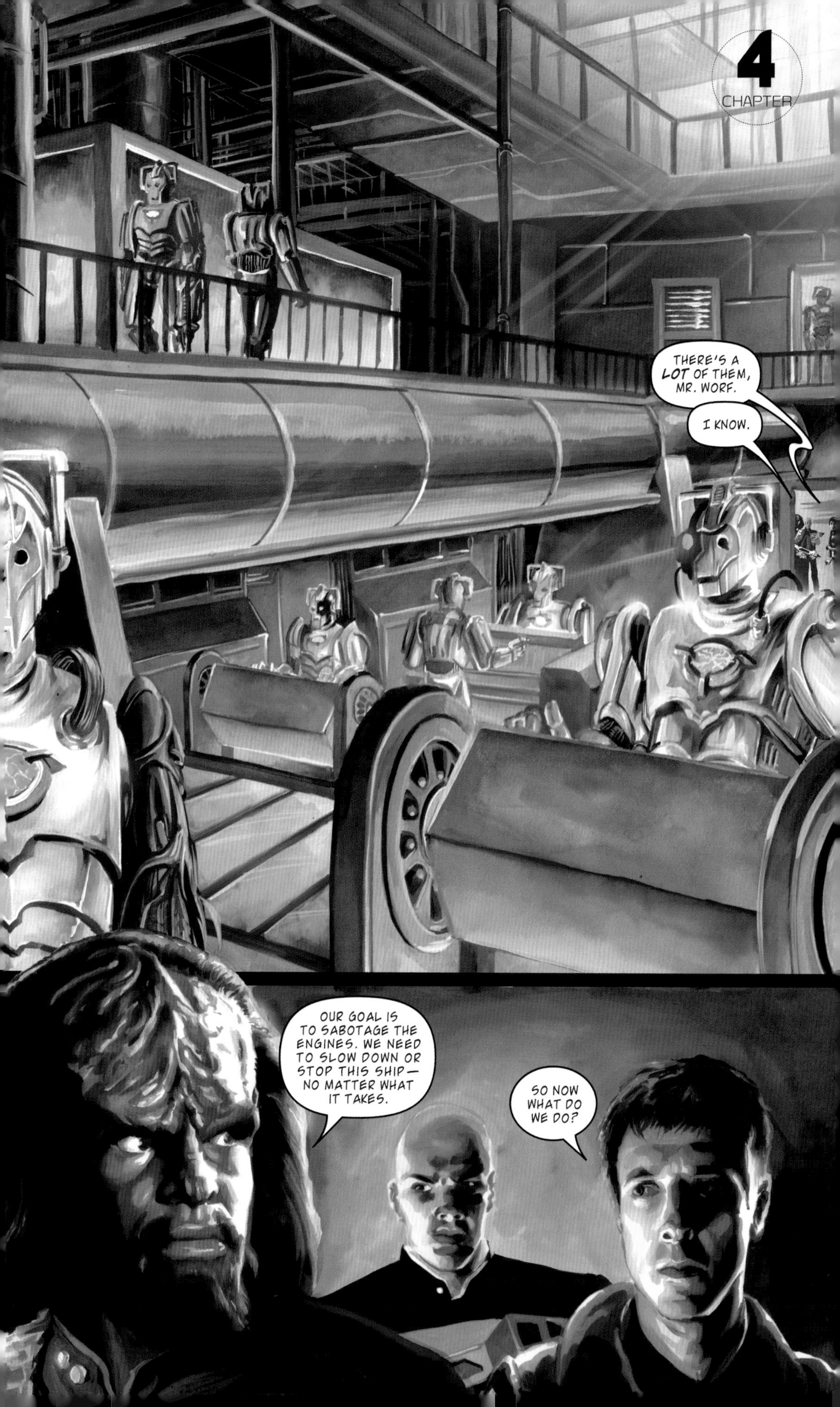
4
CHAPTER
THERE'S A LOT OF THEM, MR. WORF.
I KNOW.
OUR GOAL IS TO SABOTAGE THE ENGINES. WE NEED TO SLOW DOWN OR STOP THIS SHIP— NO MATTER WHAT IT TAKES.
SO NOW WHAT DO WE DO?

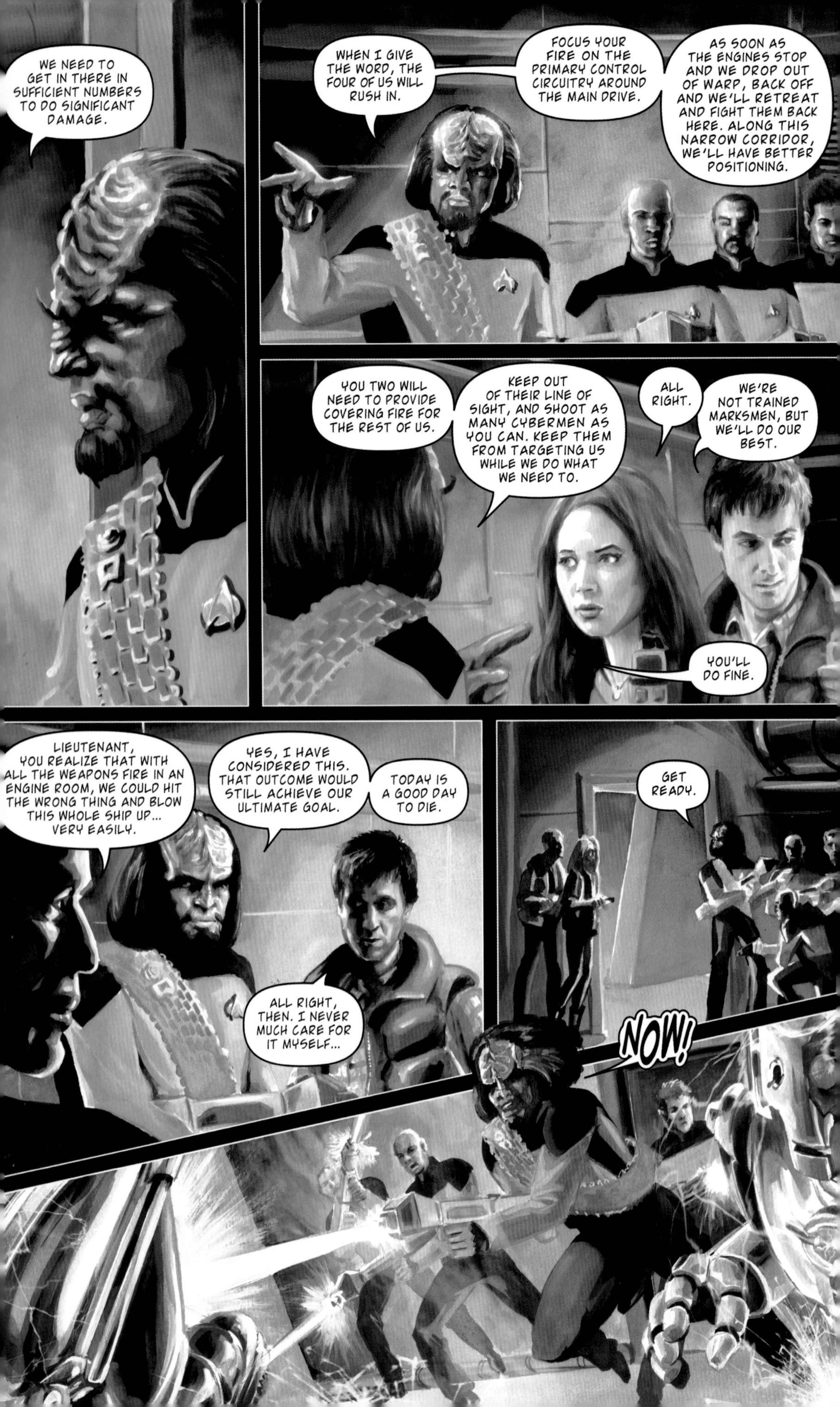
WE NEED TO GET IN THERE IN SUFFICIENT NUMBERS TO DO SIGNIFICANT DAMAGE.
WHEN I GIVE THE WORD, THE FOUR OF US WILL RUSH IN.
FOCUS YOUR FIRE ON THE PRIMARY CONTROL CIRCUITRY AROUND THE MAIN DRIVE.
AS SOON AS THE ENGINES STOP AND WE DROP OUT OF WARP, BACK OFF AND WE'LL RETREAT AND FIGHT THEM BACK HERE. ALONG THIS NARROW CORRIDOR, WE'LL HAVE BETTER POSITIONING.
YOU TWO WILL NEED TO PROVIDE COVERING FIRE FOR THE REST OF US.
KEEP OUT OF THEIR LINE OF SIGHT, AND SHOOT AS MANY CYBERMEN AS YOU CAN. KEEP THEM FROM TARGETING US WHILE WE DO WHAT WE NEED TO.
ALL RIGHT.
WE'RE NOT TRAINED MARKSMEN, BUT WE'LL DO OUR BEST.
YOU'LL DO FINE.
LIEUTENANT, YOU REALIZE THAT WITH ALL THE WEAPONS FIRE IN AN ENGINE ROOM, WE COULD HIT THE WRONG THING AND BLOW THIS WHOLE SHIP UP... VERY EASILY.
YES, I HAVE CONSIDERED THIS. THAT OUTCOME WOULD STILL ACHIEVE OUR ULTIMATE GOAL.
TODAY IS A GOOD DAY TO DIE.
ALL RIGHT, THEN. I NEVER MUCH CARE FOR IT MYSELF...
GET READY.
NOW!

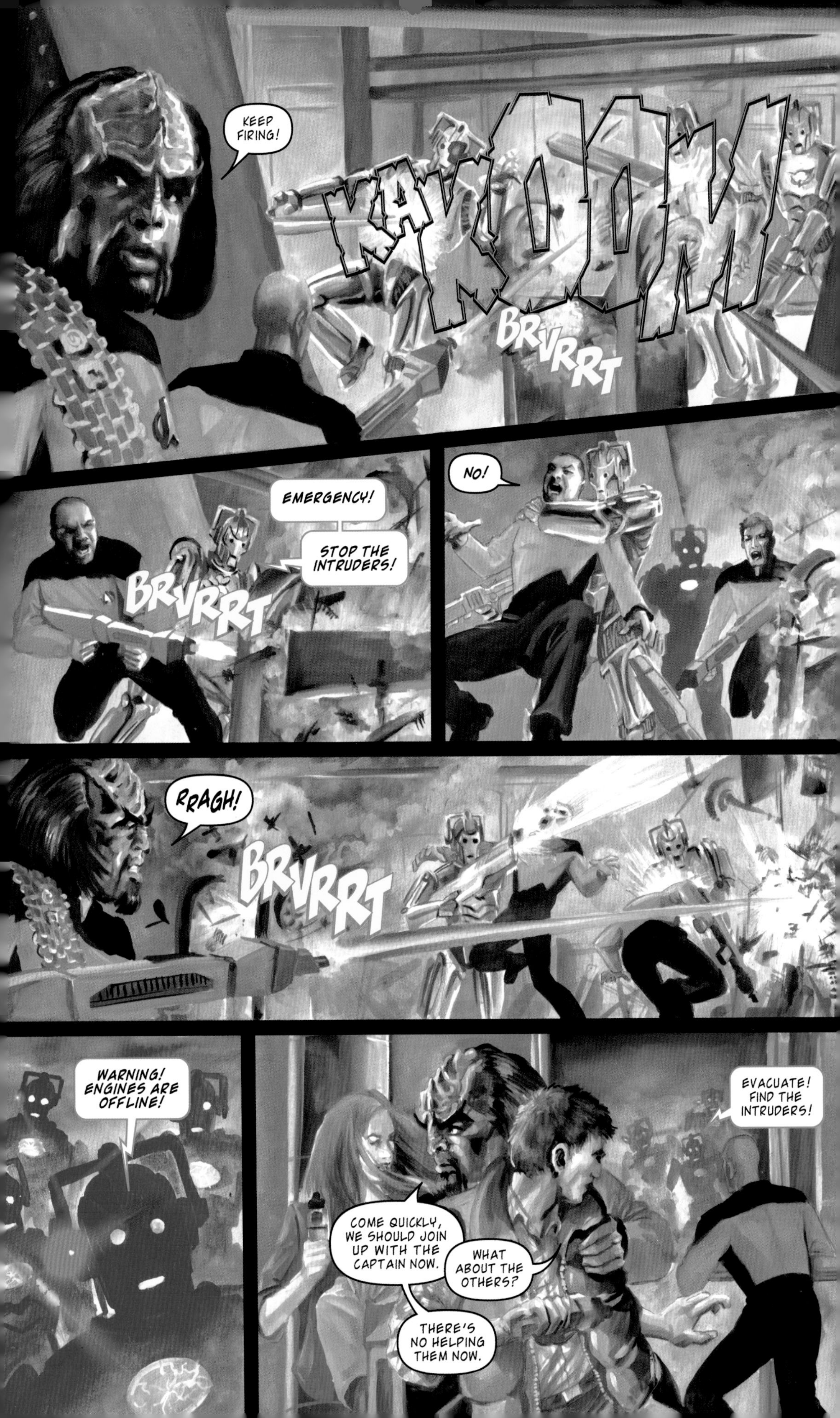
KEEP FIRING!
KAVOOOM!
BRVRRT
EMERGENCY!
STOP THE INTRUDERS!
BRVRRT
NO!
RRAGH!
BRVRRT
WARNING! ENGINES ARE OFFLINE!
EVACUATE! FIND THE INTRUDERS!
COME QUICKLY, WE SHOULD JOIN UP WITH THE CAPTAIN NOW.
WHAT ABOUT THE OTHERS?
THERE'S NO HELPING THEM NOW.

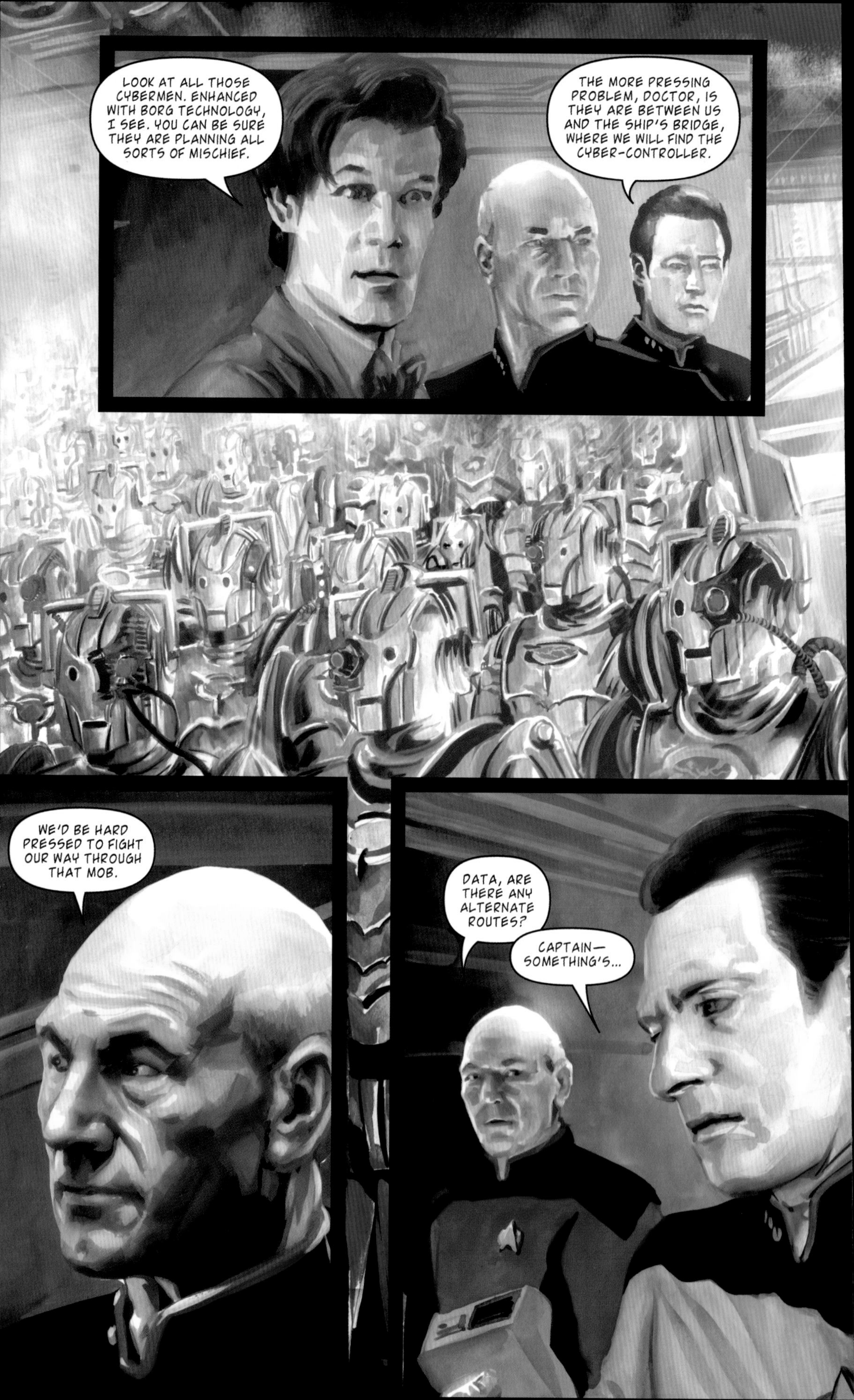
LOOK AT ALL THOSE CYBERMEN. ENHANCED WITH BORG TECHNOLOGY, I SEE. YOU CAN BE SURE THEY ARE PLANNING ALL SORTS OF MISCHIEF.
THE MORE PRESSING PROBLEM, DOCTOR, IS THEY ARE BETWEEN US AND THE SHIP'S BRIDGE, WHERE WE WILL FIND THE CYBER-CONTROLLER.
WE'D BE HARD PRESSED TO FIGHT OUR WAY THROUGH THAT MOB.
DATA, ARE THERE ANY ALTERNATE ROUTES?
CAPTAIN— SOMETHING'S...

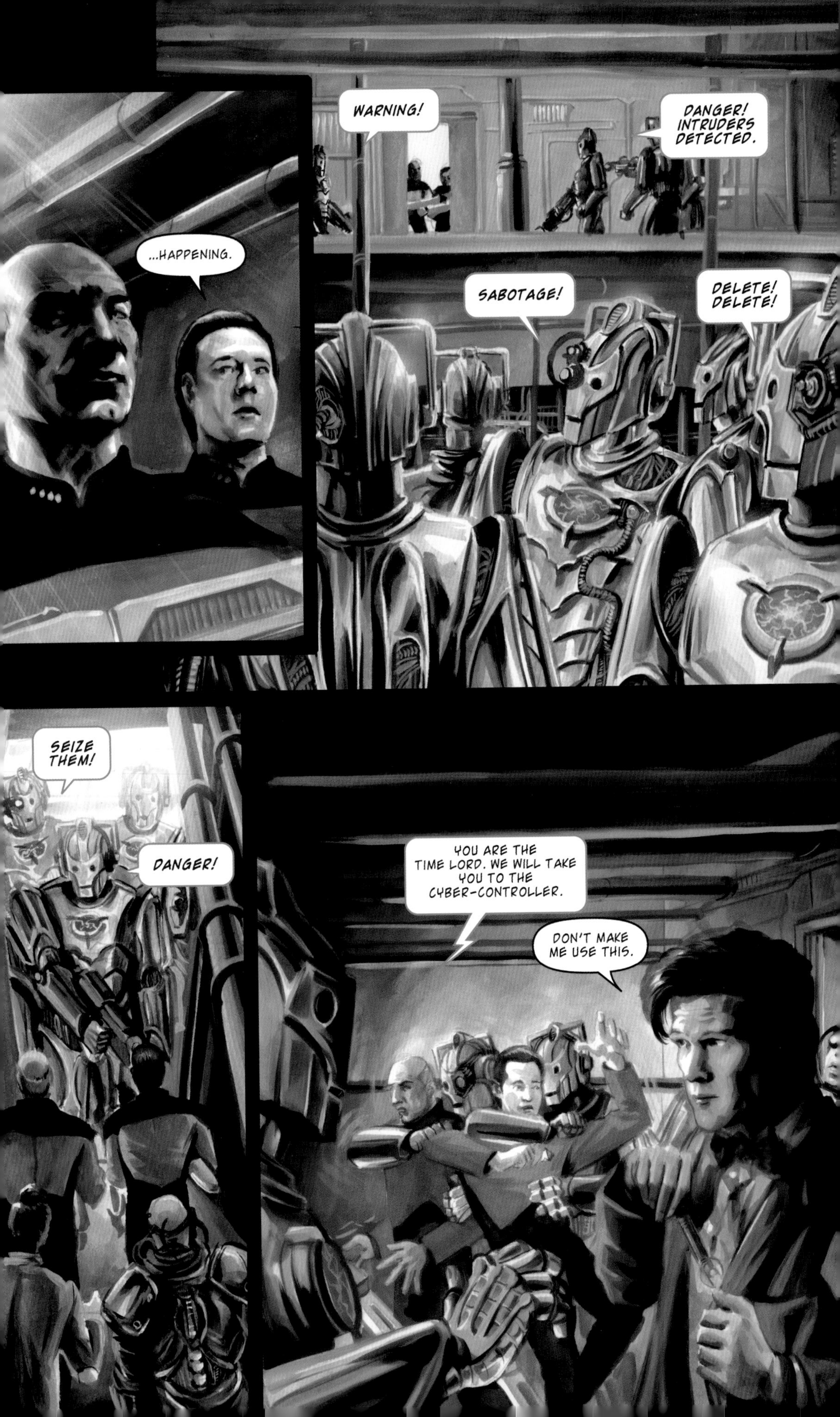
...HAPPENING.
WARNING!
DANGER! INTRUDERS DETECTED.
SABOTAGE!
DELETE! DELETE!
SEIZE THEM!
DANGER!
YOU ARE THE TIME LORD. WE WILL TAKE YOU TO THE CYBER-CONTROLLER.
DON'T MAKE ME USE THIS.

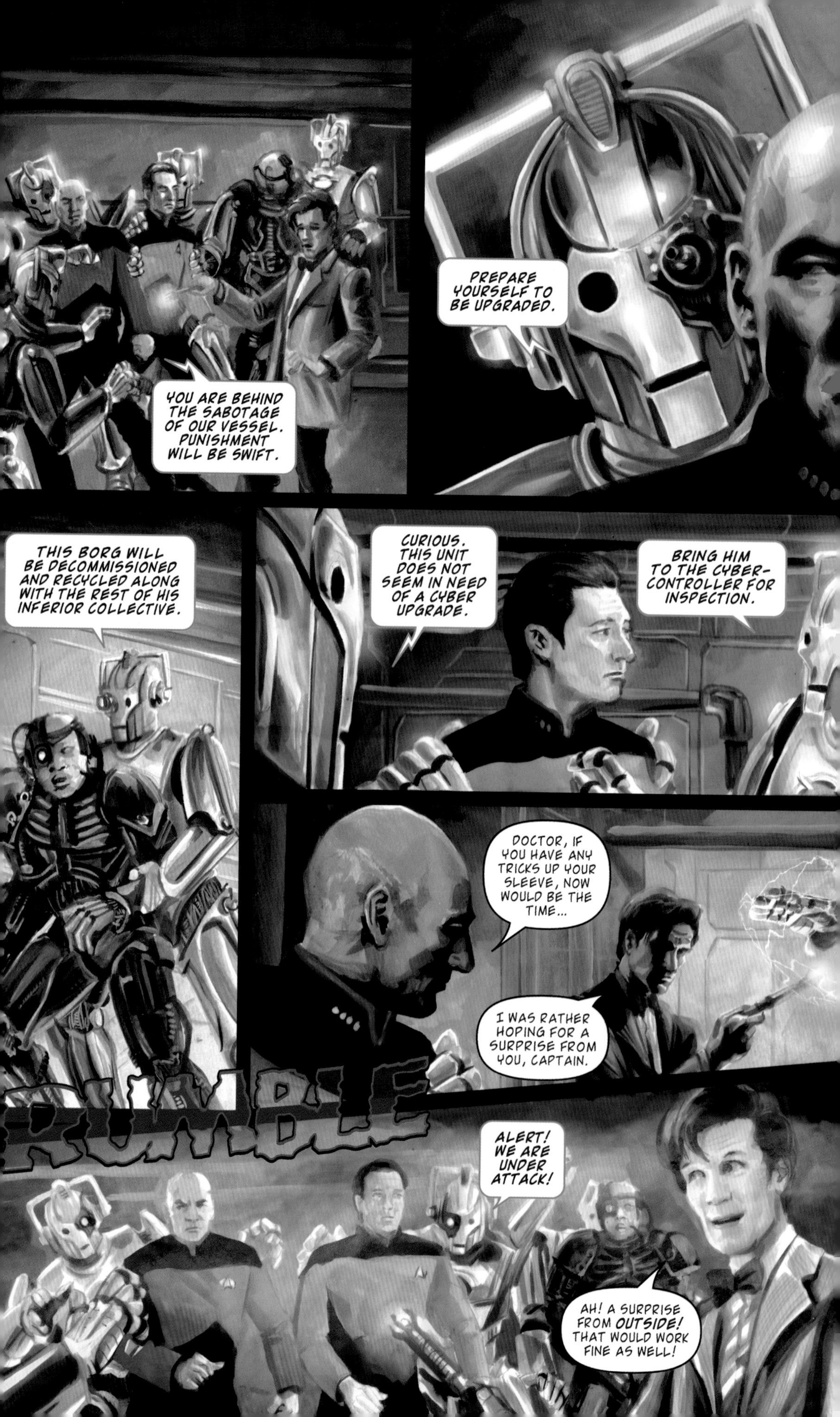
YOU ARE BEHIND THE SABOTAGE OF OUR VESSEL. PUNISHMENT WILL BE SWIFT.
PREPARE YOURSELF TO BE UPGRADED.
THIS BORG WILL BE DECOMMISSIONED AND RECYCLED ALONG WITH THE REST OF HIS INFERIOR COLLECTIVE.
CURIOUS. THIS UNIT DOES NOT SEEM IN NEED OF A CYBER UPGRADE.
BRING HIM TO THE CYBER-CONTROLLER FOR INSPECTION.
DOCTOR, IF YOU HAVE ANY TRICKS UP YOUR SLEEVE, NOW WOULD BE THE TIME...
I WAS RATHER HOPING FOR A SURPRISE FROM YOU, CAPTAIN.
RUMBLE
ALERT! WE ARE UNDER ATTACK!
AH! A SURPRISE FROM OUTSIDE! THAT WOULD WORK FINE AS WELL!

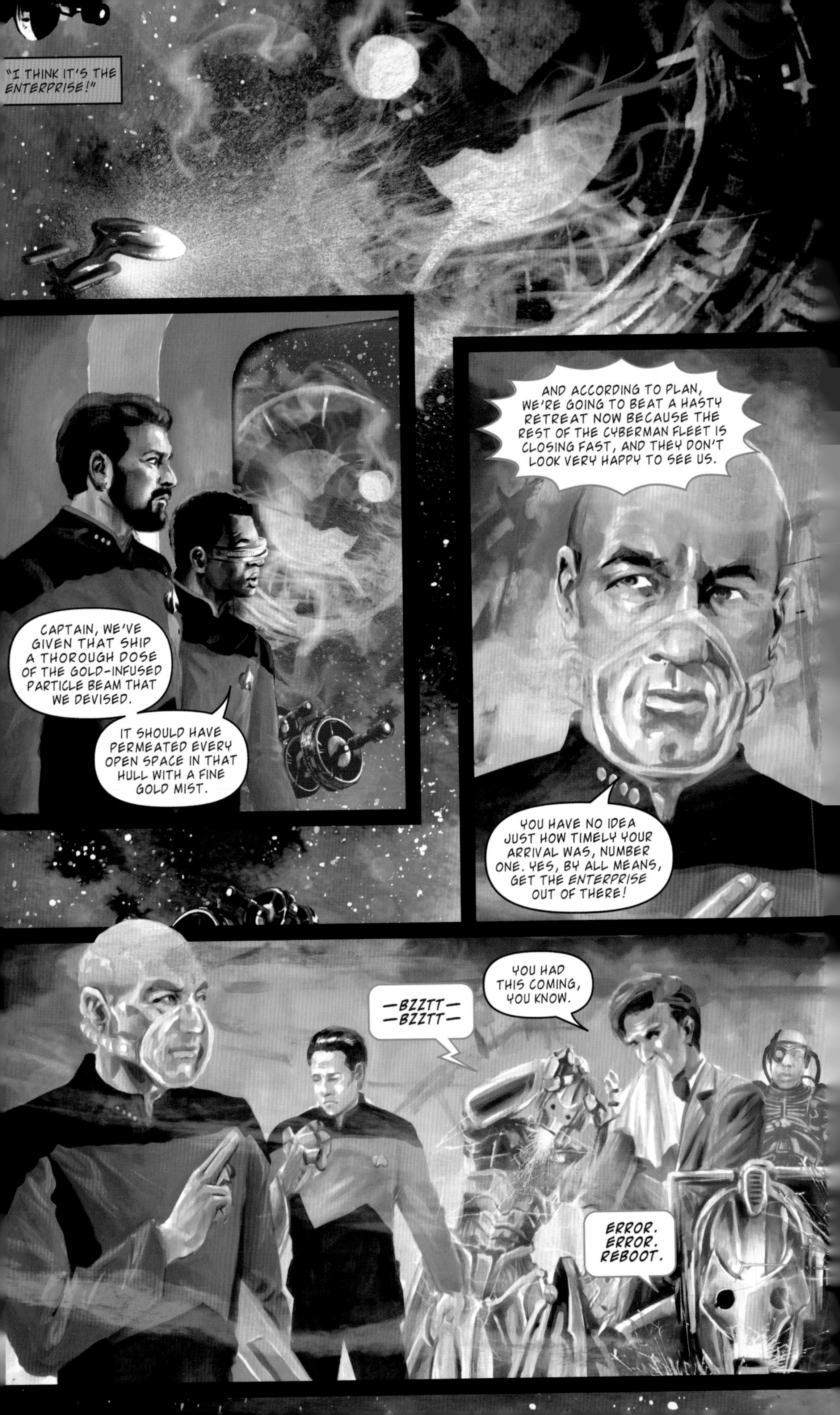
"I THINK IT'S THE *ENTERPRISE!*"
CAPTAIN, WE'VE GIVEN THAT SHIP A THOROUGH DOSE OF THE GOLD-INFUSED PARTICLE BEAM THAT WE DEVISED.
IT SHOULD HAVE PERMEATED EVERY OPEN SPACE IN THAT HULL WITH A FINE GOLD MIST.
AND ACCORDING TO PLAN, WE'RE GOING TO BEAT A HASTY RETREAT NOW BECAUSE THE REST OF THE CYBERMAN FLEET IS CLOSING FAST, AND THEY DON'T LOOK VERY HAPPY TO SEE US.
YOU HAVE NO IDEA JUST HOW TIMELY YOUR ARRIVAL WAS, NUMBER ONE. YES, BY ALL MEANS, GET THE *ENTERPRISE* OUT OF THERE!
—BZZTT— —BZZTT—
YOU HAD THIS COMING, YOU KNOW.
ERROR. ERROR. REBOOT.

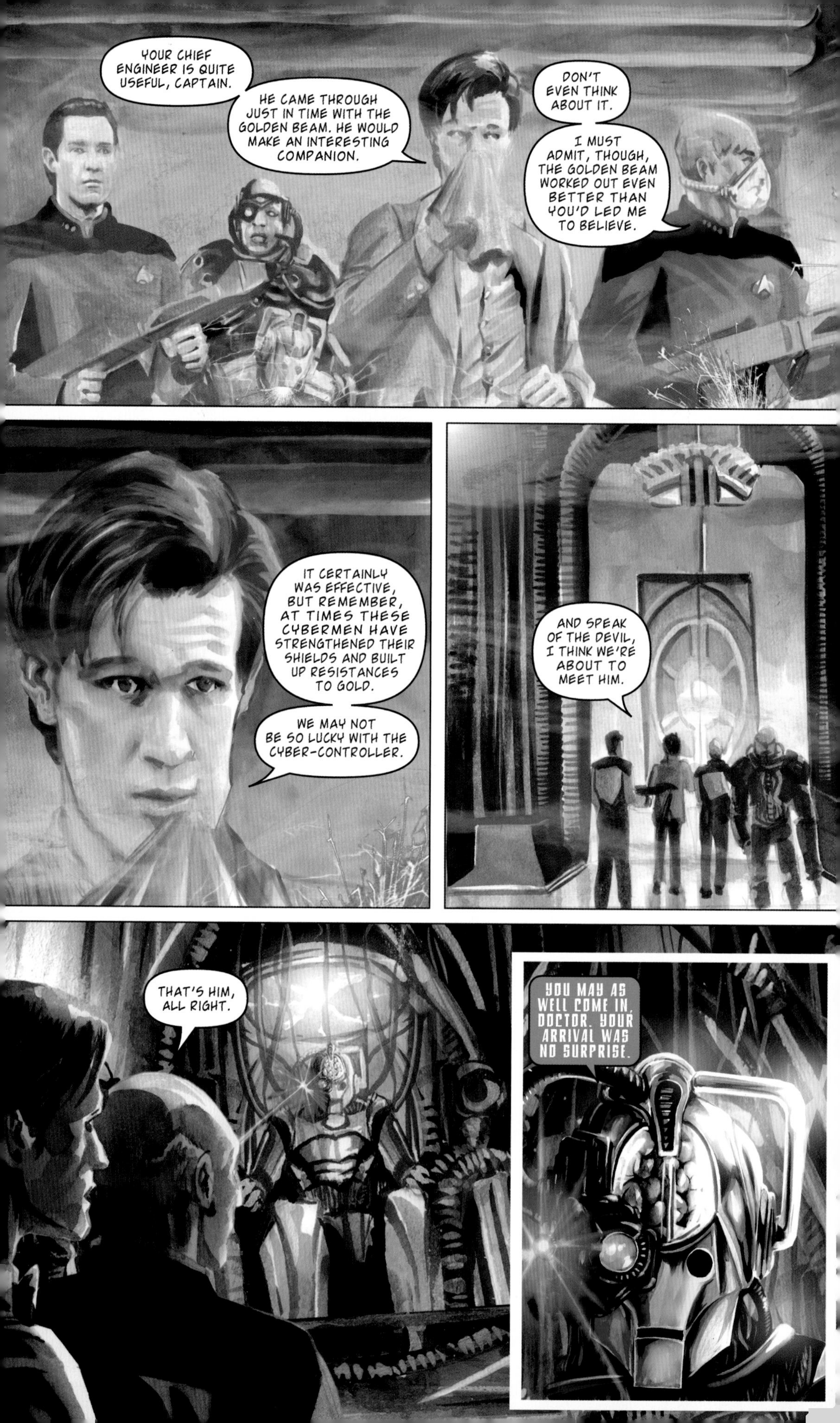

YOUR CHIEF ENGINEER IS QUITE USEFUL, CAPTAIN.
HE CAME THROUGH JUST IN TIME WITH THE GOLDEN BEAM. HE WOULD MAKE AN INTERESTING COMPANION.
DON'T EVEN THINK ABOUT IT.
I MUST ADMIT, THOUGH, THE GOLDEN BEAM WORKED OUT EVEN BETTER THAN YOU'D LED ME TO BELIEVE.
IT CERTAINLY WAS EFFECTIVE, BUT REMEMBER, AT TIMES THESE CYBERMEN HAVE STRENGTHENED THEIR SHIELDS AND BUILT UP RESISTANCES TO GOLD.
WE MAY NOT BE SO LUCKY WITH THE CYBER-CONTROLLER.
AND SPEAK OF THE DEVIL, I THINK WE'RE ABOUT TO MEET HIM.
THAT'S HIM, ALL RIGHT.
YOU MAY AS WELL COME IN, DOCTOR. YOUR ARRIVAL WAS NO SURPRISE.

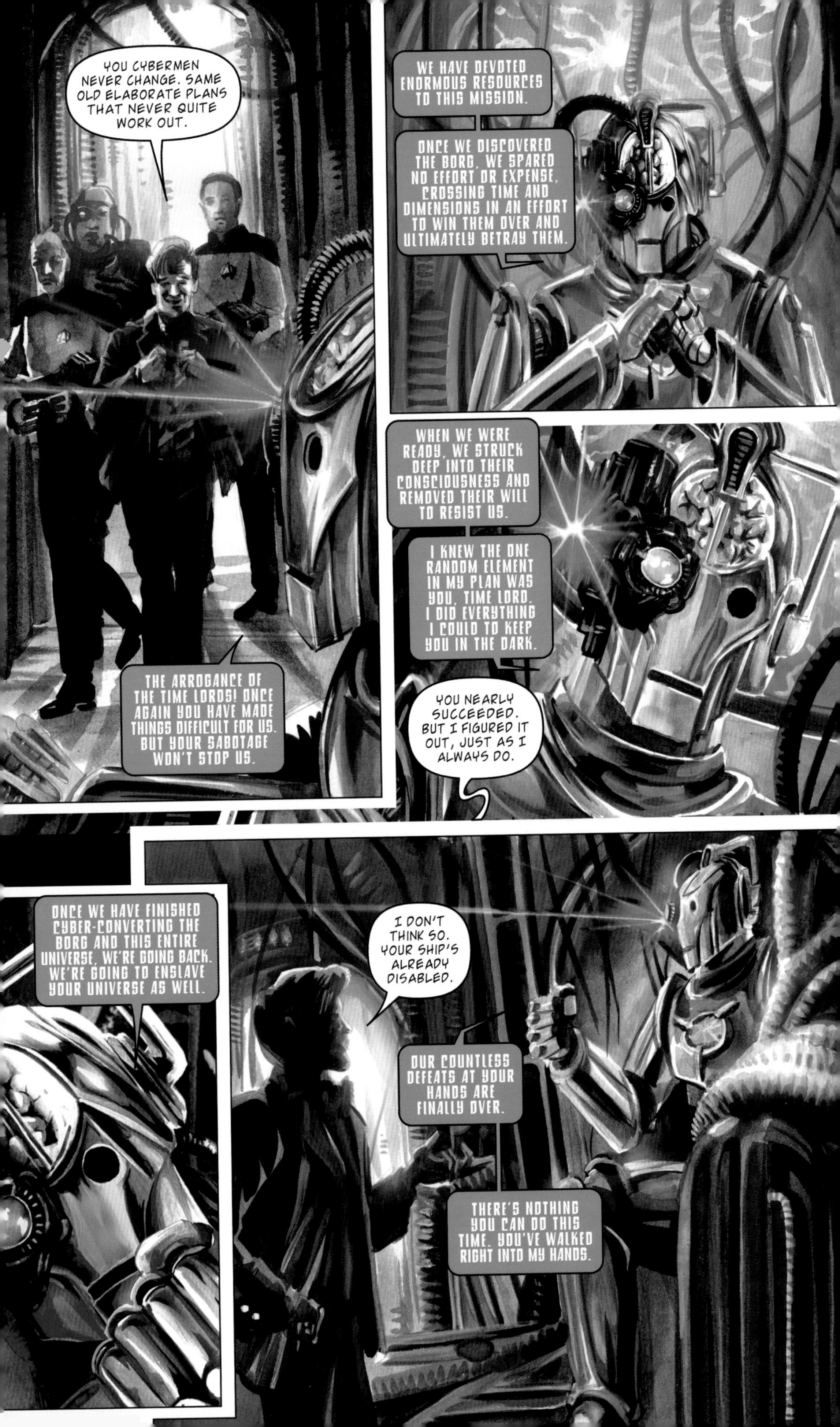

YOU CYBERMEN NEVER CHANGE. SAME OLD ELABORATE PLANS THAT NEVER QUITE WORK OUT.
THE ARROGANCE OF THE TIME LORDS! ONCE AGAIN YOU HAVE MADE THINGS DIFFICULT FOR US. BUT YOUR SABOTAGE WON'T STOP US.
WE HAVE DEVOTED ENORMOUS RESOURCES TO THIS MISSION.
ONCE WE DISCOVERED THE BORG, WE SPARED NO EFFORT OR EXPENSE, CROSSING TIME AND DIMENSIONS IN AN EFFORT TO WIN THEM OVER AND ULTIMATELY BETRAY THEM.
WHEN WE WERE READY, WE STRUCK DEEP INTO THEIR CONSCIOUSNESS AND REMOVED THEIR WILL TO RESIST US.
I KNEW THE ONE RANDOM ELEMENT IN MY PLAN WAS YOU, TIME LORD. I DID EVERYTHING I COULD TO KEEP YOU IN THE DARK.
YOU NEARLY SUCCEEDED. BUT I FIGURED IT OUT, JUST AS I ALWAYS DO.
ONCE WE HAVE FINISHED CYBER-CONVERTING THE BORG AND THIS ENTIRE UNIVERSE, WE'RE GOING BACK. WE'RE GOING TO ENSLAVE YOUR UNIVERSE AS WELL.
I DON'T THINK SO. YOUR SHIP'S ALREADY DISABLED.
OUR COUNTLESS DEFEATS AT YOUR HANDS ARE FINALLY OVER.
THERE'S NOTHING YOU CAN DO THIS TIME. YOU'VE WALKED RIGHT INTO MY HANDS.

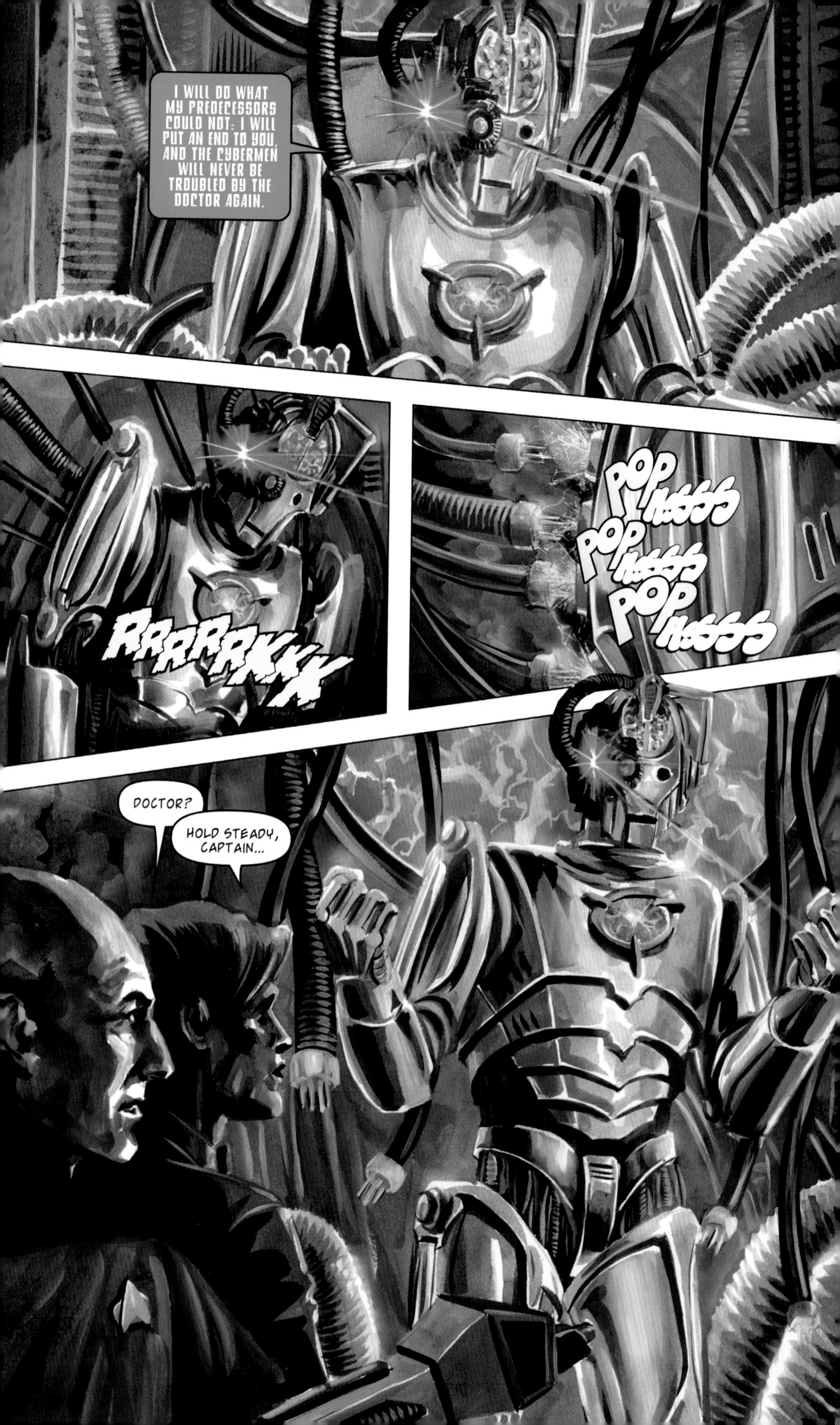
I WILL DO WHAT MY PREDECESSORS COULD NOT: I WILL PUT AN END TO YOU, AND THE CYBERMEN WILL NEVER BE TROUBLED BY THE DOCTOR AGAIN.
RRRRRKKKK
POP HSSSS
POP HSSSS
POP HSSSS
DOCTOR?
HOLD STEADY, CAPTAIN...

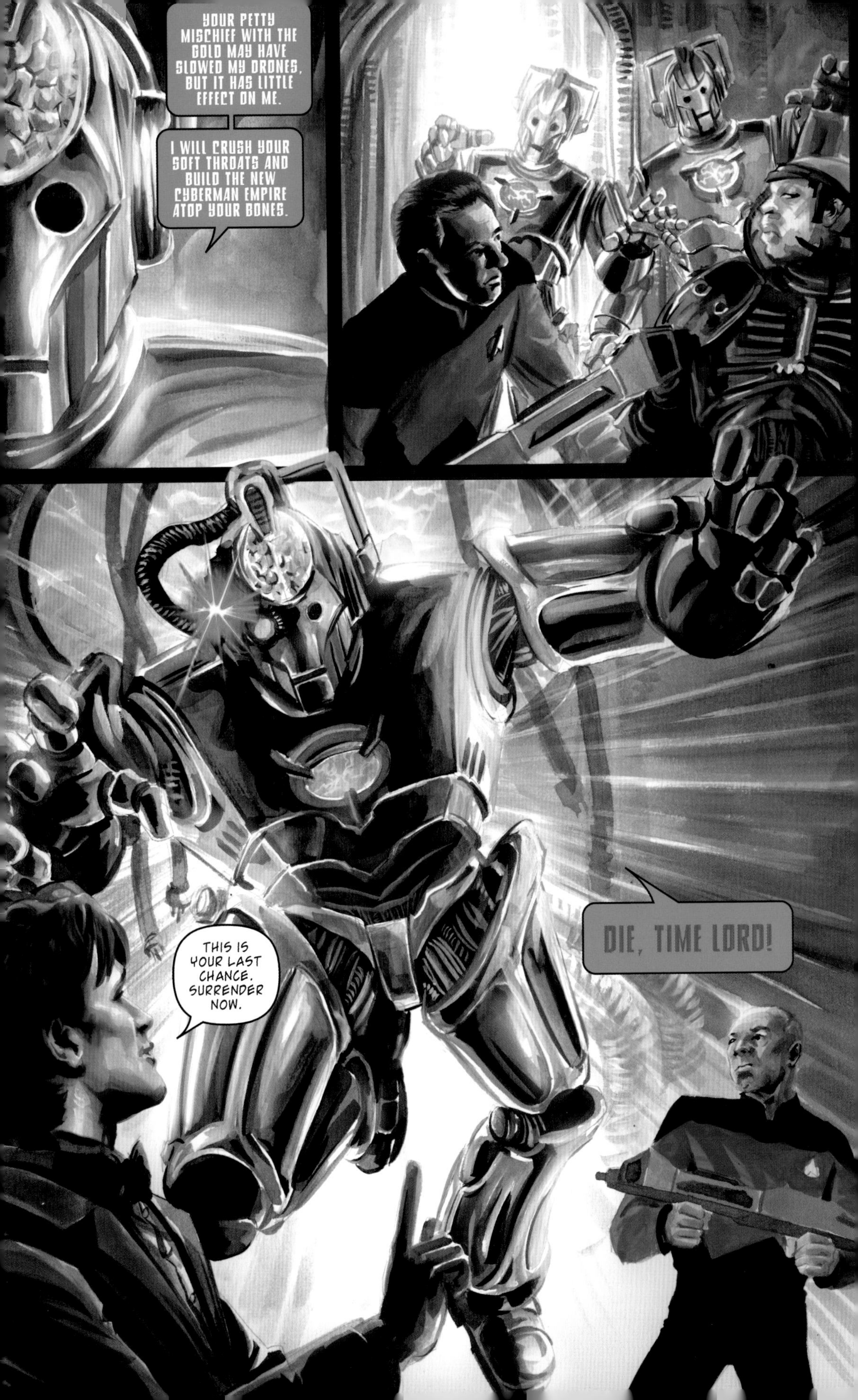
YOUR PETTY MISCHIEF WITH THE GOLD MAY HAVE SLOWED MY DRONES, BUT IT HAS LITTLE EFFECT ON ME.
I WILL CRUSH YOUR SOFT THROATS AND BUILD THE NEW CYBERMAN EMPIRE ATOP YOUR BONES.
THIS IS YOUR LAST CHANCE. SURRENDER NOW.
DIE, TIME LORD!

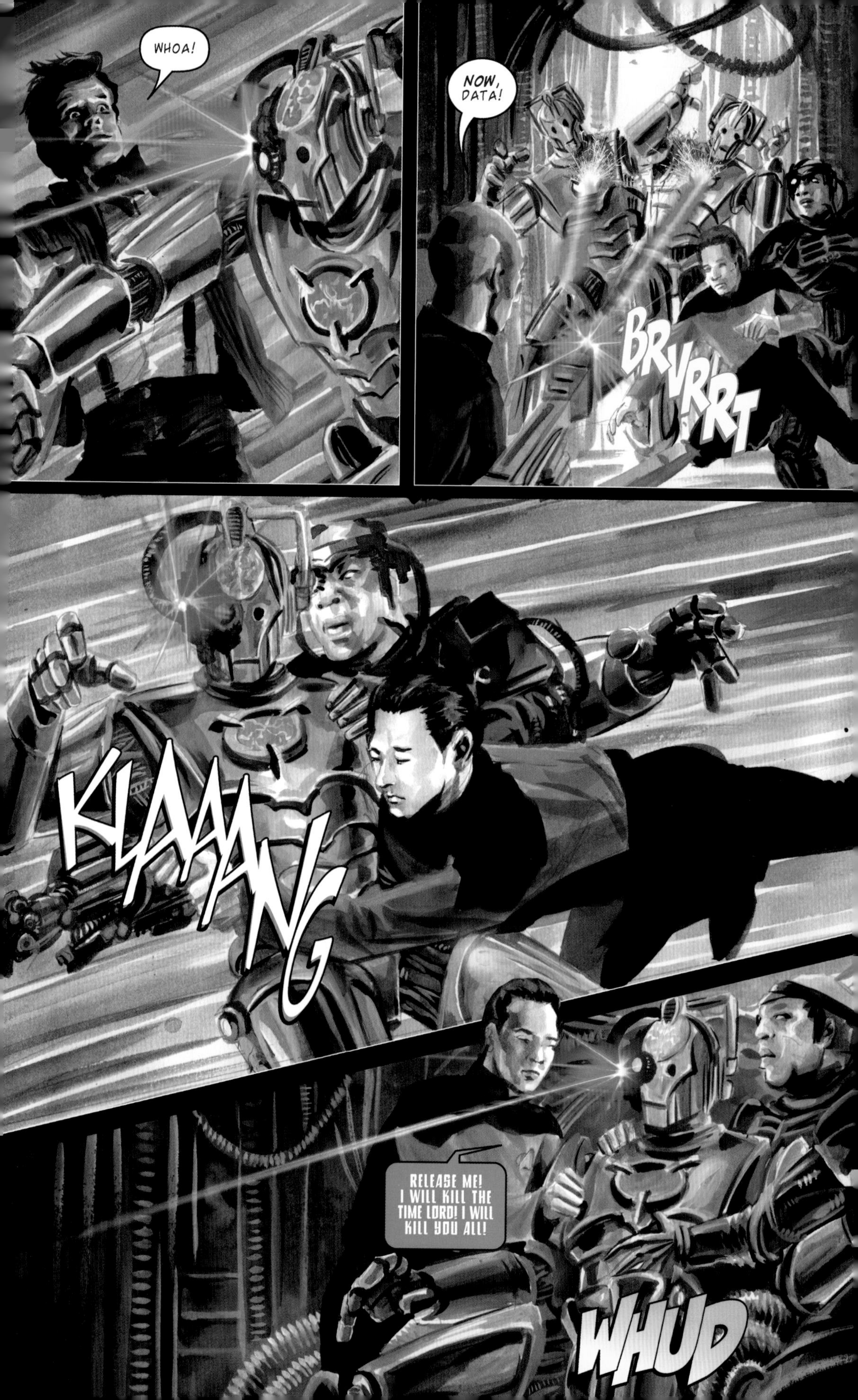
WHOA!
NOW, DATA!
BRVRRT
KLAAAANG
RELEASE ME! I WILL KILL THE TIME LORD! I WILL KILL YOU ALL!
WHUD

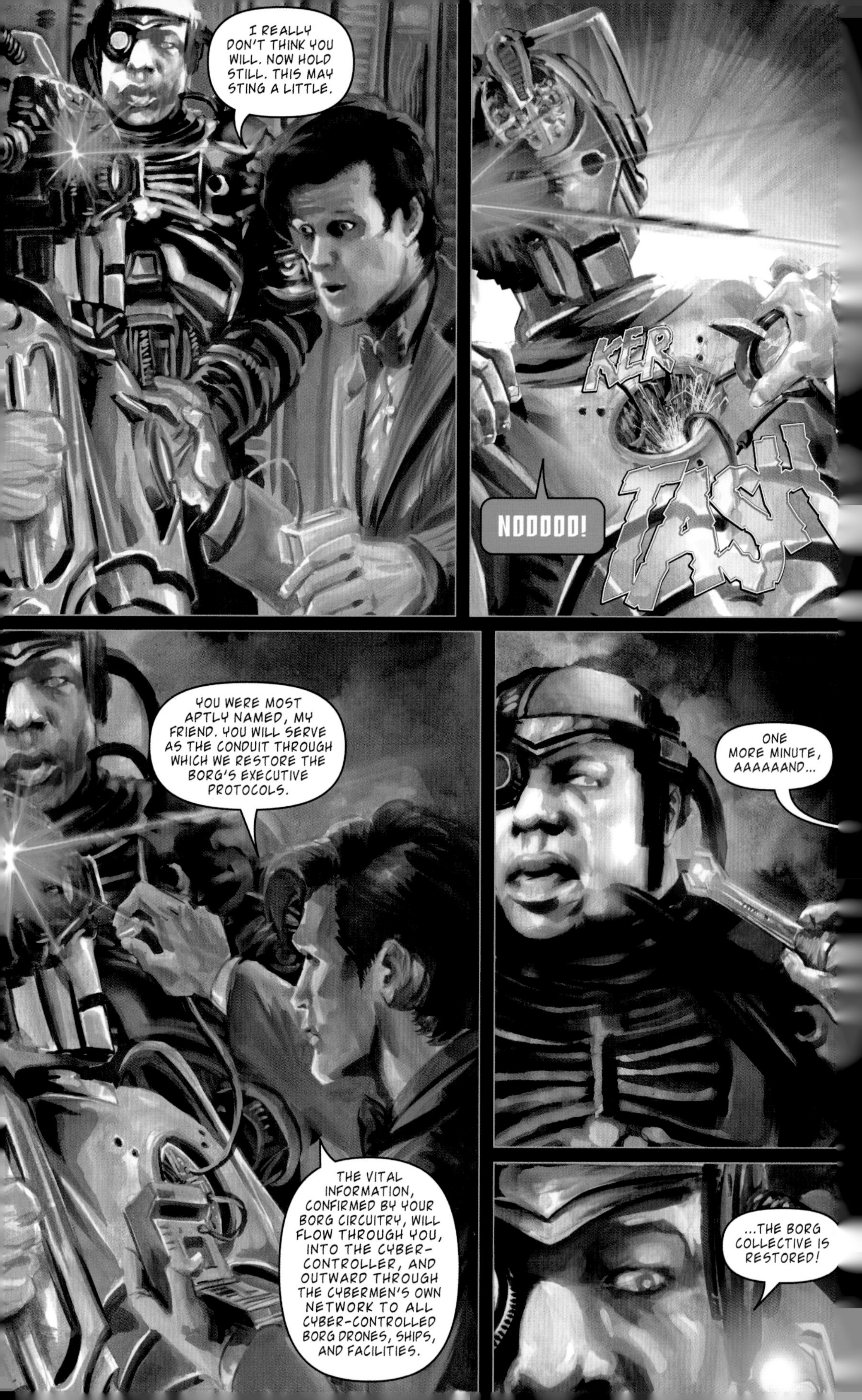
I REALLY DON'T THINK YOU WILL. NOW HOLD STILL. THIS MAY STING A LITTLE.
KER
TASH
NOOOOO!
YOU WERE MOST APTLY NAMED, MY FRIEND. YOU WILL SERVE AS THE CONDUIT THROUGH WHICH WE RESTORE THE BORG'S EXECUTIVE PROTOCOLS.
THE VITAL INFORMATION, CONFIRMED BY YOUR BORG CIRCUITRY, WILL FLOW THROUGH YOU, INTO THE CYBER-CONTROLLER, AND OUTWARD THROUGH THE CYBERMEN'S OWN NETWORK TO ALL CYBER-CONTROLLED BORG DRONES, SHIPS, AND FACILITIES.
ONE MORE MINUTE, AAAAAAND...
...THE BORG COLLECTIVE IS RESTORED!

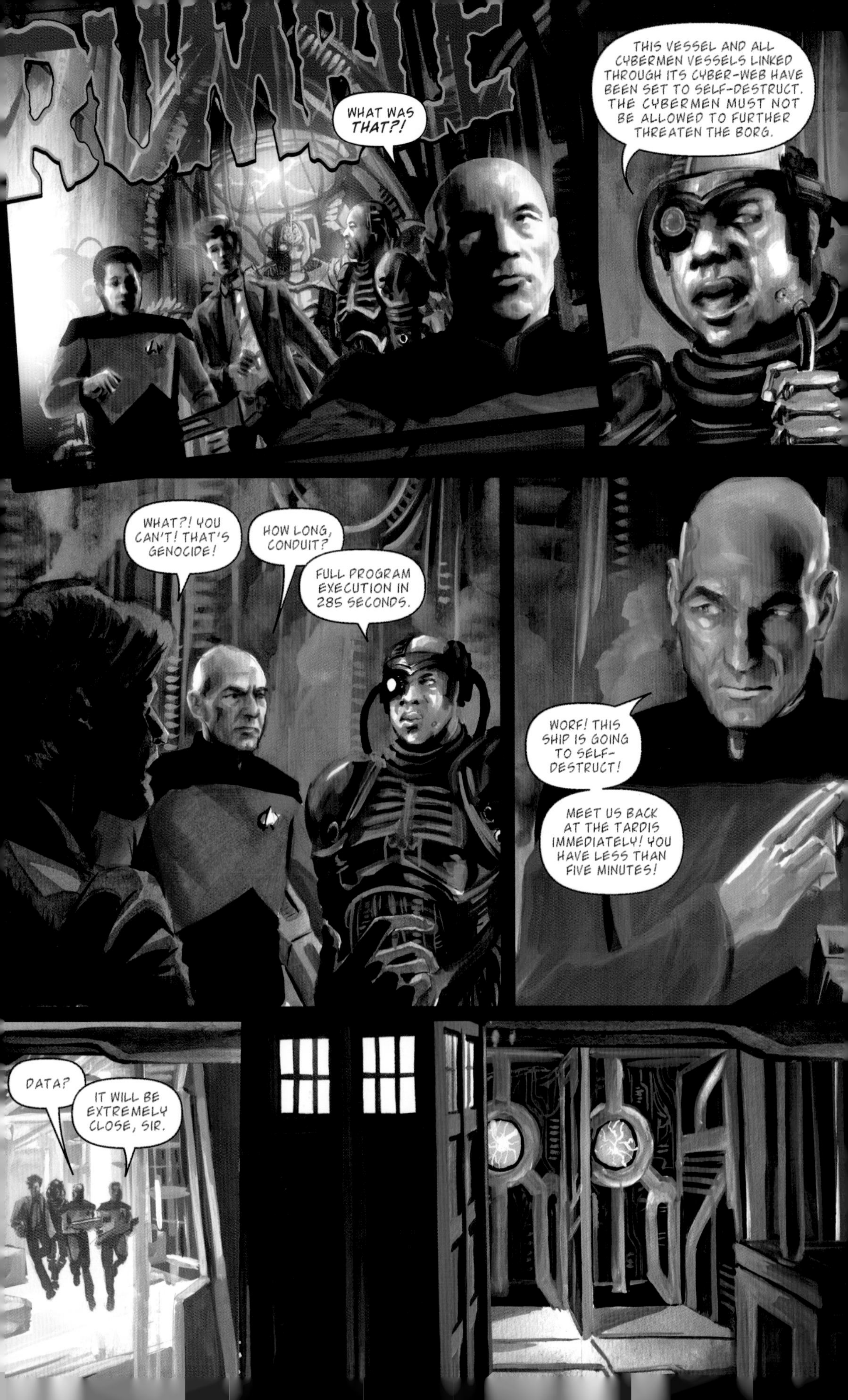
WHAT WAS THAT?!
THIS VESSEL AND ALL CYBERMEN VESSELS LINKED THROUGH ITS CYBER-WEB HAVE BEEN SET TO SELF-DESTRUCT. THE CYBERMEN MUST NOT BE ALLOWED TO FURTHER THREATEN THE BORG.
WHAT?! YOU CAN'T! THAT'S GENOCIDE!
HOW LONG, CONDUIT?
FULL PROGRAM EXECUTION IN 285 SECONDS.
WORF! THIS SHIP IS GOING TO SELF-DESTRUCT!
MEET US BACK AT THE TARDIS IMMEDIATELY! YOU HAVE LESS THAN FIVE MINUTES!
DATA?
IT WILL BE EXTREMELY CLOSE, SIR.

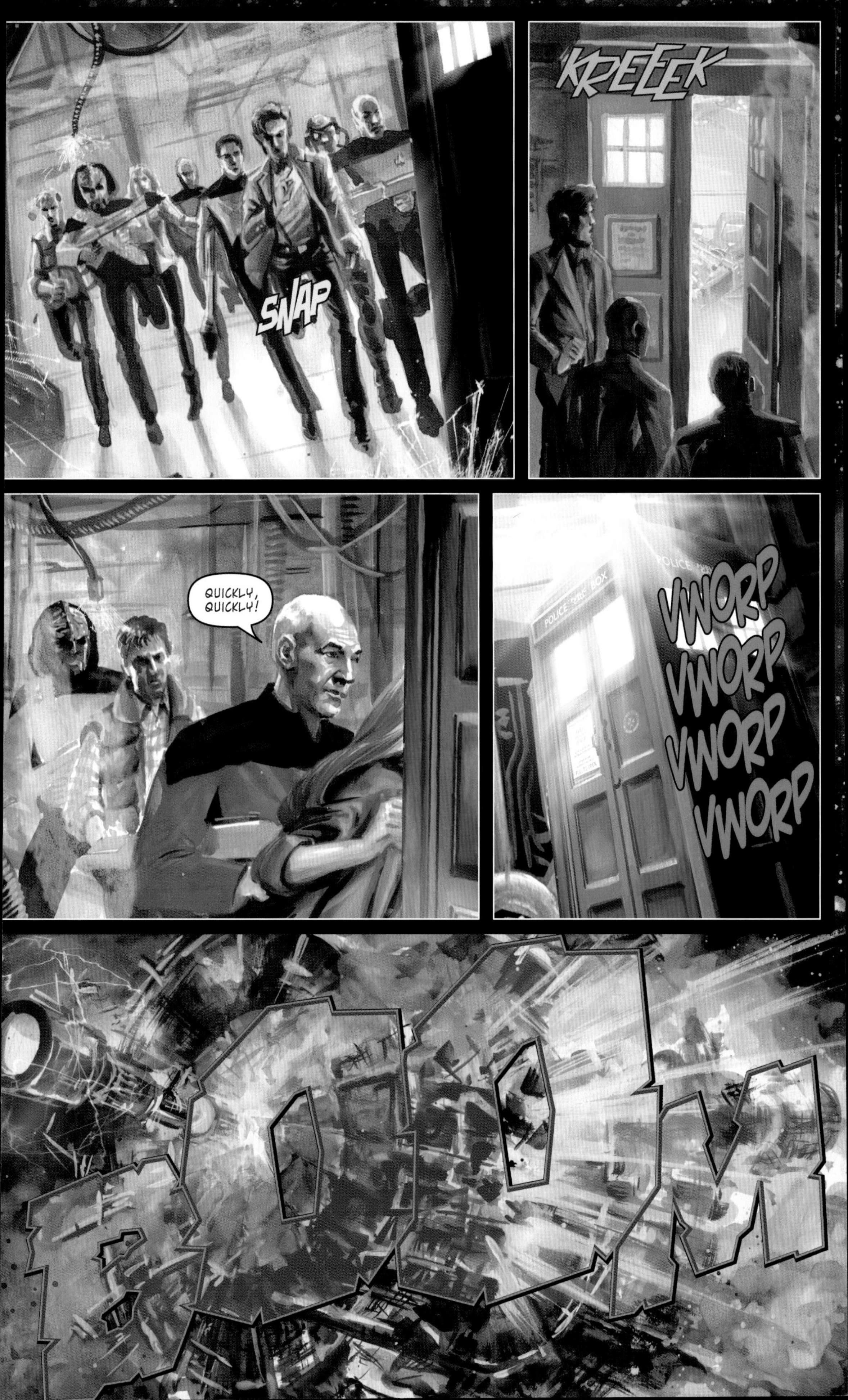
SNAP
KREEEK
QUICKLY, QUICKLY!
POLICE BOX
VWORP VWORP VWORP VWORP

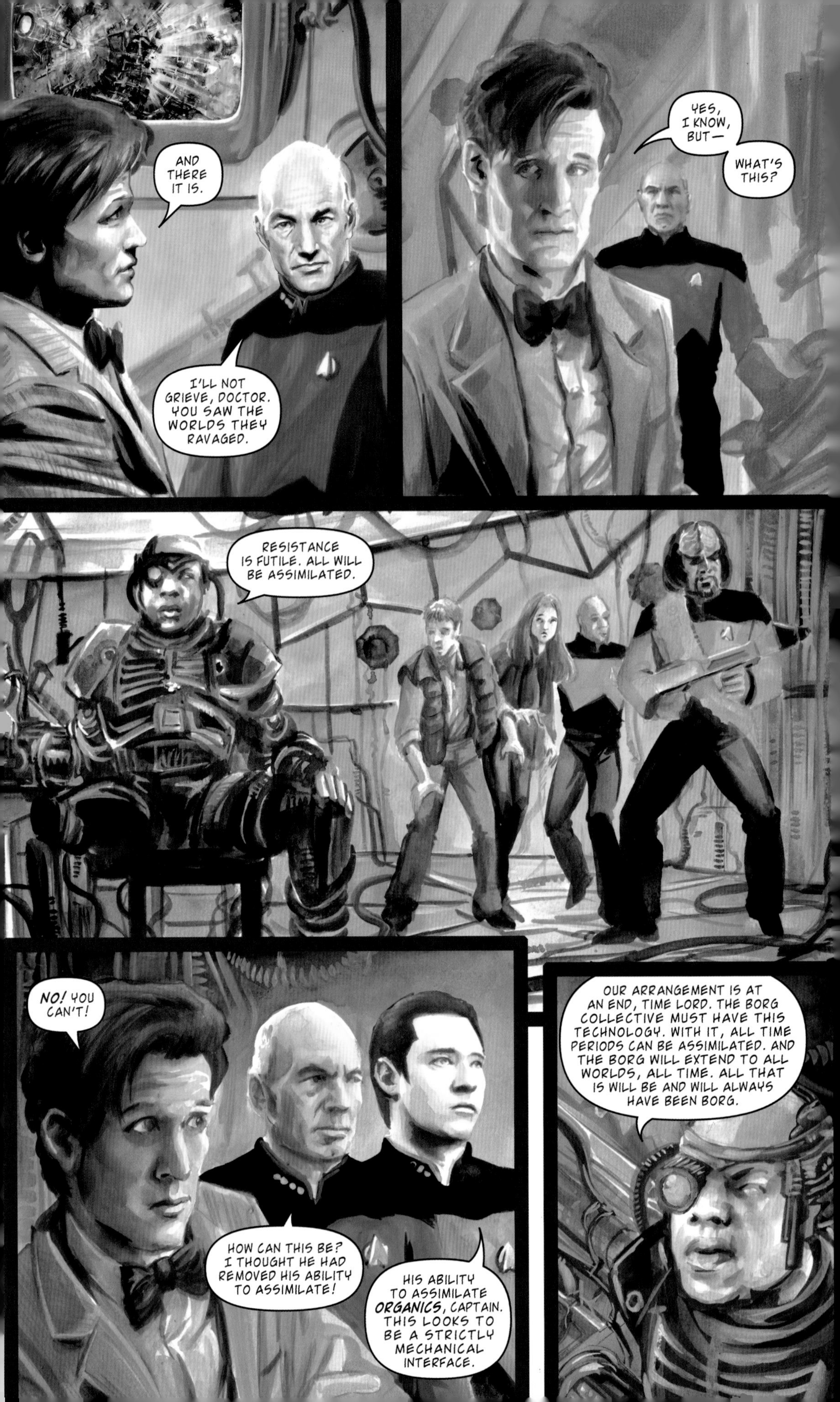
AND THERE IT IS.
I'LL NOT GRIEVE, DOCTOR. YOU SAW THE WORLDS THEY RAVAGED.
YES, I KNOW, BUT—
WHAT'S THIS?
RESISTANCE IS FUTILE. ALL WILL BE ASSIMILATED.
NO! YOU CAN'T!
HOW CAN THIS BE? I THOUGHT HE HAD REMOVED HIS ABILITY TO ASSIMILATE!
HIS ABILITY TO ASSIMILATE ORGANICS, CAPTAIN. THIS LOOKS TO BE A STRICTLY MECHANICAL INTERFACE.
OUR ARRANGEMENT IS AT AN END, TIME LORD. THE BORG COLLECTIVE MUST HAVE THIS TECHNOLOGY. WITH IT, ALL TIME PERIODS CAN BE ASSIMILATED. AND THE BORG WILL EXTEND TO ALL WORLDS, ALL TIME. ALL THAT IS WILL BE AND WILL ALWAYS HAVE BEEN BORG.

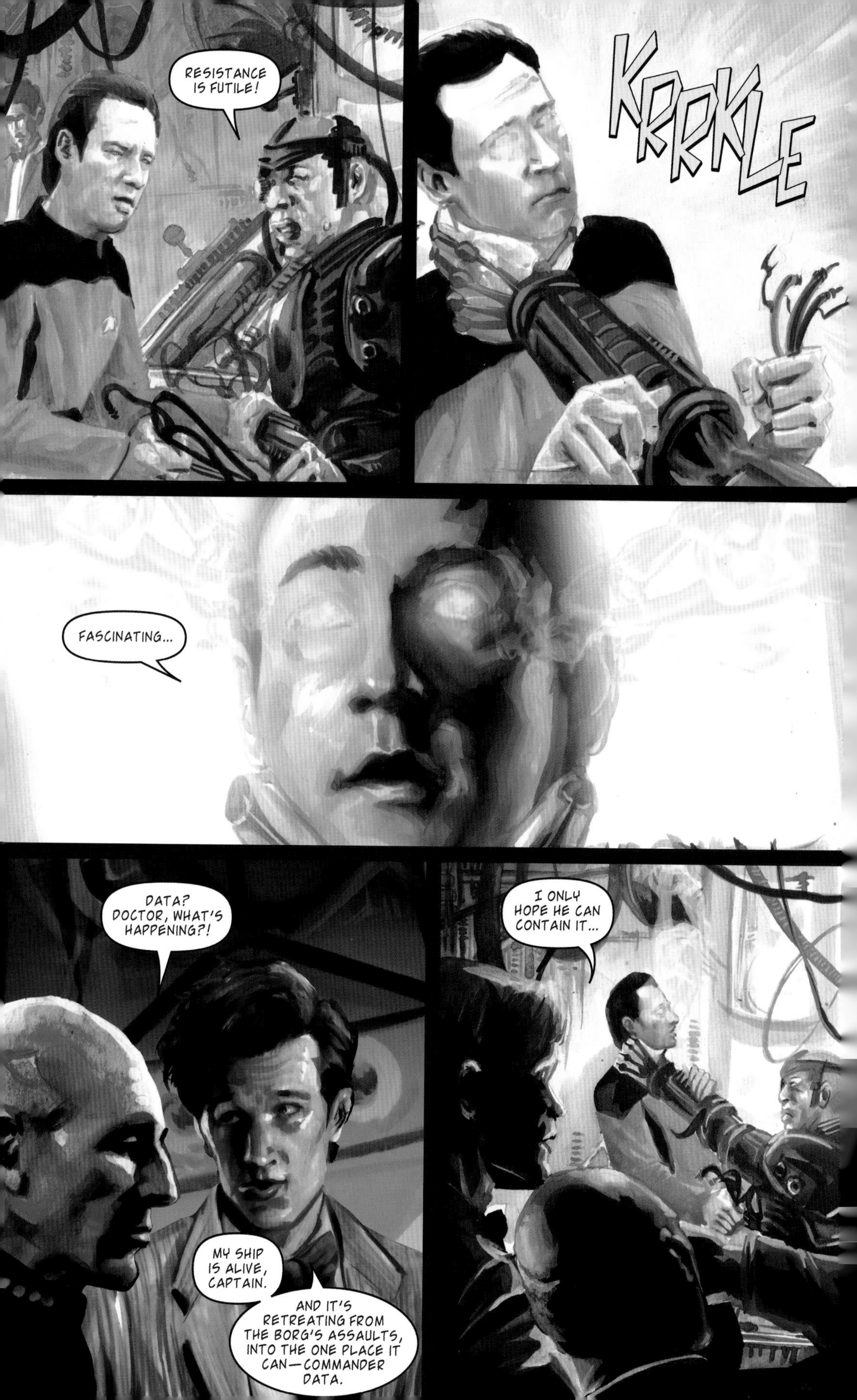

RESISTANCE IS FUTILE!
KRRKKLE
FASCINATING...
DATA? DOCTOR, WHAT'S HAPPENING?!
MY SHIP IS ALIVE, CAPTAIN.
AND IT'S RETREATING FROM THE BORG'S ASSAULTS, INTO THE ONE PLACE IT CAN—COMMANDER DATA.
I ONLY HOPE HE CAN CONTAIN IT...

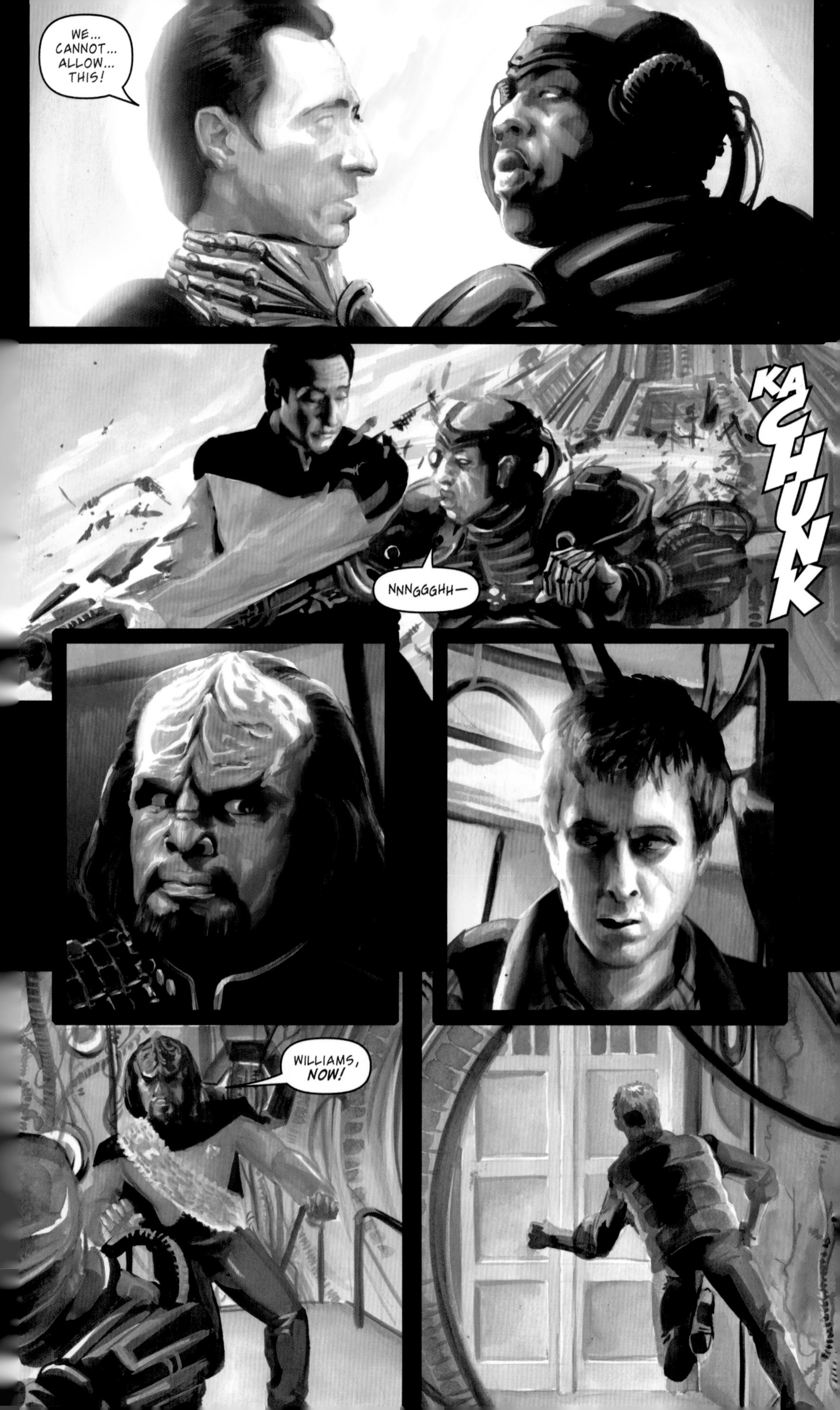
WE... CANNOT... ALLOW... THIS!
KA-CHUNK
NNNGGGHH—
WILLIAMS, NOW!

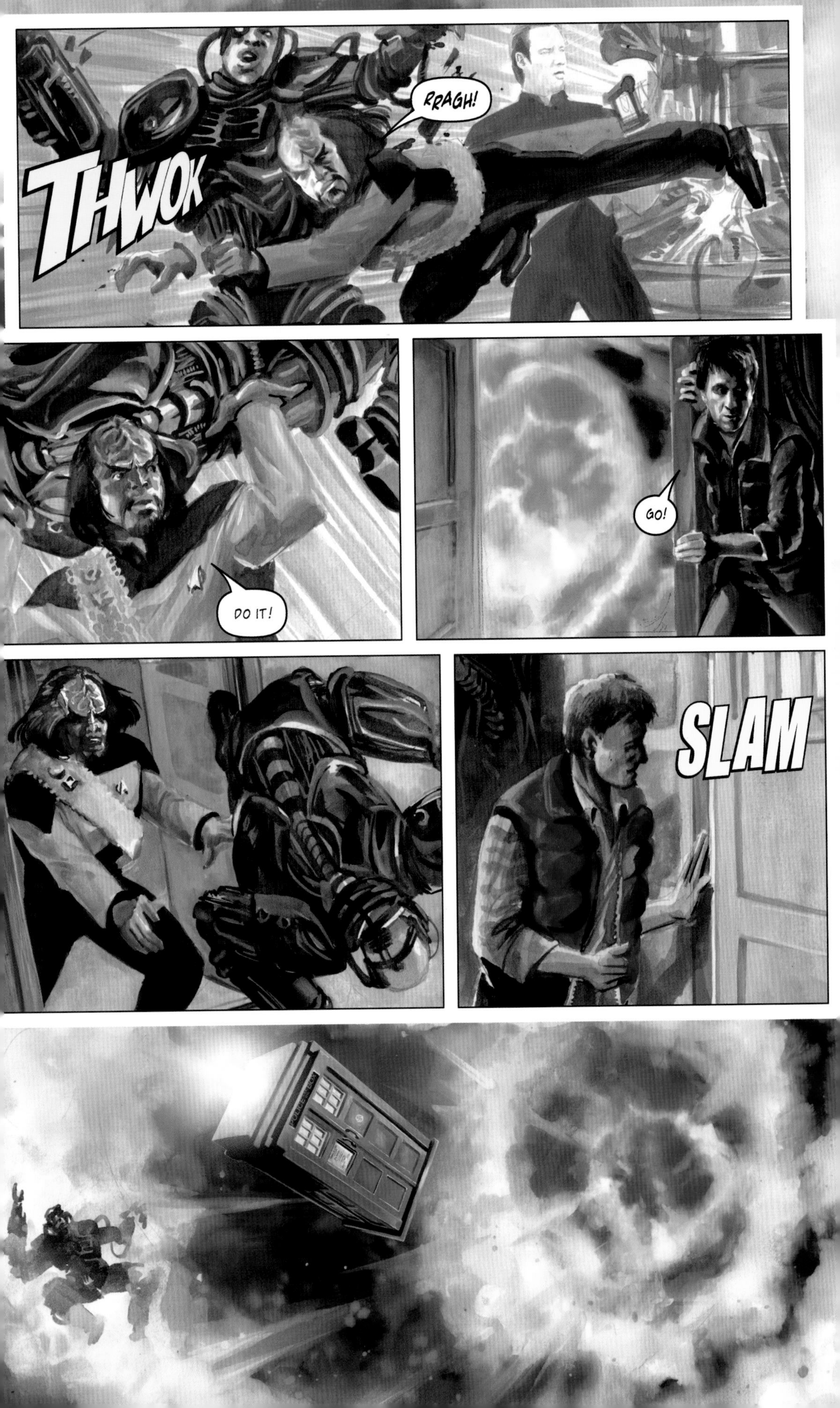
RRAGH!
THWOK
DO IT!
GO!
SLAM

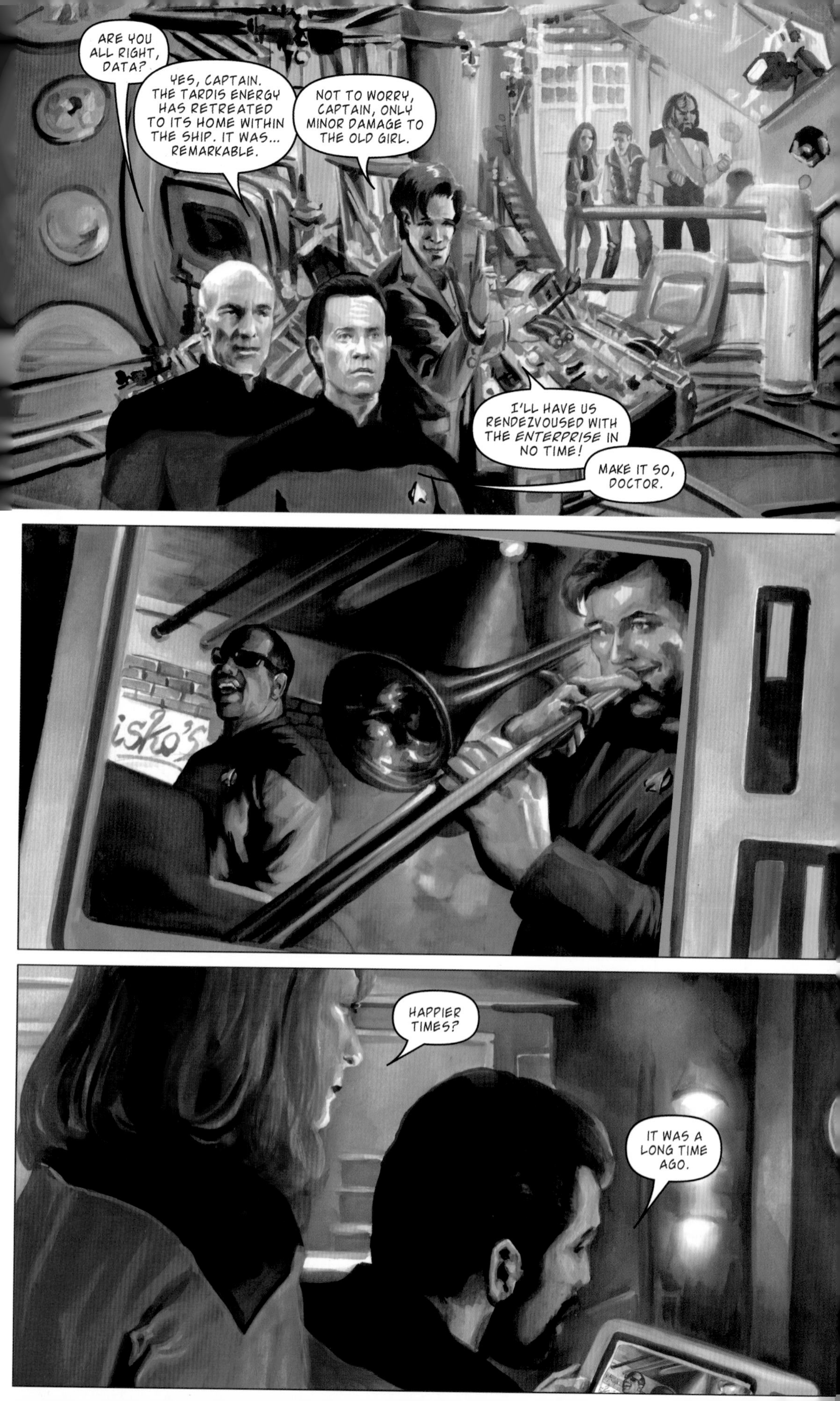
ARE YOU ALL RIGHT, DATA?
YES, CAPTAIN. THE TARDIS ENERGY HAS RETREATED TO ITS HOME WITHIN THE SHIP. IT WAS... REMARKABLE.
NOT TO WORRY, CAPTAIN, ONLY MINOR DAMAGE TO THE OLD GIRL.
I'LL HAVE US RENDEZVOUSED WITH THE *ENTERPRISE* IN NO TIME!
MAKE IT SO, DOCTOR.
isko's
HAPPIER TIMES?
IT WAS A LONG TIME AGO.

I DON'T UNDERSTAND. HE WAS A STRONG, FIERCELY INDEPENDENT MAN. I THOUGHT HE MIGHT BE ABLE TO FREE HIMSELF FROM THE COLLECTIVE.

I NEVER EXPECTED THAT HE WOULD GO SO FAR AS TO BETRAY US TO THE BORG LIKE THAT.

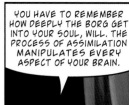

YOU HAVE TO REMEMBER HOW DEEPLY THE BORG GET INTO YOUR SOUL, WILL. THE PROCESS OF ASSIMILATION MANIPULATES EVERY ASPECT OF YOUR BRAIN.

IT DOESN'T TAKE LONG BEFORE YOUR ENTIRE PERSONALITY, YOUR VERY ESSENCE, IS TIED DIRECTLY INTO THE WILL OF THE COLLECTIVE.

MY ONLY CONSOLATION IS THAT WHATEVER WAS LEFT OF BERTRAND DID HELP US DEFEAT THE CYBERMEN.

I'D LIKE TO THINK THAT THERE WAS AT LEAST A PART OF HIM LEFT THAT ALLOWED HIM SOME SATISFACTION IN HELPING US.

I THINK HE WOULD LIKE YOU TO REMEMBER THAT PART OF HIM.

COMMANDER, WE SHOULD PROBABLY BE ON OUR WAY.

DOCTOR, A QUESTION—ONCE YOU DEPART, WILL ALL TRACES OF YOUR UNIVERSE'S INCURSION HERE REMAIN?

AN EXCELLENT QUESTION, COMMANDER! I'D SAY MY DEFINITIVE ANSWER IS A FIRM "YES AND NO." WITH THE TOTAL DESTRUCTION OF THE CYBERMEN FROM THIS UNIVERSE, ALL OF THE CHANGES MADE TO YOUR HISTORY IN THEIR WAKE HAVE PROBABLY ALREADY UNWOUND THEMSELVES.

I'D WAGER A LOOK AT YOUR COMPUTER BANKS WILL FIND NO SIGN OF MY PREVIOUS ENCOUNTER WITH YOUR PREDECESSOR. HOWEVER, THE THINGS WE OURSELVES HAVE EXPERIENCED, THOSE MEMORIES—AHH, THOSE ARE OURS TO KEEP, FOR GOOD AND ILL.

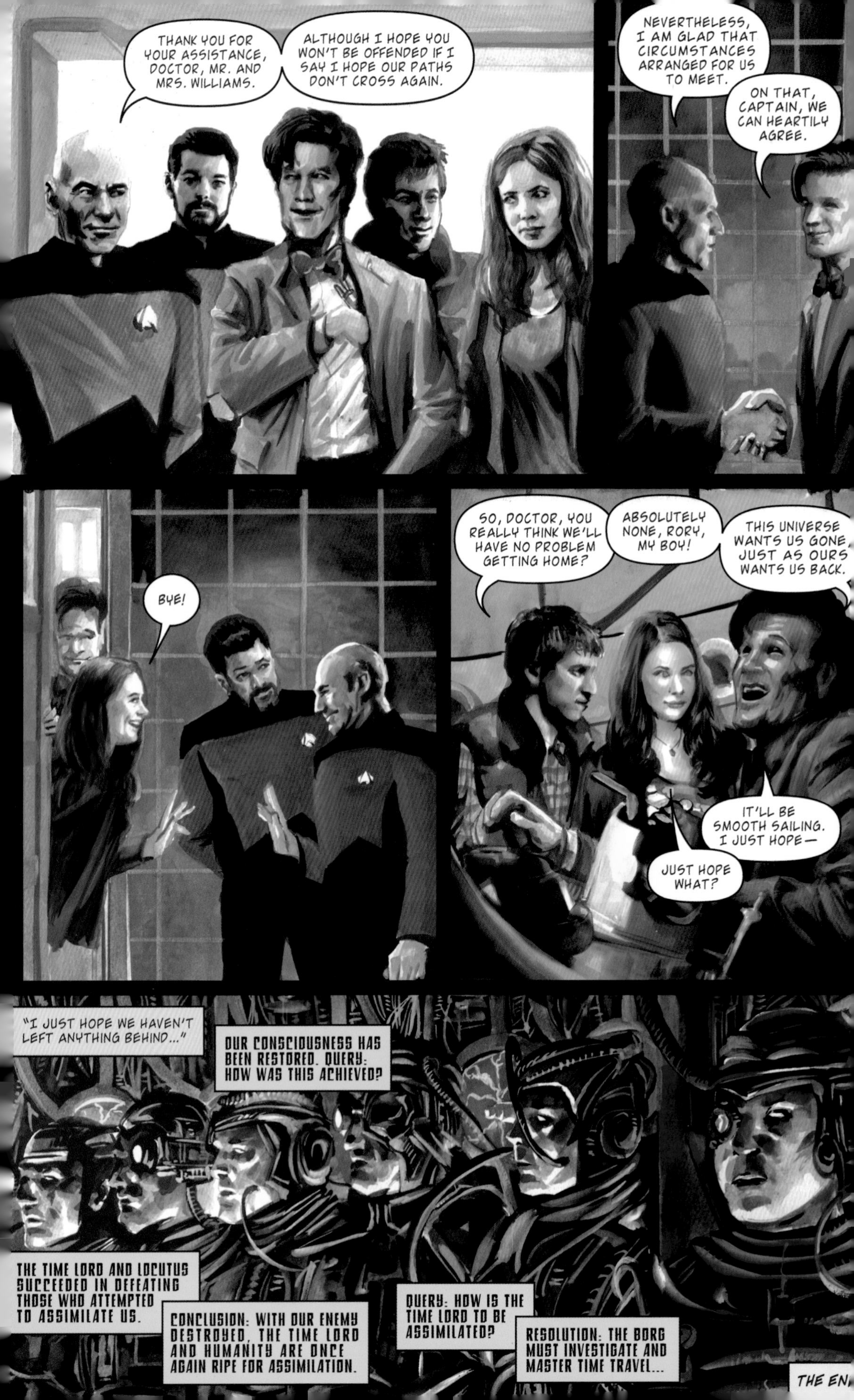
THANK YOU FOR YOUR ASSISTANCE, DOCTOR, MR. AND MRS. WILLIAMS.
ALTHOUGH I HOPE YOU WON'T BE OFFENDED IF I SAY I HOPE OUR PATHS DON'T CROSS AGAIN.
NEVERTHELESS, I AM GLAD THAT CIRCUMSTANCES ARRANGED FOR US TO MEET.
ON THAT, CAPTAIN, WE CAN HEARTILY AGREE.
BYE!
SO, DOCTOR, YOU REALLY THINK WE'LL HAVE NO PROBLEM GETTING HOME?
ABSOLUTELY NONE, RORY, MY BOY!
THIS UNIVERSE WANTS US GONE, JUST AS OURS WANTS US BACK.
IT'LL BE SMOOTH SAILING. I JUST HOPE—
JUST HOPE WHAT?
"I JUST HOPE WE HAVEN'T LEFT ANYTHING BEHIND..."
OUR CONSCIOUSNESS HAS BEEN RESTORED. QUERY: HOW WAS THIS ACHIEVED?
THE TIME LORD AND LOCUTUS SUCCEEDED IN DEFEATING THOSE WHO ATTEMPTED TO ASSIMILATE US.
CONCLUSION: WITH OUR ENEMY DESTROYED, THE TIME LORD AND HUMANITY ARE ONCE AGAIN RIPE FOR ASSIMILATION.
QUERY: HOW IS THE TIME LORD TO BE ASSIMILATED?
RESOLUTION: THE BORG MUST INVESTIGATE AND MASTER TIME TRAVEL...
THE EN

ART GALLERY

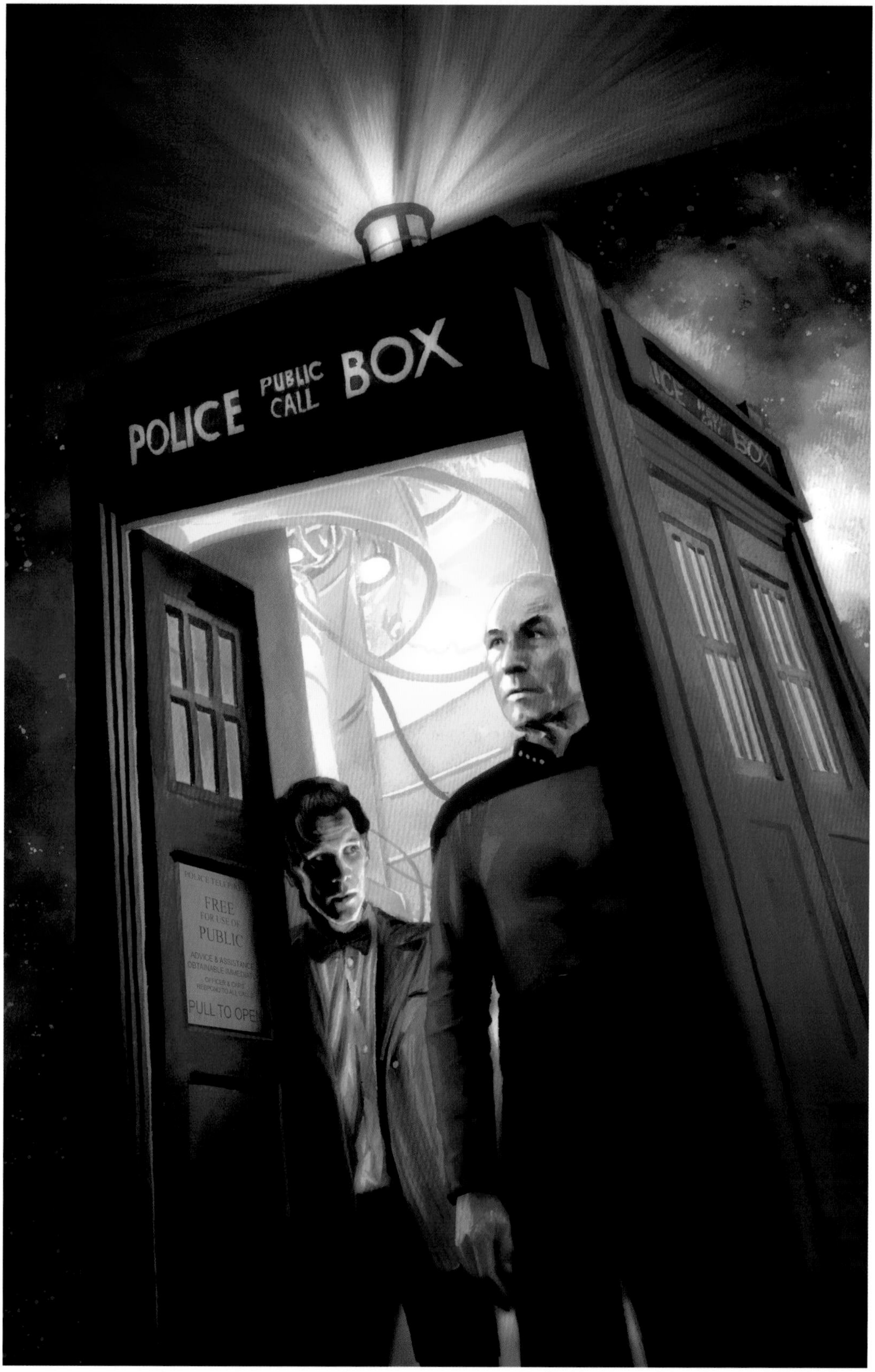
POLICE PUBLIC CALL BOX
POLICE PUBLIC CALL BOX
FREE
FOR USE OF
PUBLIC
ADVICE & ASSISTANCE
PULL TO OPEN

art by J.K. Woodward

opposite page: art by The Sharp Brothers

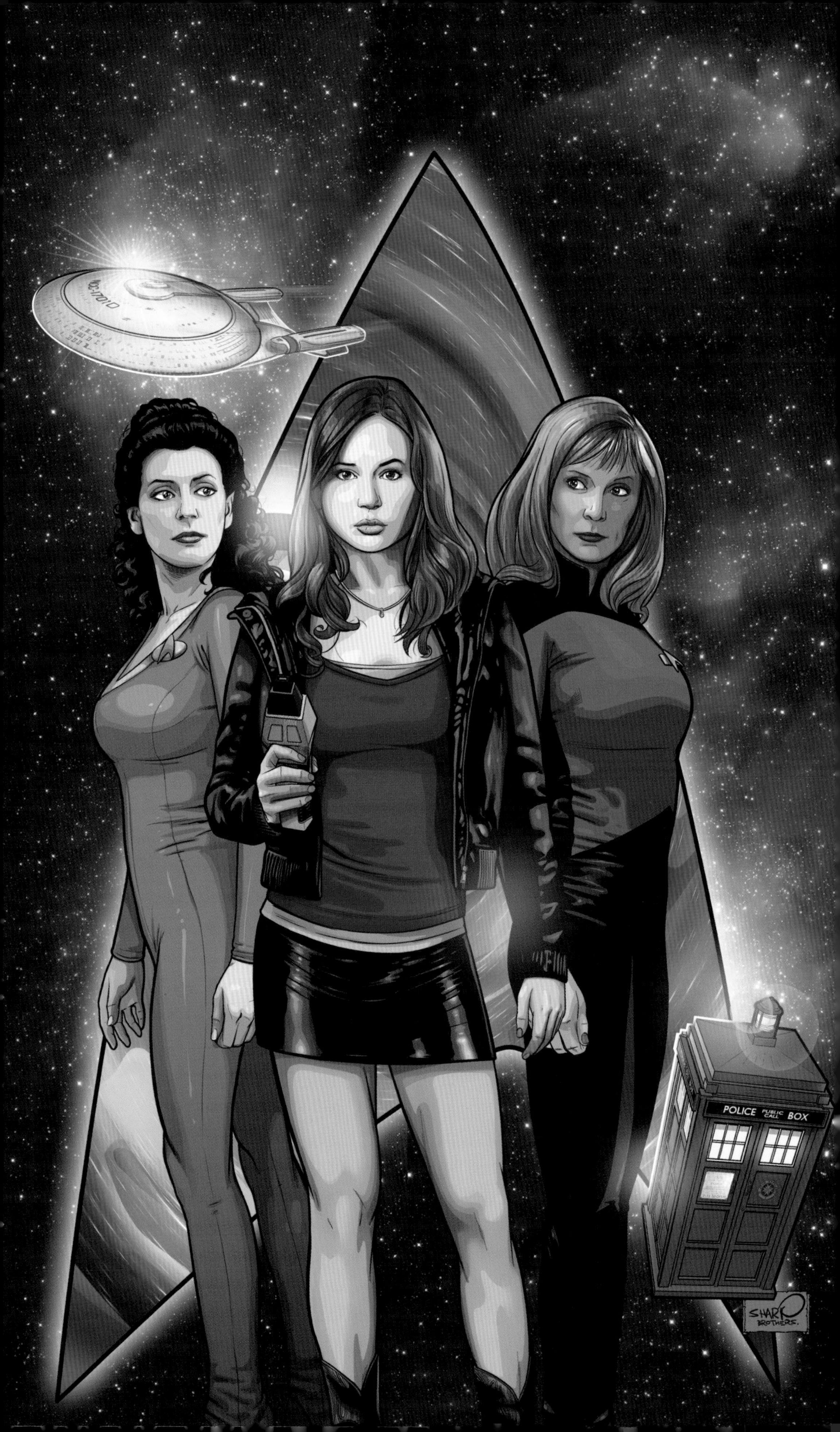
POLICE PUBLIC CALL BOX
SHARP BROTHERS.

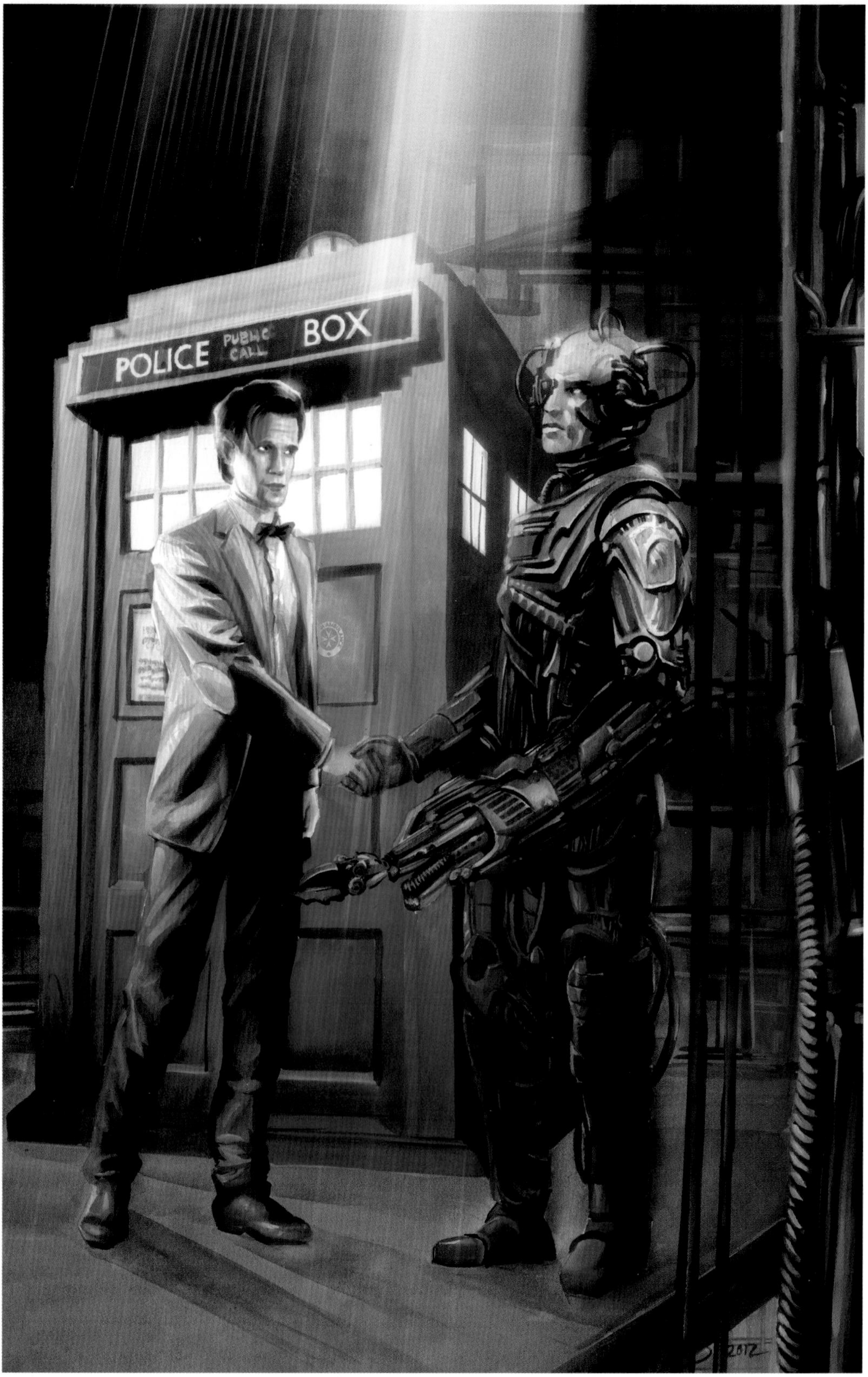
POLICE
PUBLIC CALL
BOX

art by J.K. Woodward

opposite page: art by Emanuela Lupacchino, Colors by Fabio Mantovani

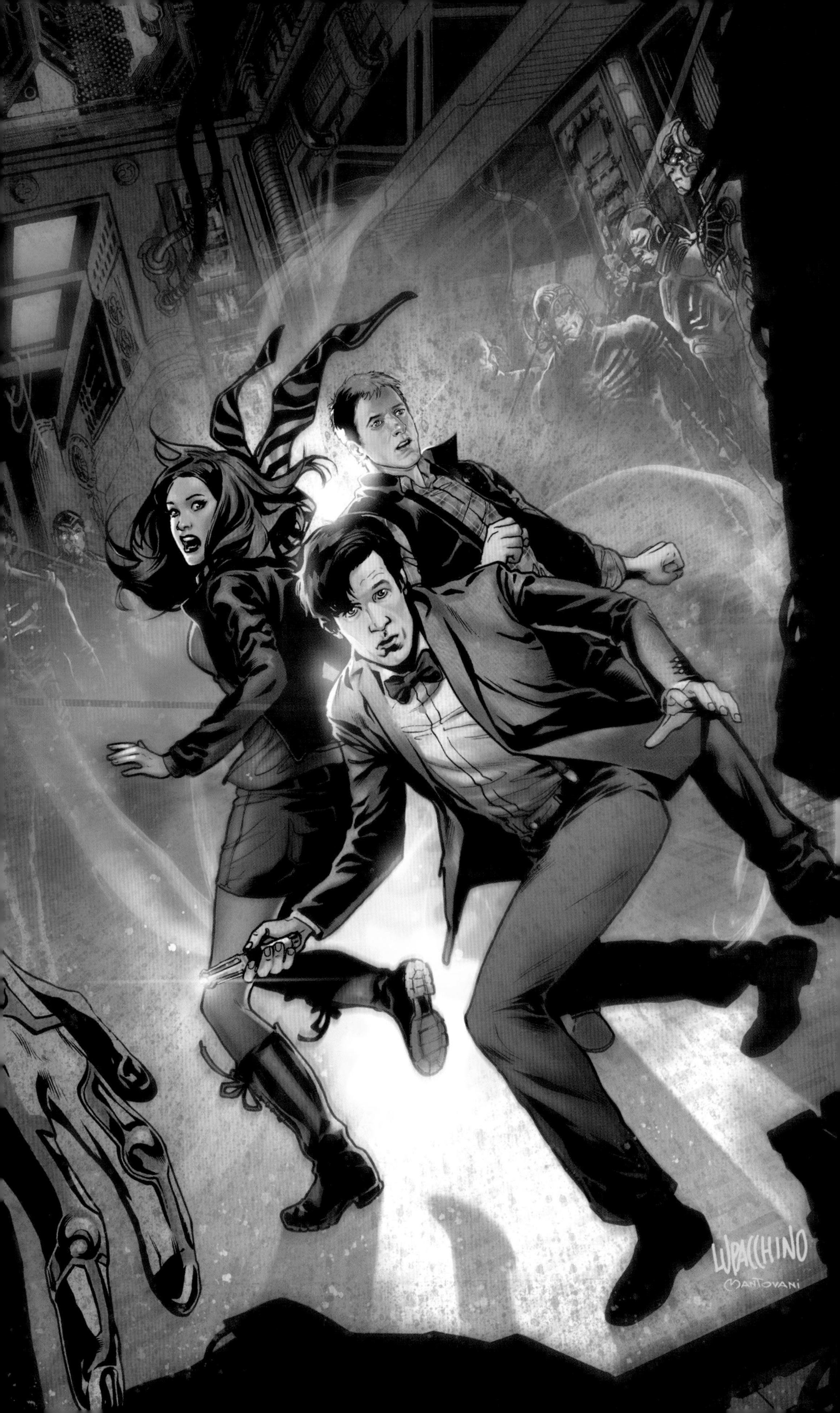
LUPACCHINO
MANTOVANI

art by J.K. Woodward

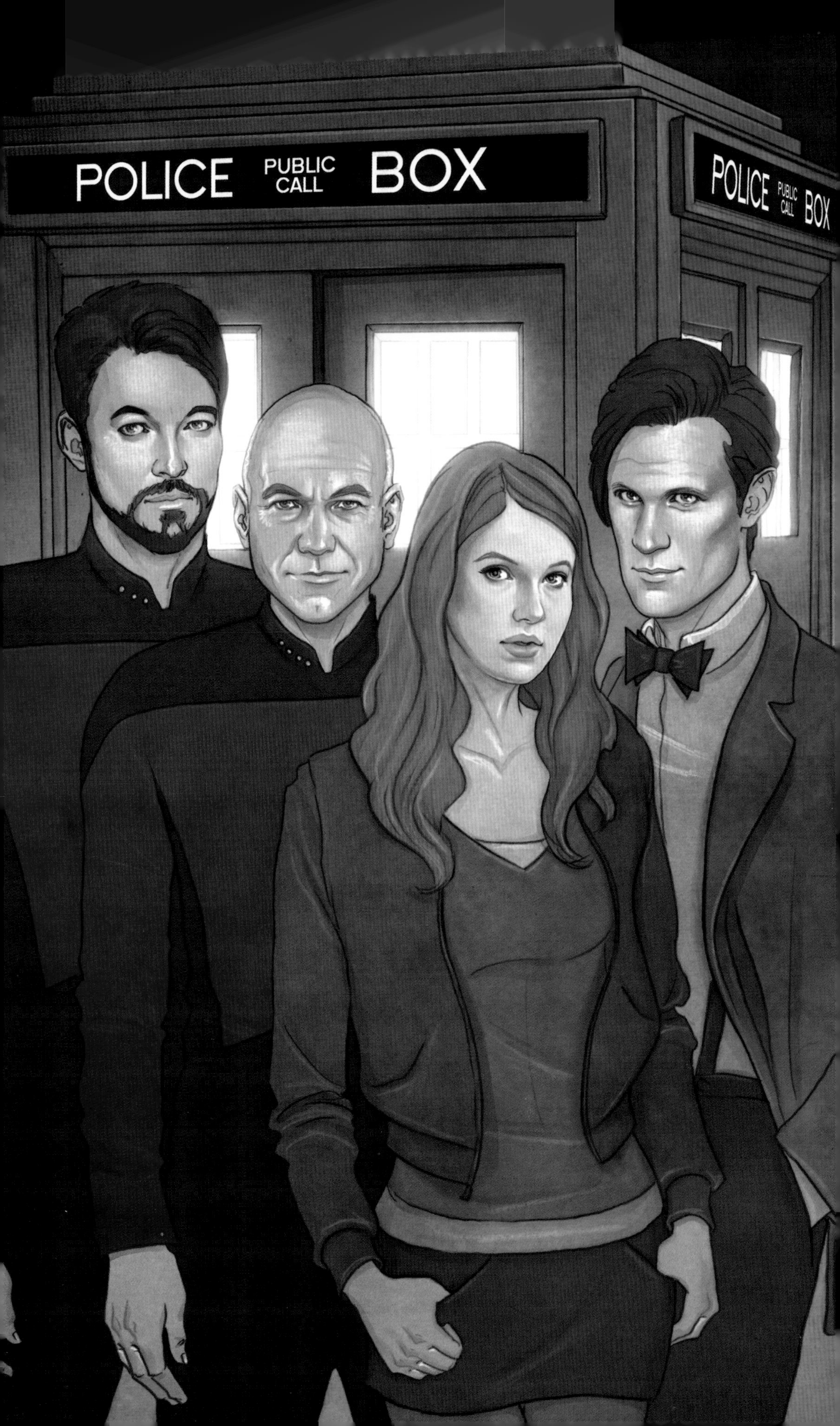
POLICE PUBLIC CALL BOX
POLICE PUBLIC CALL BOX

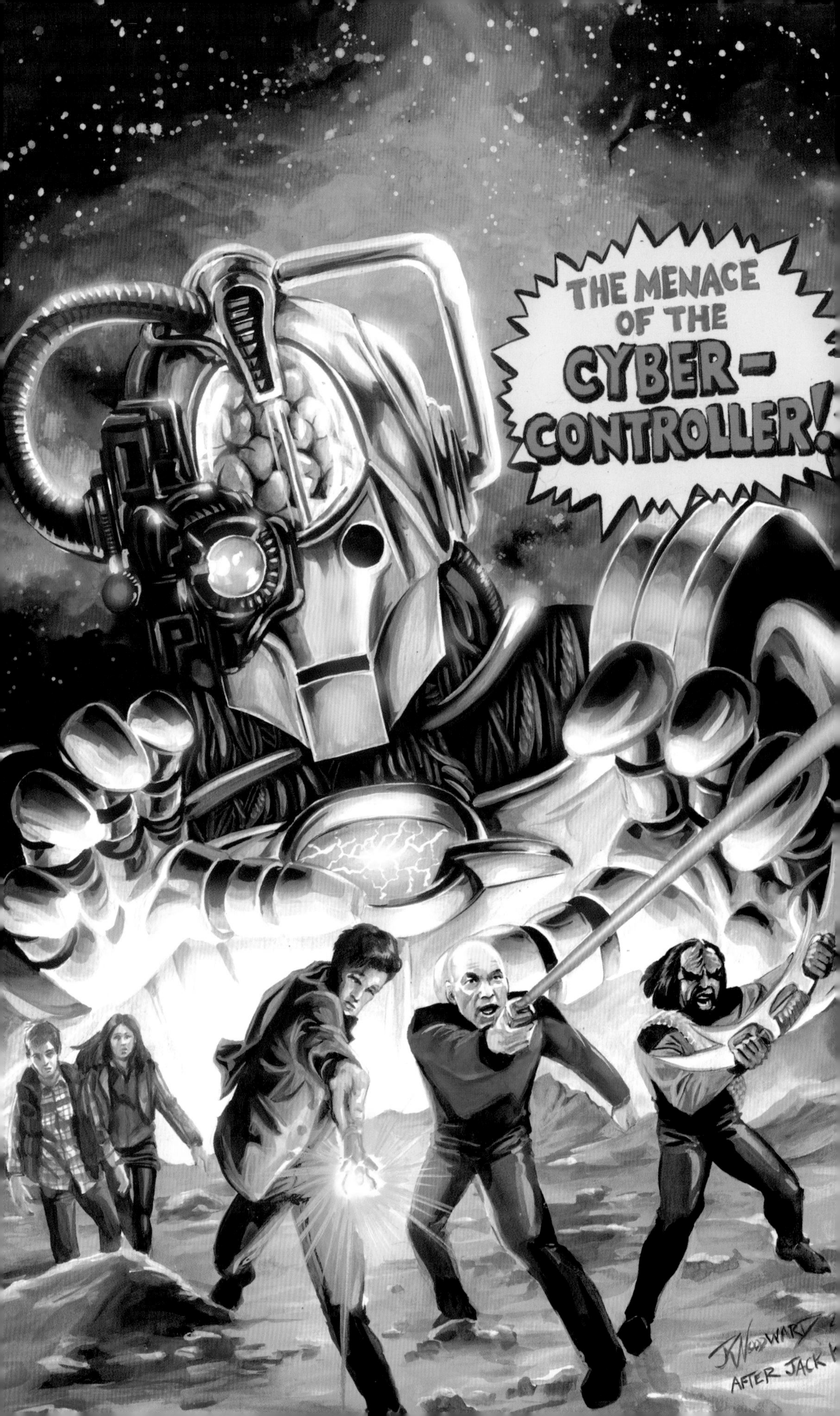
THE MENACE OF THE CYBER-CONTROLLER!
JK WOODWARD
AFTER JACK

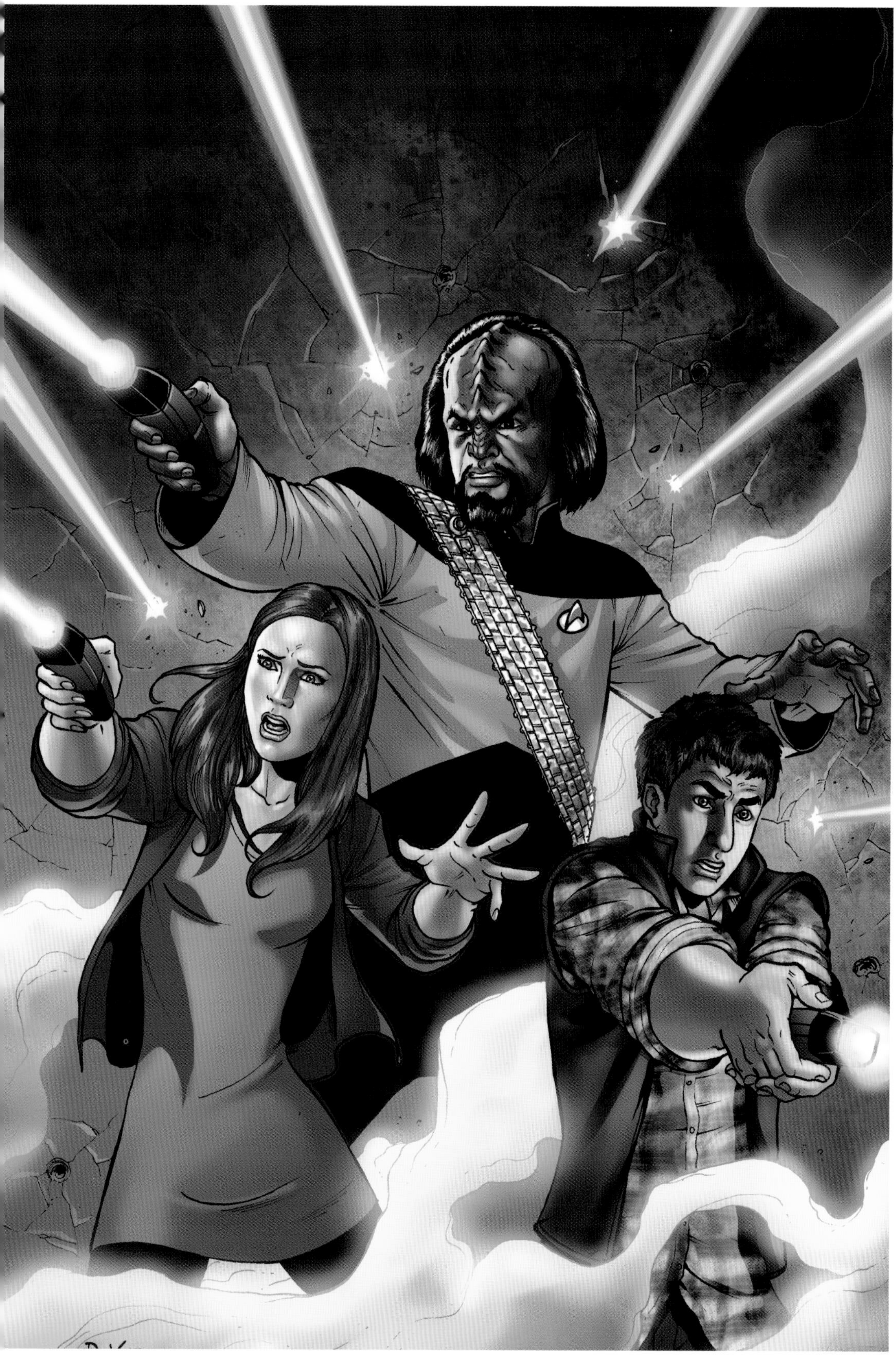

art by Andrea Di Vito, Colors by Laura Villari

opposite page: art by J.K. Woodward

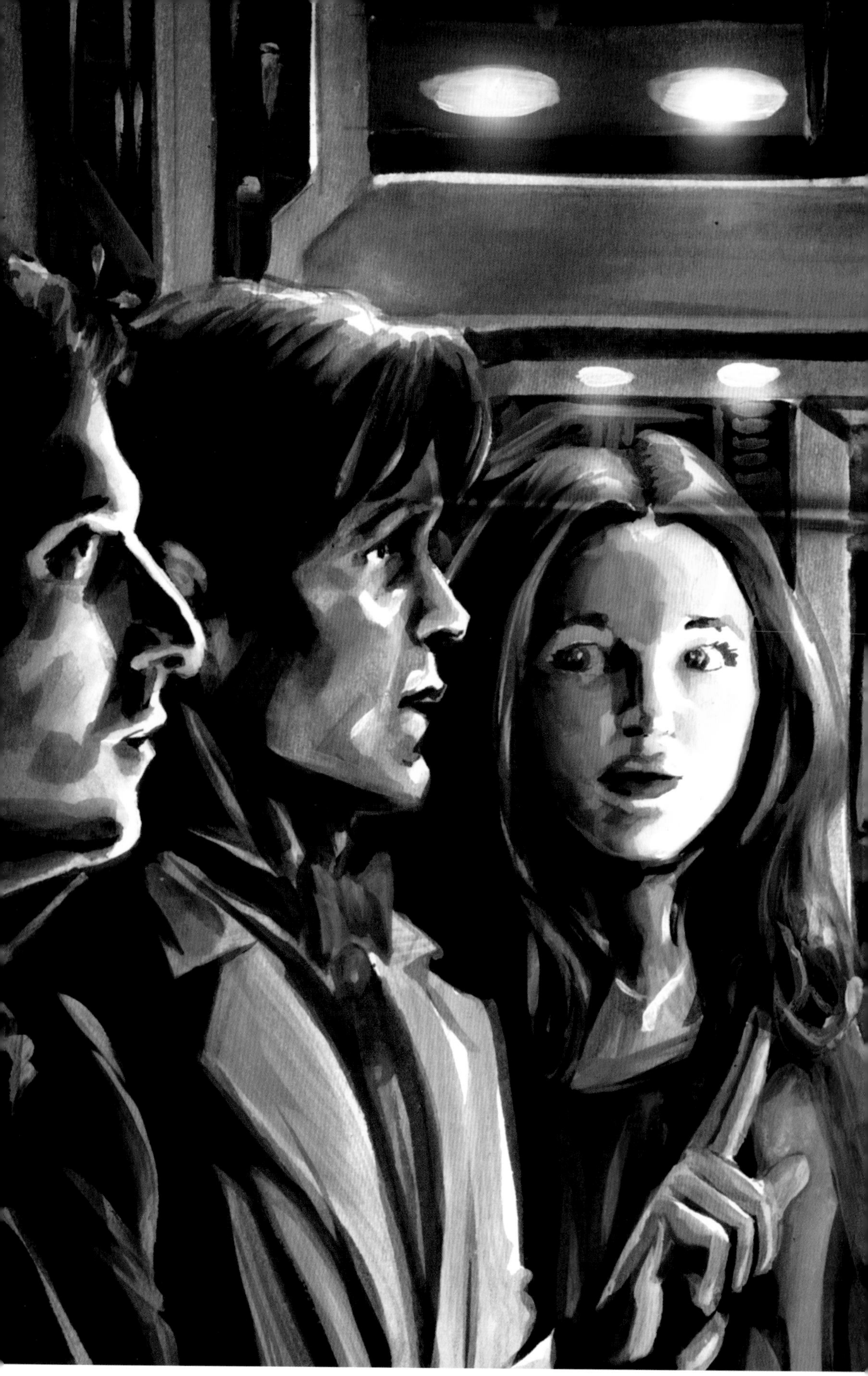

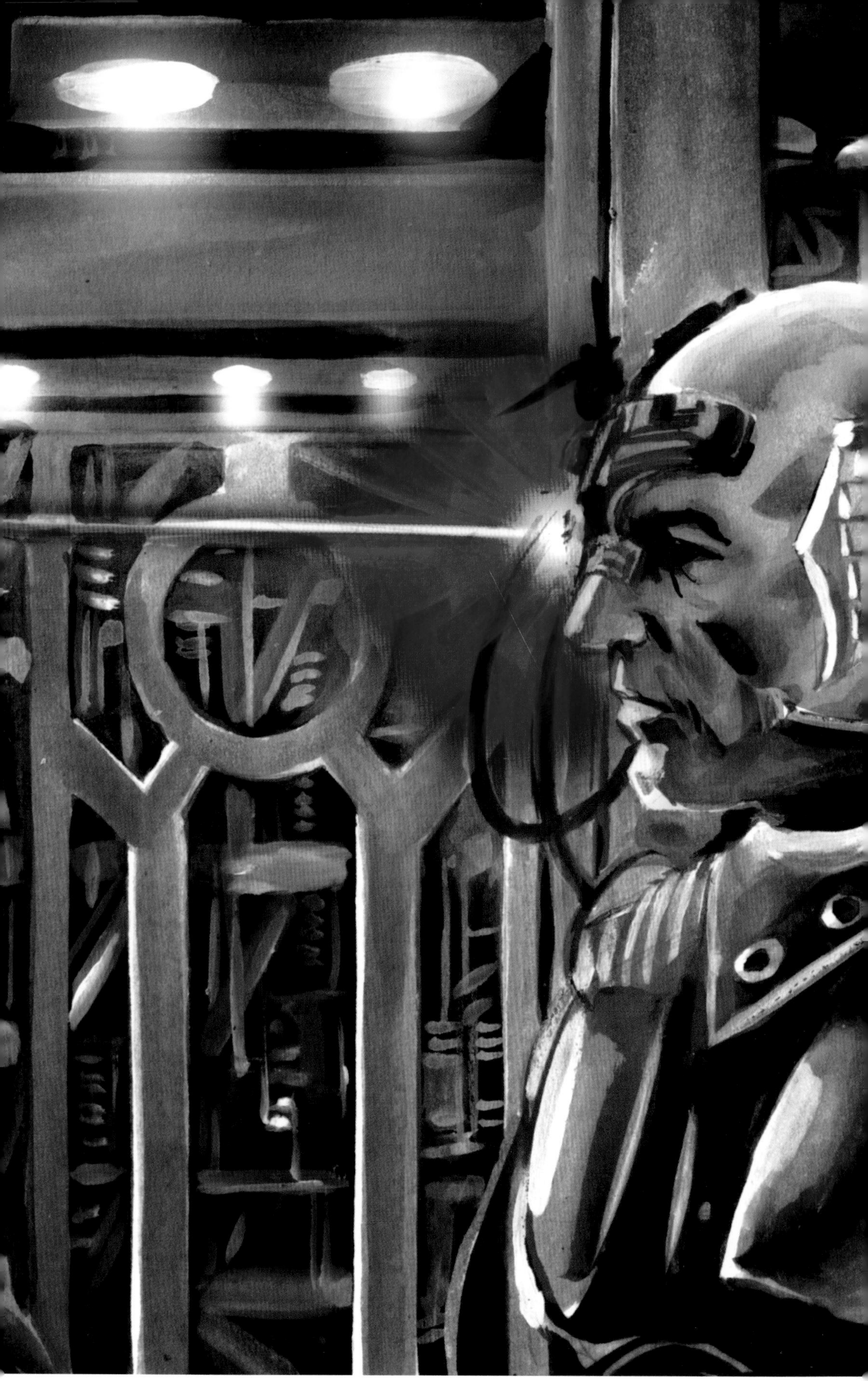

pencils by Gordon Purcell, painted art by J.K. Woodward

More Star Trek and Doctor Who titles from

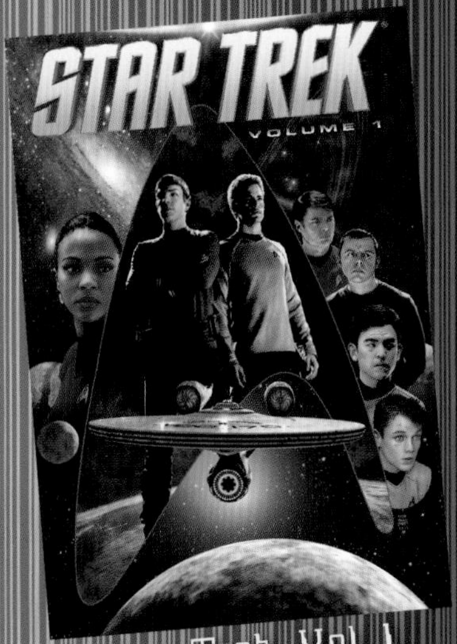
STAR TREK
VOLUME 1

Star Trek, Vol. 1

ISBN: 978-1-61377-150-1

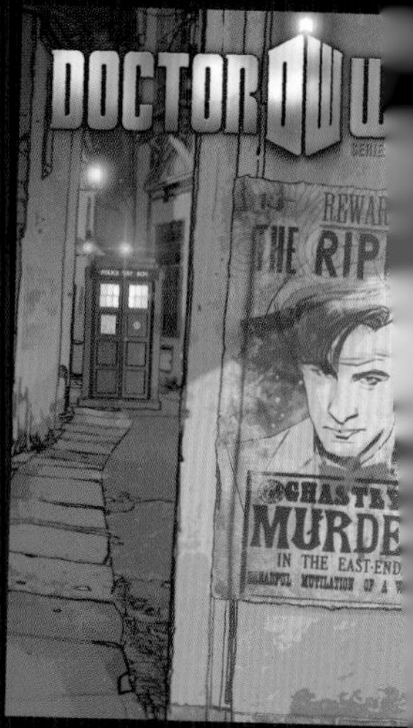
IN THE EAST-END

Doctor Who
Series 2, Vol. 1

ISBN: 978-1-60010-974-

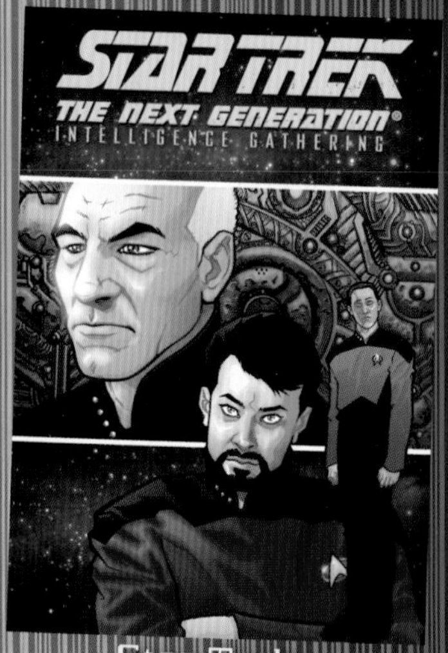
STAR TREK
THE NEXT GENERATION
INTELLIGENCE GATHERING

Star Trek:
The Next Generation:
Intelligence Gathering

ISBN: 978-1-60010-199-1

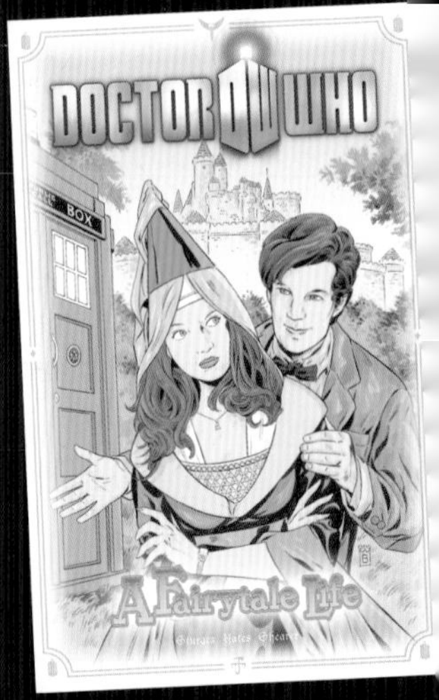
DOCTOR WHO
A Fairytale Life

Doctor Who:
A Fairytale Life

ISBN: 978-1-61377-022-1

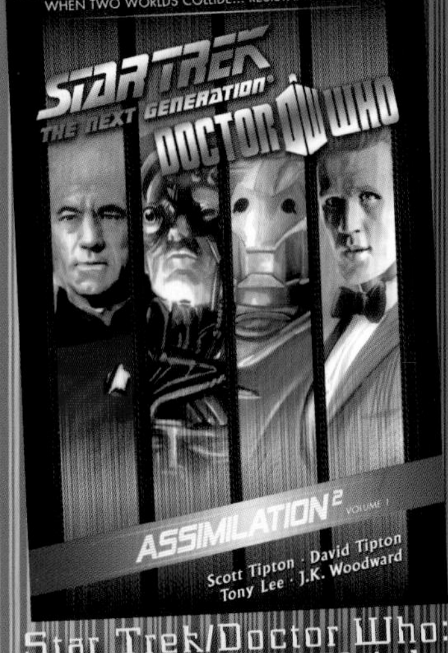
WHEN TWO WORLDS COLLIDE... RESISTANCE IS FUTILE.
STAR TREK
THE NEXT GENERATION
DOCTOR WHO
ASSIMILATION² VOLUME 1
Scott Tipton · David Tipton
Tony Lee · J.K. Woodward

Star Trek/Doctor Who:
Assimilation², Vol. 1

ISBN: 978-1-61377-403-8

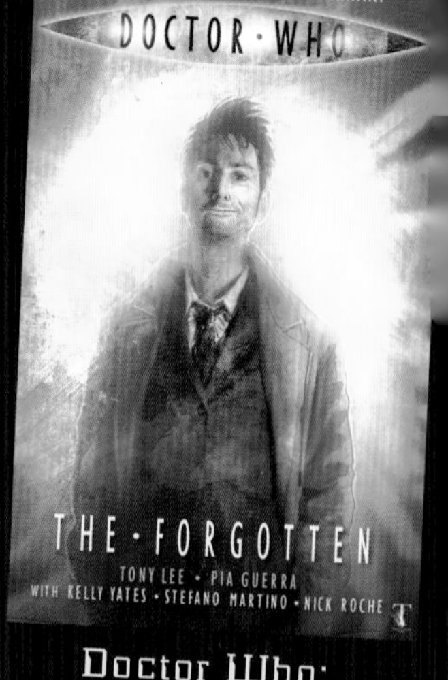
"BEAUTIFULLY DONE." — DAVID TENNANT
DOCTOR · WHO
THE · FORGOTTEN
TONY LEE · PIA GUERRA
WITH KELLY YATES · STEFANO MARTINO · NICK ROCHE

Doctor Who:
The Forgotten

ISBN: 978-1-60010-396-4